CHELMSFORD
IN 50 BUILDINGS

JIM REEVE

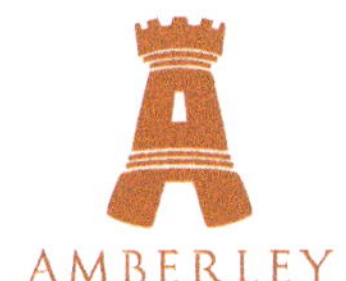

AMBERLEY

First published 2021

Amberley Publishing, The Hill, Stroud
Gloucestershire GL5 4EP

www.amberley-books.com

British Library Cataloguing in Publication Data.
A catalogue record for this book is available from the British Library.

ISBN 978 1 3981 0685 7 (print)
ISBN 978 1 3981 0686 4 (ebook)

Typesetting by SJmagic DESIGN SERVICES, India.
Printed in Great Britain.

Contents

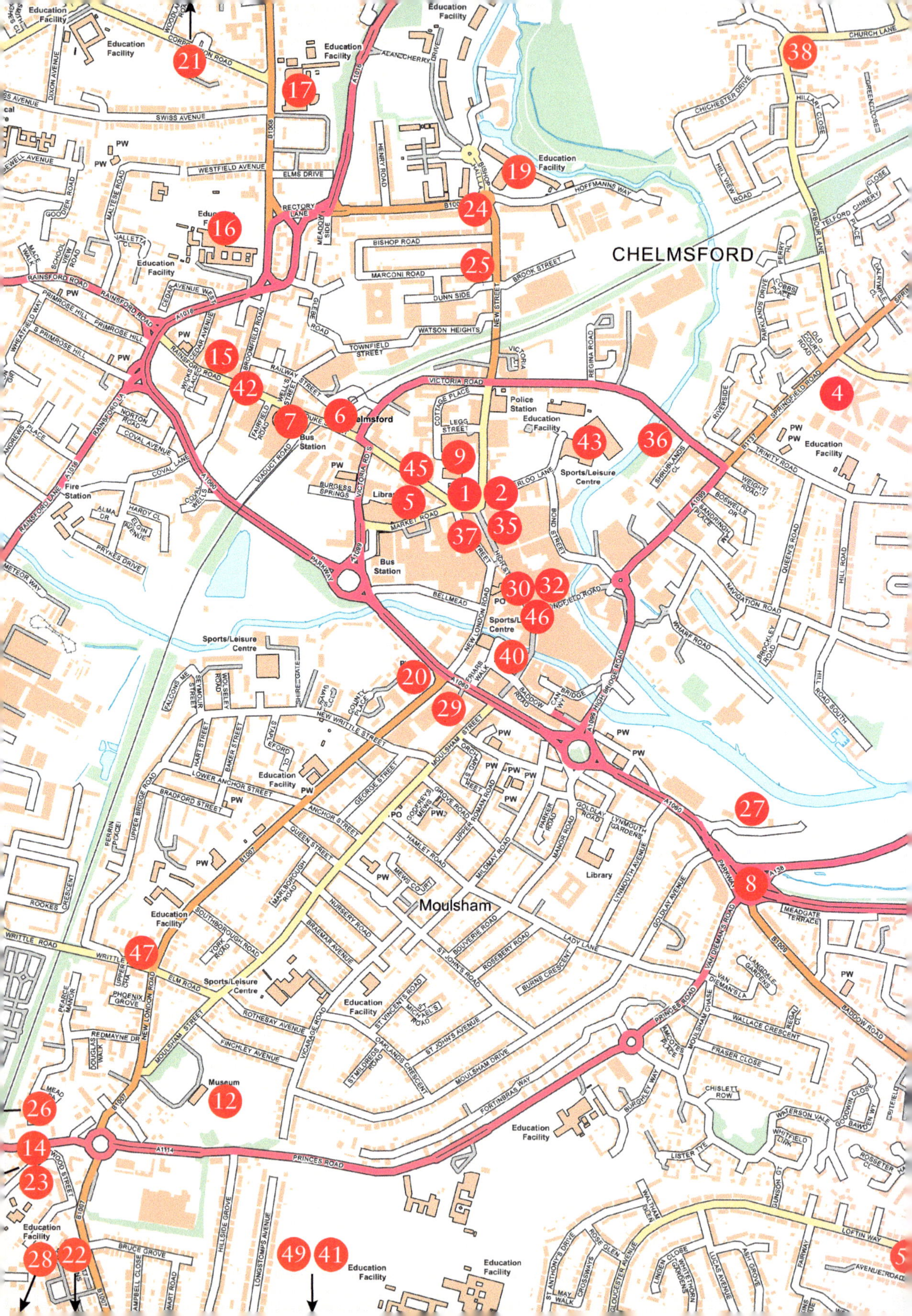

CHELMSFORD
Moulsham
Education Facility
Police Station
Sports/Leisure Centre
Bus Station
Library
Museum
Fire Station
SWISS AVENUE
WESTFIELD AVENUE
RAINSFORD ROAD
PRIMROSE HILL
CEDAR AVENUE WEST
BROOMFIELD ROAD
RAILWAY STREET
VICTORIA ROAD
NEW STREET
BISHOP ROAD
MARCONI ROAD
DUNN SIDE
BROOK STREET
TOWNFIELD STREET
WATSON HEIGHTS
VICTORIA
MARKET ROAD
COVAL AVENUE
COVAL LANE
PARKWAY
NEW WRITTLE STREET
MOULSHAM STREET
BAKER STREET
HART STREET
LOWER ANCHOR STREET
BRADFORD STREET
ANCHOR STREET
QUEEN STREET
GEORGE STREET
GROVE ROAD
HAMLET ROAD
UPPER ROMAN ROAD
MILDMAY ROAD
MANOR ROAD
MARLBOROUGH ROAD
YORK ROAD
ELM ROAD
NURSERY ROAD
BRAEMAR AVENUE
ROTHESAY AVENUE
VICARAGE ROAD
SOUTHBOROUGH ROAD
FINCHLEY AVENUE
PRINCES ROAD
WOOD STREET
NEW LONDON ROAD
MOULSHAM DRIVE
ST JOHN'S ROAD
ST JOHN'S AVENUE
BOUVERIE ROAD
ROSEBERY ROAD
LADY LANE
BURNE CRESCENT
GOLDLAY AVENUE
LYNMOUTH AVENUE
BADDOW ROAD
WHARF ROAD
NAVIGATION ROAD
QUEEN'S ROAD
HILL ROAD
SPRINGFIELD ROAD
REGINA ROAD
RIVERSIDE
WEIGHT ROAD
TRINITY ROAD
HOFFMANNS WAY
CHURCH LANE
HILLARY CLOSE
HILL VIEW ROAD
CHICHESTER DRIVE
PARKLANDS DRIVE
BOND STREET
HIGH STREET
BELLMEAD
MEADGATE TERRACE
PRINCES ROAD
VAN DIEMAN'S ROAD
WALLACE CRESCENT
FRASER CLOSE
CHISLETT ROW
RAINSFORD LANE
PRYKES DRIVE
SEYMOUR STREET
WOLSELEY ROAD
MOULSHAM ORCHARD

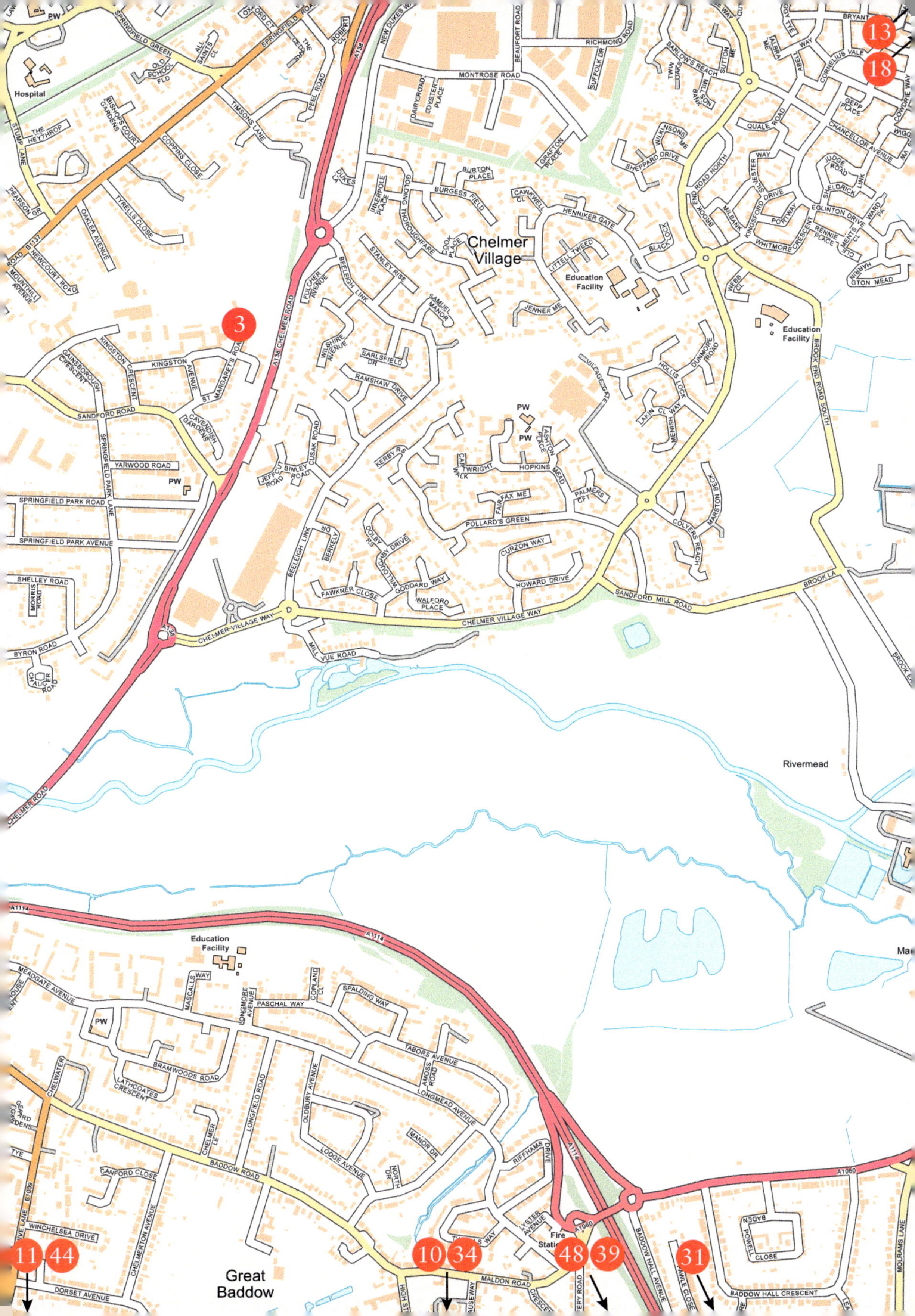

Hospital
Chelmer Village
Education Facility
Education Facility
Rivermead
Great Baddow
Fire Station
PW
13
18
3
11
44
10
34
48
39
31

Key

Introduction

The city of Chelmsford has fascinated me since I was a child, when my Grandfather used to take my hand and walk me down the market. I loved the noise and excitement generated by the crowds of milling people. Chelmsford became a city in 2012 and has a combination of interesting old and new buildings. The two rivers, the Chelmer and Can, which run through the city were paramount in its making. People were living by the rivers in the Neolithic period (10,000BC–4500 BC), as proved by the Cursus and burial ground that was discovered when they were building Springfield Business Park, which commenced in 1979. What was exciting was the discovery of an incomplete ring of post holes, a small amount of beakers, pieces of Bronze Age pottery and worked flint. The discovery of these items proved beyond doubt that the area was occupied over a very long period, but unfortunately the site now lies buried under the tarmac of the business park.

Although Julius Caesar first invaded Britain in 55 BC and then again in 54 BC, he never settled here and after several battles with the Celtic tribes, returned to France and then Rome. It was not until AD 43 that Aulus Plautius, on the instructions of Emperor Claudius, began the conquest of Britain in earnest. No evidence has been found to show that the Romans settled in Chelmsford at first but their legions must have passed through it on their way to Colchester. This all changed after Boadicea's (also known as Boudica) revolt and defeat in AD 60/61 when a Roman military post was built in Chelmsford called Caesaromagus, which means Caesar's field or market.

A bridge was constructed across the river and baths were built to give the troops some relaxation. Gradually the area built up, with houses and traders taking advantage of being on the road to the important Roman town of Colchester. Following the sacking of Rome by the Vandals in AD 410, the Romans withdrew their troops to defend their country. Chelmsford, along with the rest of Britain, fell into the Dark Ages. Lack of maintenance caused the bridge to collapse, as did the rest of what the Romans built. Luckily, there were two fords across the rivers controlled by two Saxons: Ceolmaer, after whom Chelmsford was named, and who controlled the Chelmsford side; and Muls Ham managed the Moulsham side.

When the Normans invaded Britain in 1066 there were two settlements in Chelmsford which were recorded in the Domesday Book of 1086 as 'a small rural farm of four households on the Chelmsford side and twelve households on the Moulsham side'.

Edward the Confessor (1042–66) gave Chelmsford to the Bishops of London and it remained in their hands until 1545, when it was given to Henry VIII. Chelmsford came into its own during the reign of bad King John (1166–1215) when he granted the Bishop of London, William of Sainte-Mere-Eglise, the right to hold a market in the High Street. It proved to be a great success as it took advantage of travellers passing through Chelmsford from London to Colchester. About this time a bridge was built over the River Can and soon the stalls were replaced by permanent shops, for which the Bishop charged an annual fee. The cheaper plots were smaller and down by the river, whereas the more expensive ones were at the top. A channel was dug in the centre of the High Road so that when the market had finished at the end of the day, the rubbish and waste of the market and animals were swept into it and carried down to the river, which became polluted, and caused outbreaks of diseases. In 1832 there was an outbreak of cholera and the Board of Health appointed Edward Cresy to investigate and, following his report, James Fenton was asked to produce plans to install a drainage system to remedy the problem. Thanks to him, Chelmsford today is a good, healthy place to live and at the last census, in 2011, the population had grown to 168,310.

The 50 Buildings

1. Shire Hall

Shire Hall stands majestically at the top of the High Street, surveying the hustle and bustle of the crowds below. It replaced two older buildings, the first having been built in medieval times, and when that was condemned, a new building called Tudor Market Cross or Great Cross was constructed in 1569. The ground floor was open to the elements and served as a marketplace while the upper galleries were used as a Court of Assize and Quarter Sessions, but somewhere between that being built and 1660, a civil court, called Little Cross, was constructed on the west side of Tudor Market.

In 1566, the famous witch trials were held in Tudor Market. They were instigated by Matthew Hopkins, Witch Hunter General, who, it is said, was responsible for the death of 230 witches. Three of them, Agnes Waterhouse, her daughter Joan and Elizabeth Francis, were hanged on the spurious evidence of a girl of twelve. They were accused of having a cat with a monkey's head, who had

Shire Hall, 1900s.

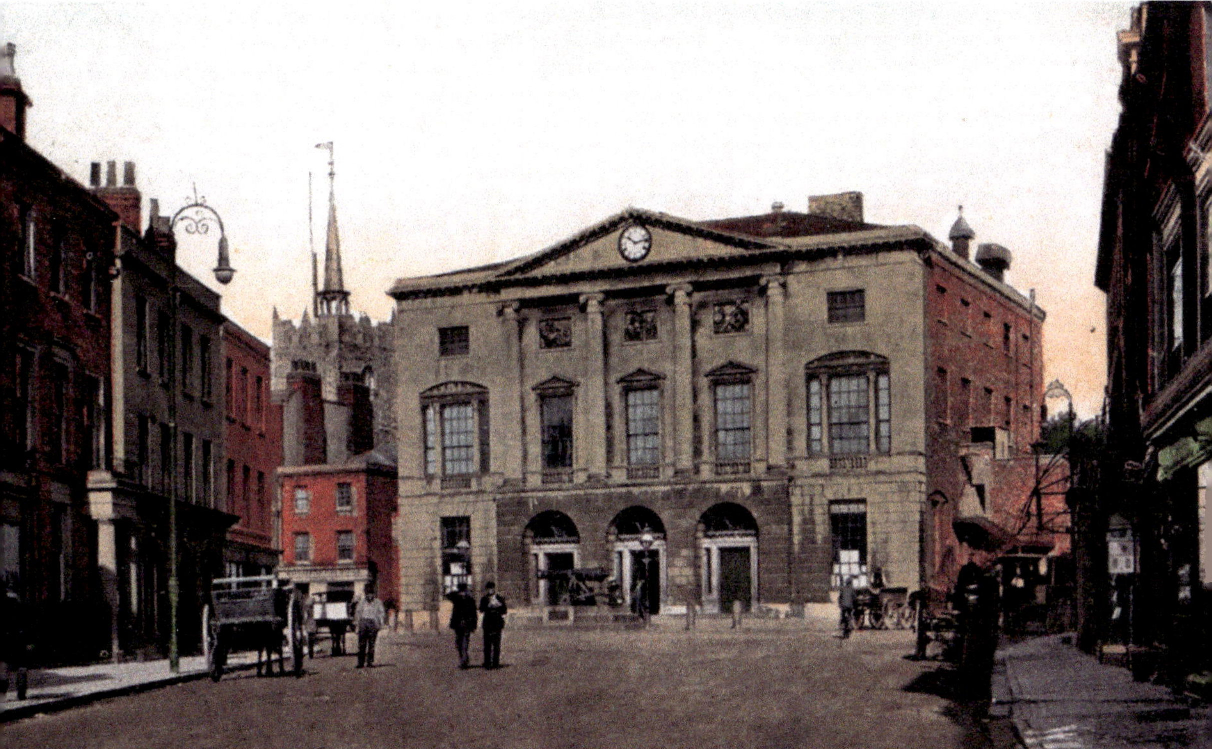

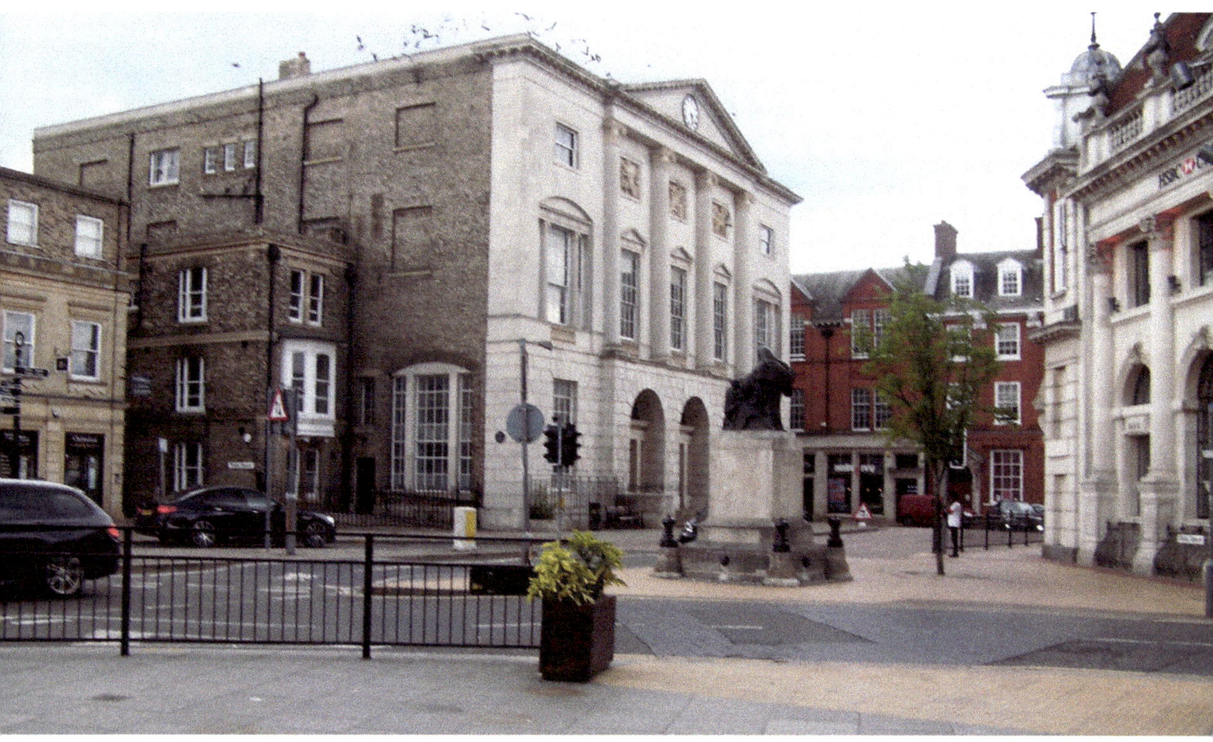

Shire Hall, 2020.

helped them cause the death of a man and his cattle. They were also charged with spoiling butter and cheese.

The original building was condemned in 1789 and Shire Hall was built under the direction of the County Surveyor, Mr Johnson. It took two years to build and cost £14,000. The ground floor was designed to be used as a corn exchange and the upper rooms were used as court premises. The building was not without its tragedies. Five men were being tried for the murder of a policeman while they were poaching. There was a tremendous interest in the case and crowds gathered. The stairs were teeming with people, all anxious to hear the trial. As they pushed and shoved, the balustrades gave way. Then, the staircase collapsed, sending everybody tumbling down to the ground floor in a great heap, killing a nineteen-year-old youth. The court was in a dilemma. Now there was no staircase, how were they going to get out? The judge, witnesses and prisoners all climbed through a window and onto the roof of a nearby building

2. Chelmsford's Old Police Station

Conveniently, the old police station is directly opposite Shire Hall in Waterloo Road and prisoners did not have to go out into the High Road to the courts,

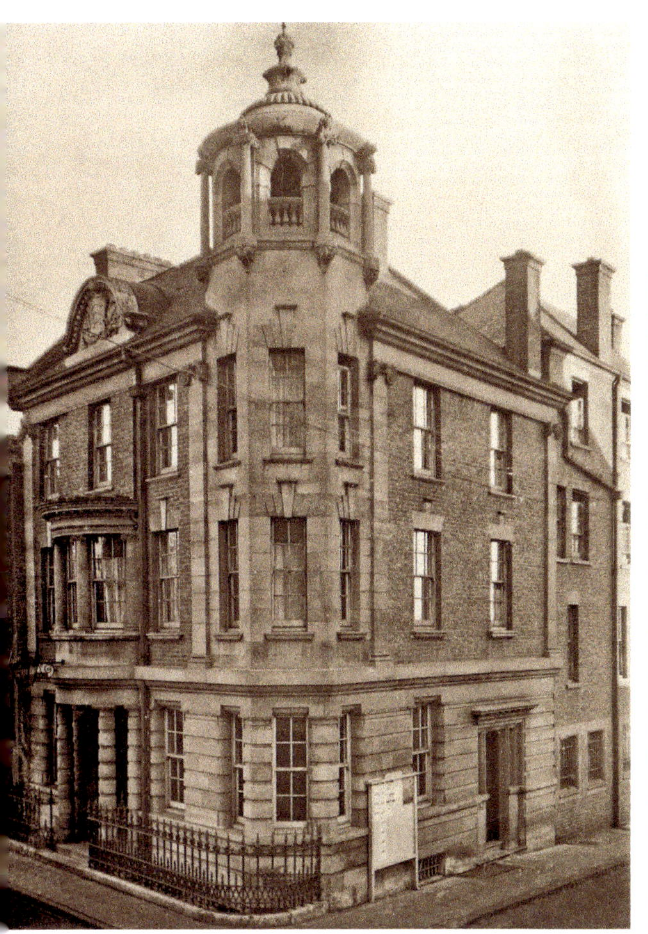

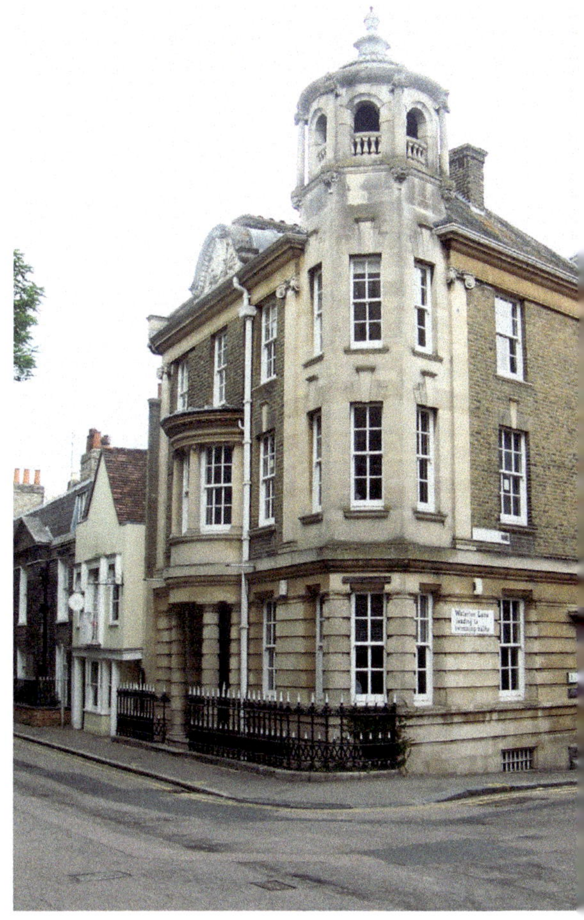

Above left: Old police station.

Above right: Restaurant, 2020.

but were lead through a tunnel which connected the two buildings, without seeing daylight and with no chance of escape. At first, the town was patrolled by nightwatchmen, but in 1839, the County Police Act was passed and within a year Essex was one of the first to establish a police force under the leadership of Captain Hardy, a retired navy captain.

The new police constables were given only four weeks' training before they were sent out to face the public. Today's police receive eighteen weeks' training plus a probationary period of two years. Life in those days, as it is today for a constable, was very tough. They had none of the equipment that the police have today and worked seven days a week, without a break, and it was not until 1910 that they were given a rest day. For their efforts they were paid the same as a farm labourer – £1. 10s a week. Their only means of summoning help was a whistle and for protection they had a truncheon. Out in the country, alone, many were assaulted and a few, like Sergeant Eves, murdered. He had his throat cut by a gang. Luckily, they were caught and one of them, John Davis, who committed the murder, was hanged from Chelmsford Prison gate before a crowd estimated at several thousand. The building today is used as a restaurant and offices. The restaurant still has the prison cells.

3. Essex Police Training College

The Essex Police Training College is situated in Arbour Lane. The force first started training there in 1840, in what had previously been an old military barracks. It was originally called New Court and is now known as Old Court. By 1900 the premises became too small and it was inconvenient to take prisoners through the streets to the law court at Shire Hall. After some deliberation it was decided to build a new headquarters in Springfield on land bought from a local farmer for just over £1,000. The new building was designed by the firm Clare and Ross and was built in a curve out of very attractive red bricks.

The police moved into the premises in 1903. It was very modern for that time and consisted of living quarters, offices and many features that the man in the street did not acquire until many years later, such as electricity, running hot water and a telephone, which saved them using messengers to communicate. The entrance to the block has a beautiful brick arch which was once the

The Essex Police Training College, 1930. (Copyright Essex Police Museum)

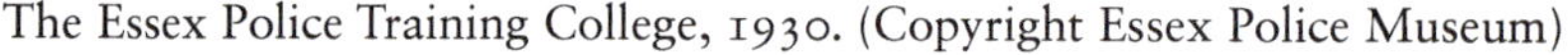

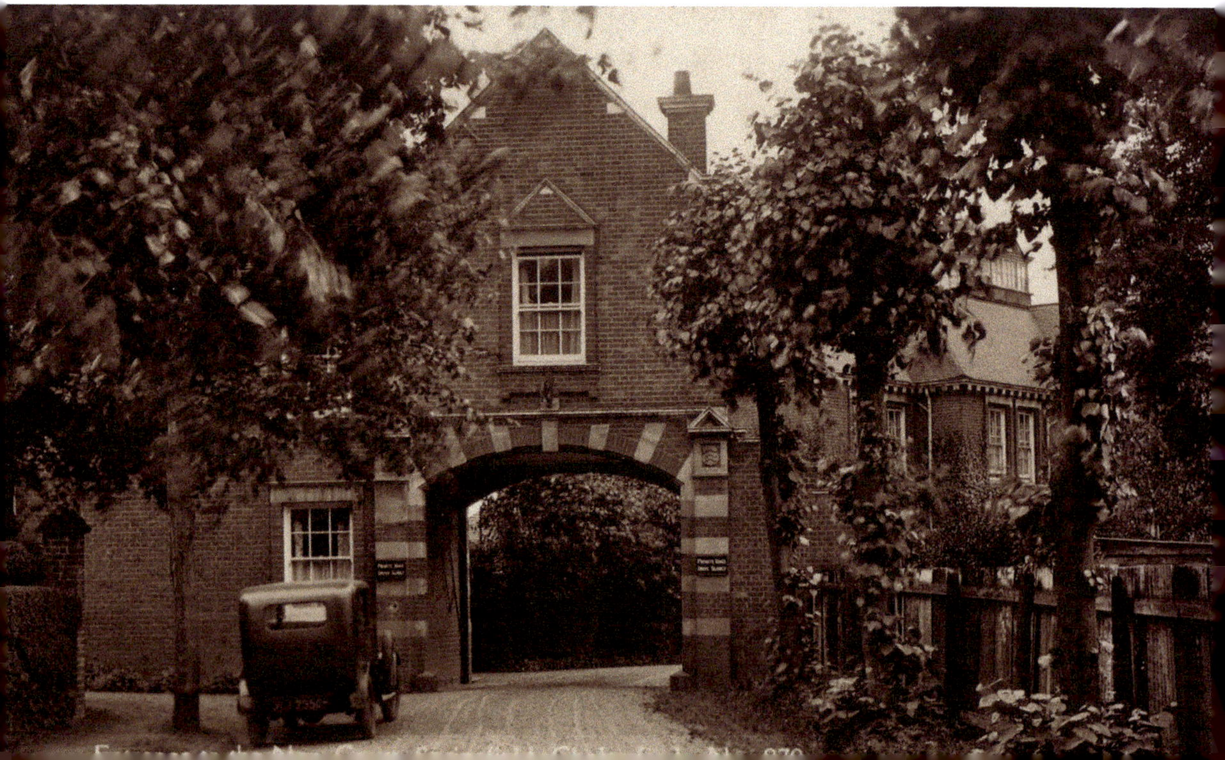

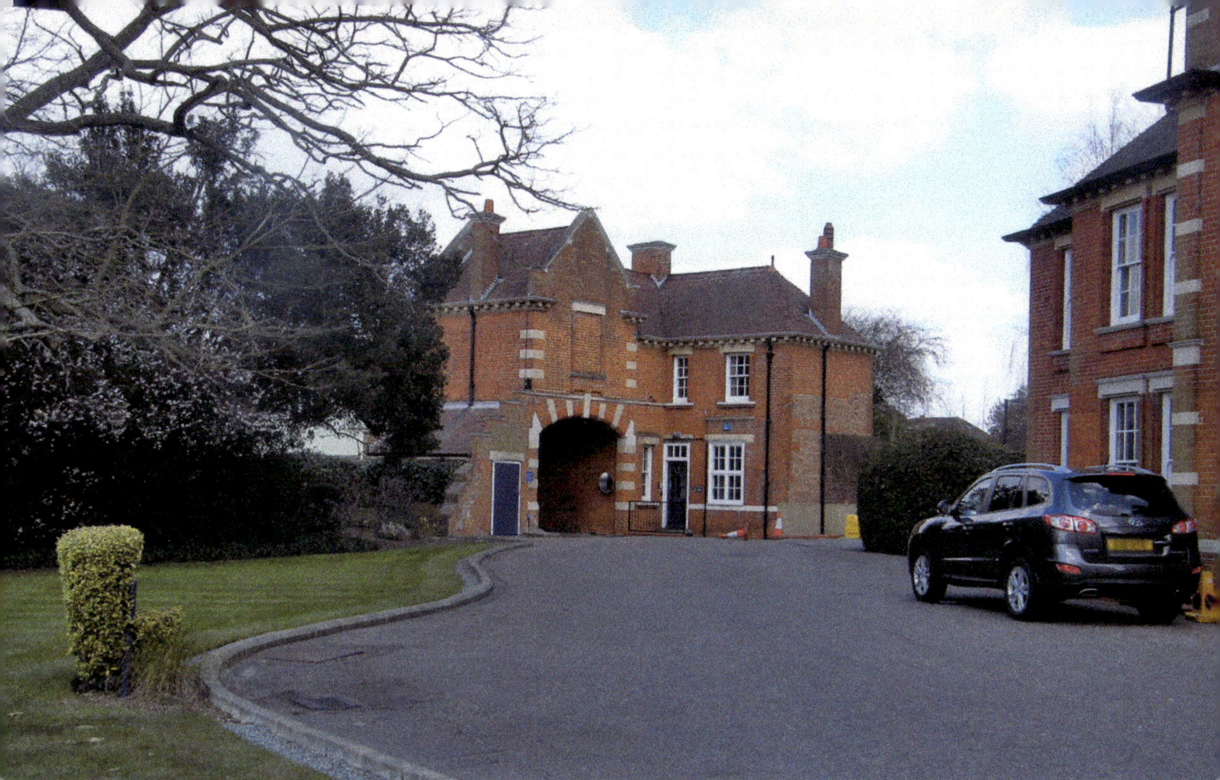

Police College today.

groom's living quarters. New Court, as it is now called, was opened by the Chief Constable, Edward Showers.

One block is for recruits and there was another one which was used as stables until 1920, when it was converted to garages, to accommodate the police becoming mechanized. I understand that even today a few horses are still kept. The college has had a number of alterations over the years, one being in 1937, when recreational resources were provided, including a cricket pavilion. In 1953 two new extensions were built. During the Second World War, in 1940, the Germans bombed the recruits' and stable blocks. Today there is an excellent police museum which is well worth a visit.

4. Springfield Prison

The authorities started building Chelmsford Prison in Springfield Road in 1822. As building progressed, the cells were occupied by the prisoners from the two old prisons, which were condemned. The first of these old prisons was constructed in 1658 at the side of the Stone Bridge, and was for prisoners who had committed petty crimes, such as prostitution and fraud. Another prison was built by the side of the river for more serious crimes, like murder, theft and, surprisingly, for stealing a man's tools of his trade. These prisons became damp and unusable and it is said that some walls became so soft that one prisoner dug his way out with a spoon.

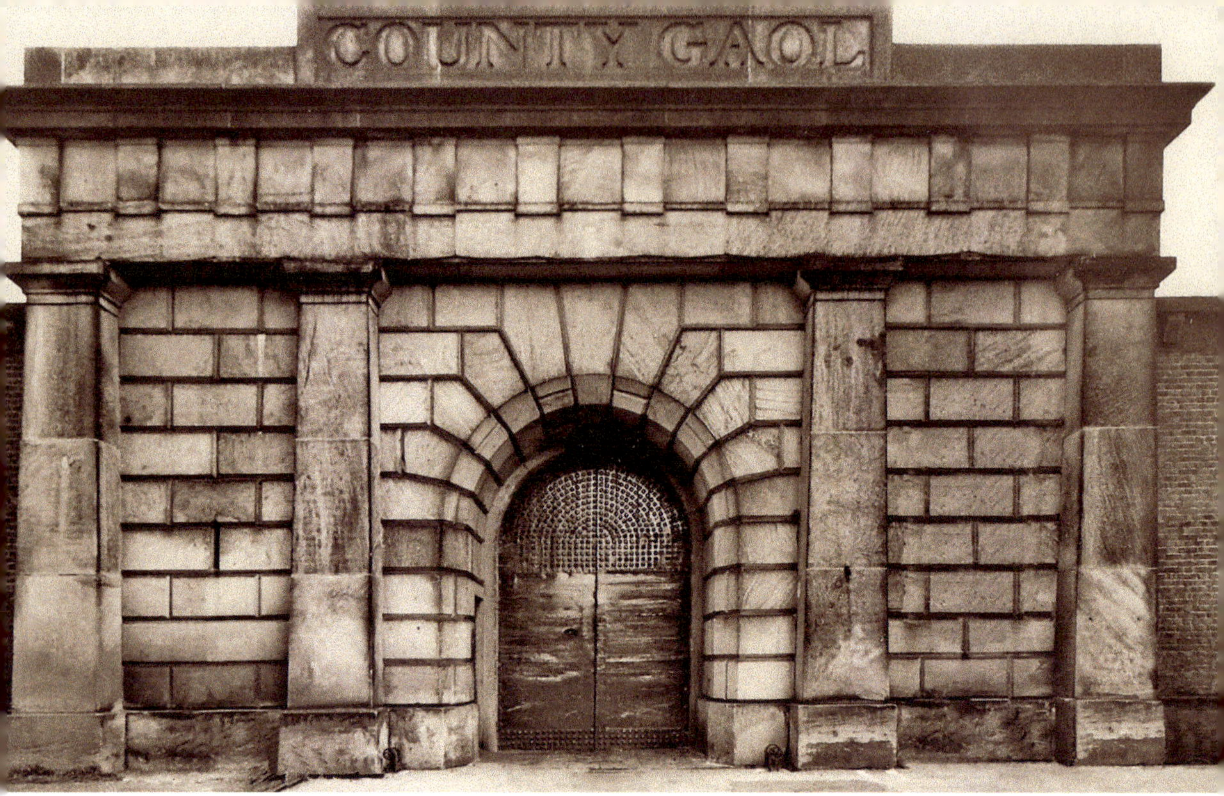

Above: Springfield Prison in the late eighteenth century.

Below: Springfield Prison today.

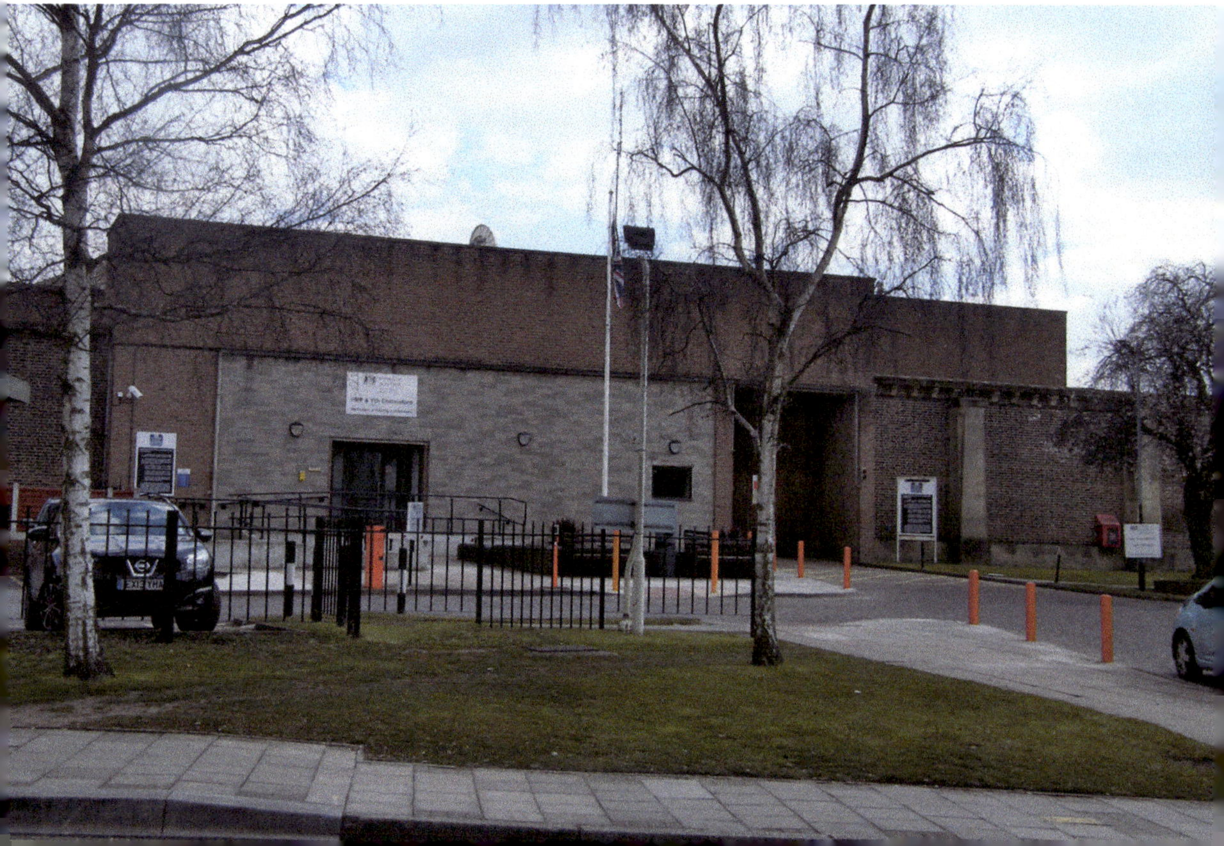

The first Governor of Chelmsford Prison was Thomas Neal, who also founded Chelmsford Museum. The prison was built to house 272 prisoners, as opposed to 695 in 2016. Prisoners were moved from the old prisons as cells became available. They slept on stone beds and had only two blankets each to keep them warm, even in winter. There was no heating of any kind. Some prisoners were punished by being whipped with the cat o' nine tails for breaking prison rules. This punishment could strip a man's flesh to the bone. Life in prison became harder when two treadmills were introduced for men or women who broke the rules. They were subjected to up to ten hours a day pounding away at the wheel. Later, this punishment was stopped for women. Prisoners had one bath a month in the open yard, even in the depths of winter. Their diet was restricted to bread and two pints of beer but after three months, relatives could bring in food to supplement their diet. From the date the prison opened until 1868, prisoners sentenced to hang were hanged from the prison gate in full view of the public, who considered the spectacle a day out, and thousands would attend. Forty-four prisoners were hanged and only one man survived. They tried to hang him several times, but failed, and so they sentenced him to life imprisonment.

In 1978 the prison caught fire and had to be refurbished. Today, the prison is a category B prison for men and young offenders. It was used to film the TV comedy *Porridge*, staring Ronnie Barker.

5. Essex Fire Brigade

The Chelmsford Fire Brigade had a station in Market Road near the old cattle market but then they moved to Springfield and then later to Rainsford Road.

When the Romans conquered Britain in AD 47 they fought fires with simple fire pumps and buckets of water, but when they left in AD 410 there appeared to be no organised way of fighting fires. If they could not extinguish it, they demolished buildings in its pathway to make a fire break.

It took the Great Fire of London in 1666 to make people realize that a firefighting service was needed. The fire had destroyed a great deal of London, including the old St Paul's Cathedral and it was obvious that some form of fire service had to be formed. A property developer, Nicholas Barton, set up an insurance company called 'The Fire Office', which would attend fires provided the firm had joined their insurance company and had a plaque on the building to say so. If there was not a plaque the firefighters would stand and watch the building burn. Later, the Hand in Hand Fire Insurance Company took over from The Fire Office. Many villages and towns throughout Britain had small teams of firefighters. In 1823 James Braidwood set up the first city fire brigade in Edinburgh and then, in 1833, he helped to set up the London Fire Brigade and became their Chief Officer.

During the First World War firemen were called up as firefighting was not considered a protected occupation, and many of the men were killed in action.

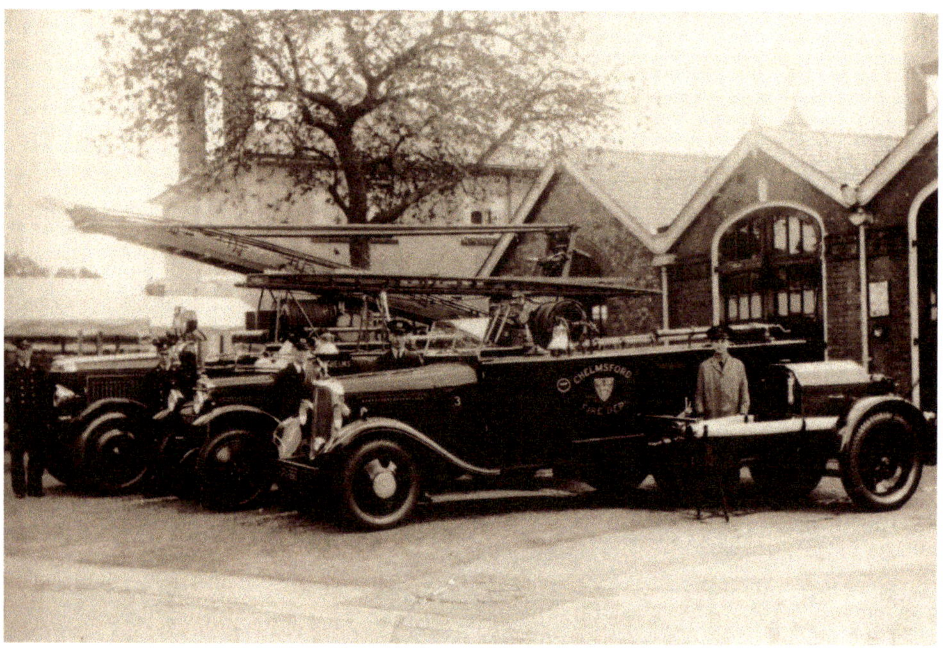

Above: The old fire station in Market Street, 1930. (Copyright Essex Fire Brigade)

Below: Firemen outside the fire station in Threadneedle Street in the 1930s. (Copyright Essex Fire Brigade)

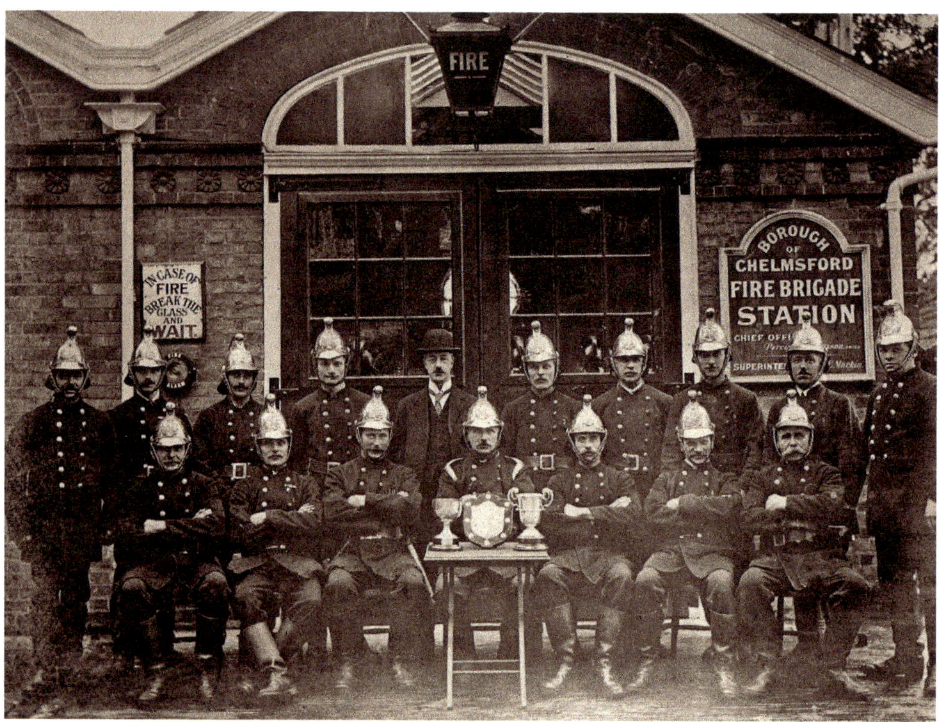

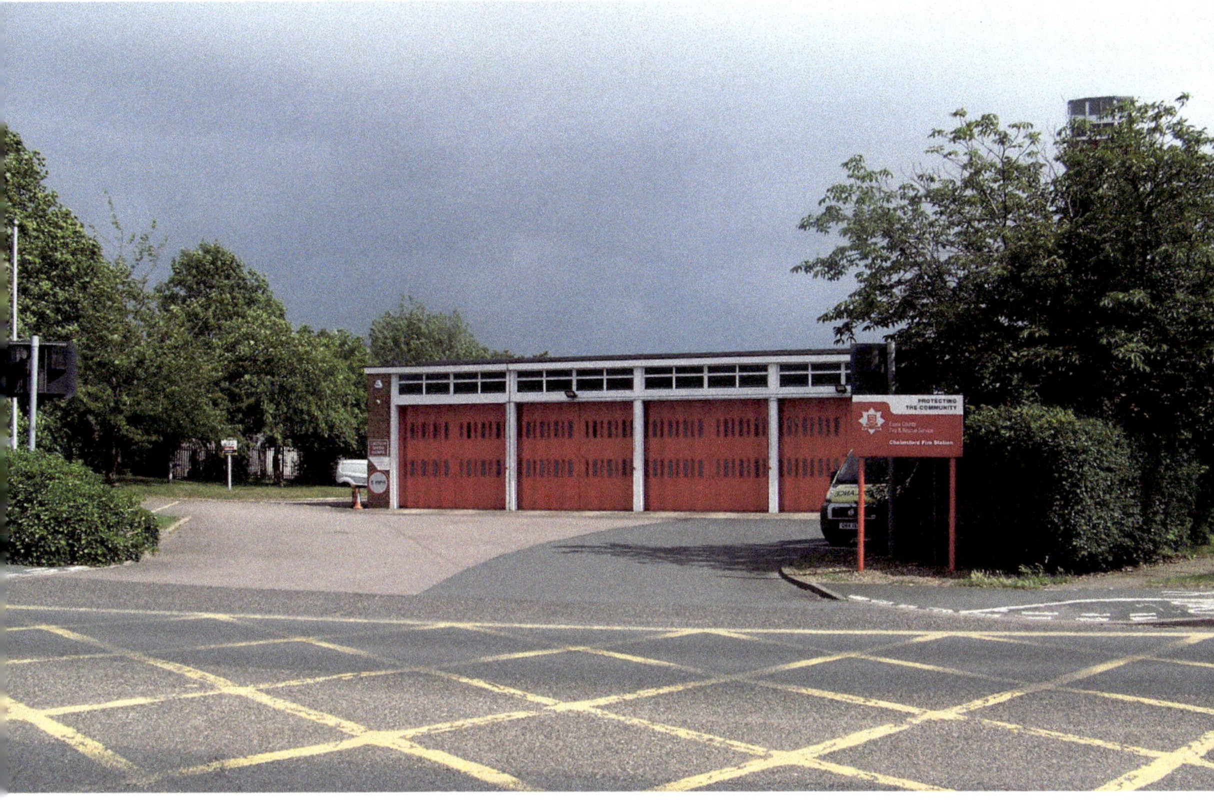

Fire station in Rainsford Road, 2020.

In 1938 the Auxiliary Fire Brigade was set up before Britain went to war. Later, they changed their name to the National Fire Service. After the war, the government brought in the 1947 Fire Services Act, which gave county authorities the right to form their own fire service, and 148 fire organisations were formed throughout the country.

6. Chelmsford Railway Station

Chelmsford have the Mildmay family and other notable people of the city to thank for the railway in Chelmsford. They sold a corridor of land to the Eastern Counties Railway, which enabled the company to build the railway. Their first task was to build three viaducts. The longest of these is supported by the eighteen arches in Central Park and one of them spans the River Chelmer. The first station was built in 1885 by the Great Eastern Railway and was slightly north of the current one, and it was not refurbished until 1985. The railway played a major part in the development of Chelmsford, as manufactured goods could be transported all over the country and abroad.

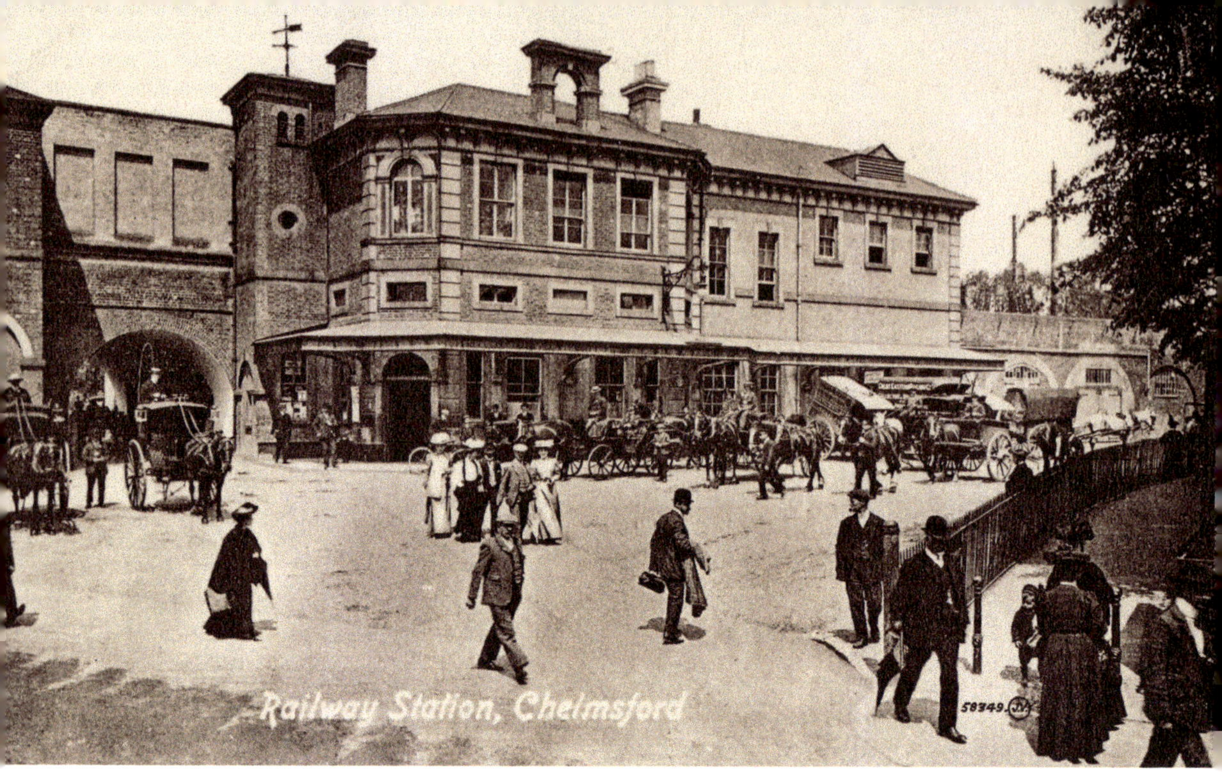

Above: Chelmsford railway station around 1900.

Below: Chelmsford railway station, 2020.

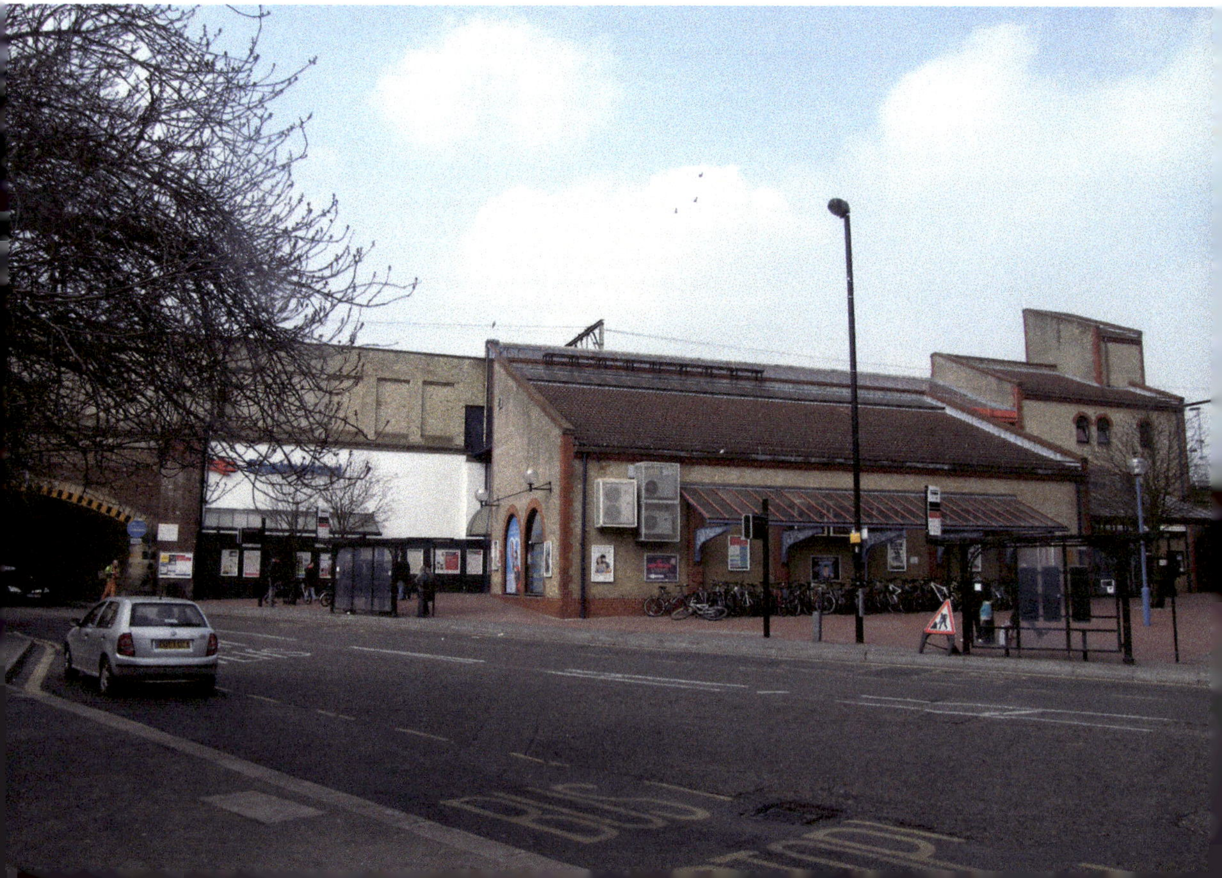

Chelmsford station is only 29 miles from London and in the year 2018/19, 8,927 million passengers passed through the station, mainly travelling to London, but others travelled to Ipswich, Clacton, Harwich and Norwich.

In the early days, the carriages were open to the elements and the smoke from the engines blew back on the passengers and smothered them in soot. At first, there were no first- or second-class carriages but as time went on, first and second class was introduced, and for these customers the carriages were enclosed and had more comfortable seats. The third-class passengers travelled in open carriages and sat on wooden seats. As far as I can establish, there has been only one serious accident. It happened on 2 March 1901, while drivers were shunting carriages around. A truck was accidentally left on the main line and an express train, racing through, struck it. Luckily, the train was not derailed or else there would have been serious injuries.

7. Chelmsford Bus Station

The bus station is situated in Duke Street, next to the Council Offices and was opened in 1931. On 14 May 1943, at the height of the Second World War, a bomb dropped through the roof, causing a fire which destroyed thirteen buses and spread to adjoining houses. It took the fire brigade over two hours to extinguish the blaze.

In 2004 the old garage was demolished and the new one erected. Before the trains and bus services, in 1720, there was a horse-drawn coach service travelling to London on a regular basis, but one had to get up very early to catch it. The introduction of a railway in 1885 and the steam bus service in 1903 tolled the

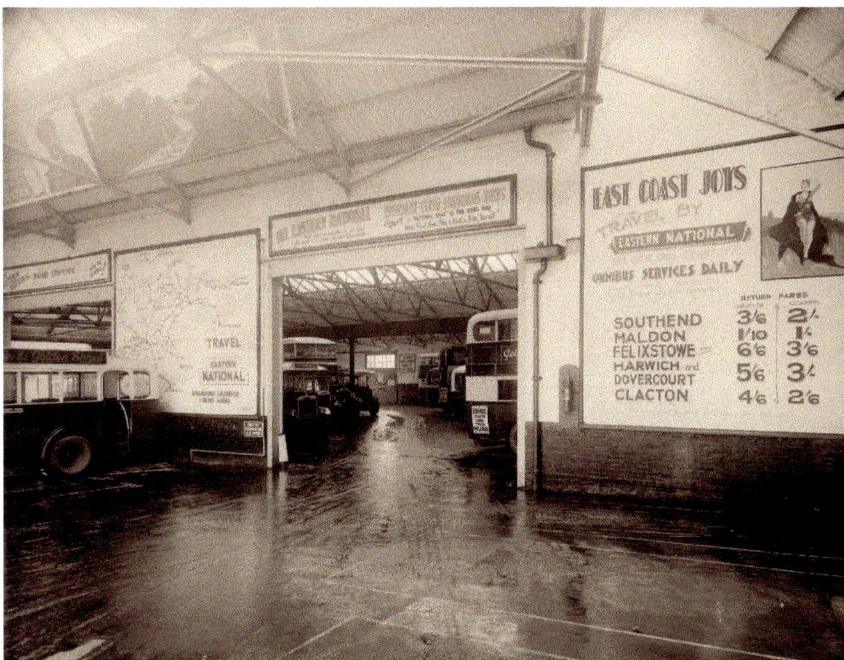

Chelmsford's old
bus station, 1940.

death knell of this coach service. The roads were not tarmacked in those far-off days but were clay, which turned into a quagmire in the depths of winter and a dust bowl at the height of summer.

Steam buses first put in an appearance on the streets of Chelmsford in 1903, although they were first used in other parts of the country from 1830. There was very strong opposition to this form of transport because of the noise that frightened the horses. People threw stones and laid boulders in the road to stop them. At first, the red flag laws of 1865 applied to buses. This required a man to walk in front of the bus with a red flag, walking at 4mph in the country and 2mph in town. This law was repealed in 1896, long before Chelmsford got its first steam bus. The steam buses were run by the National Steam Car Company. They were double-decker, with the upper deck open to the elements and it must have been very uncomfortable for the driver because he had no windscreen. In 1912, the Great Eastern Bus Company took over and in the 1930s, gradually started using diesel.

As a child during the Second World War, I remember catching the single-decker buses into Chelmsford with my grandfather and I will never forget how hard the wooden seats were.

Bus station, 2020.

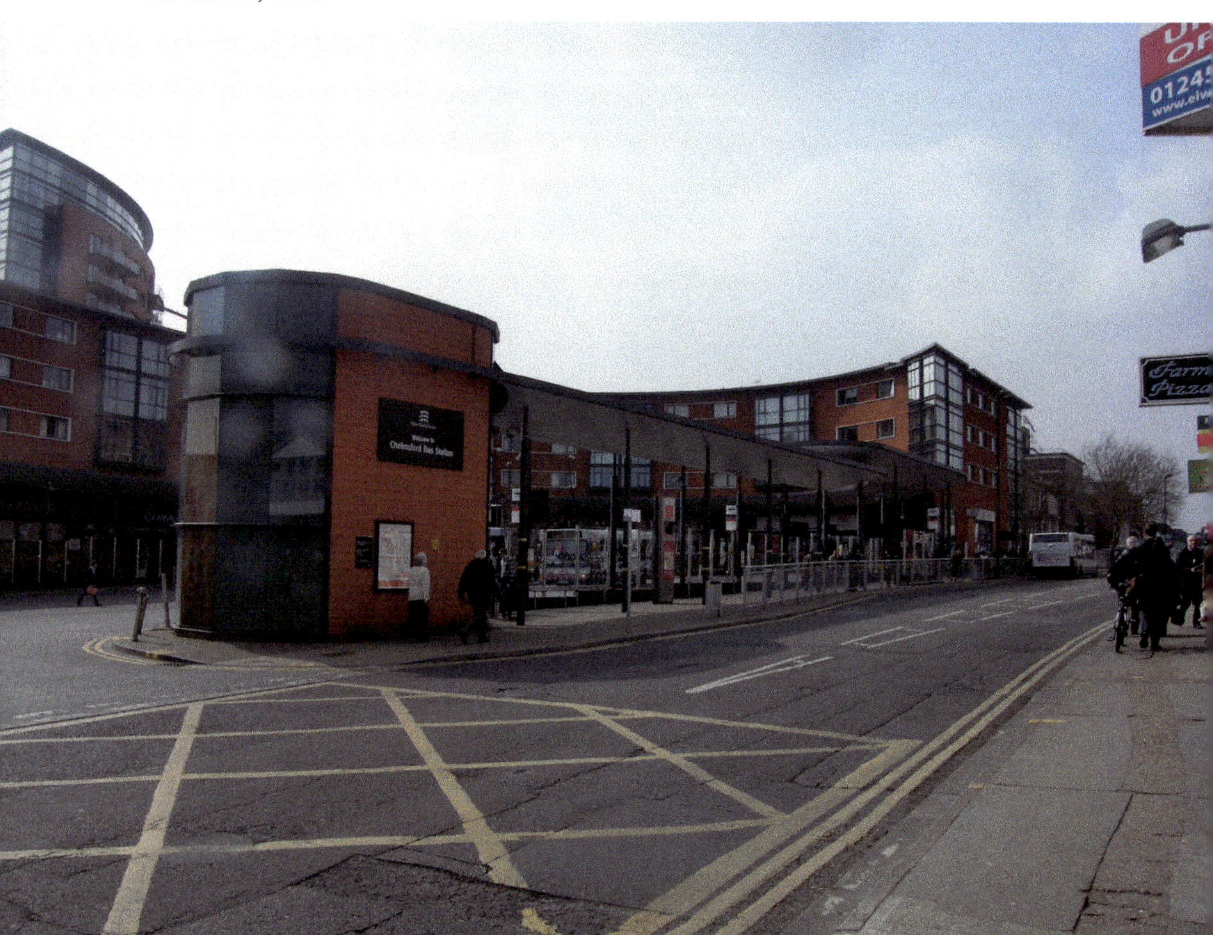

8. Army and Navy Flyover

Nothing has caused so much controversy in Chelmsford as the Army and Navy Flyover. In 1976, the population were clamouring to have it built to ease the A12 traffic going through the roundabout and causing chaos. There was an intense debate as to whether the A12 should go via Boreham or through the town. At that time people were concerned about cars breaking down or crashing on the bridge, as the type of automatic signs that were used to warn traffic that the bridge was closed had not been invented. There were talks of constructing a double bridge, but after much discussion they came to nothing. Finally, in May 1978, it was decided to build a single, temporary bridge at an estimated cost of £400,000.

When the surveyors started carrying out soil tests, before they started to build, they discovered, to their horror, that there were a large number of drains, water pipes and electric cables running through the bridge site that had to be rerouted before building could commence, and of course this added to the cost. When the flyover was finally built it cost £630,000. The first car to drive over it was a blue Jaguar, which crossed the bridge on 10 December 1988. It was said that the bridge would be temporary and only last four years, but it lasted forty before it started to show its age and bits of concrete started falling off and it became dangerous. There was talk of repairing it but finally it was decided to demolish it.

Army and Navy Flyover before being demolished.

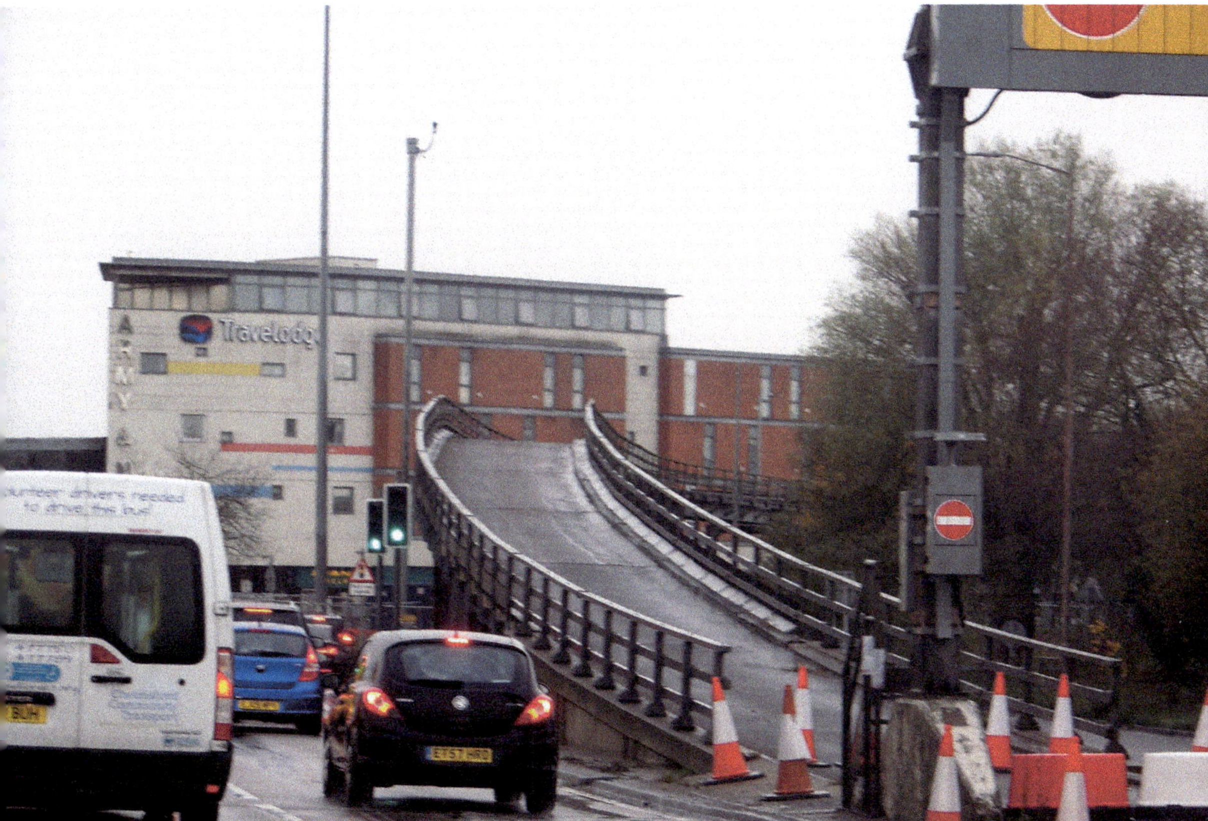

Over the years there have been a number of crashes on the bridge, one involving as many as ten cars. Sadly there have been two deaths. On 16 January 1999, a man was killed and then, on 27 June 2012, during a torrential storm, a woman driver crossing the bridge became confused and drove down the wrong way when she came off the flyover and for half a mile drove on the wrong side of the road, hitting a BMW which killed her.

9. Chelmsford Cathedral

Chelmsford's Cathedral of St Mary, St Peter and St Cedd is the second smallest in Britain but it serves one of the biggest dioceses in the country, taking in the whole of Essex and five London boroughs. Much of the building is fifteenth century and replaced an earlier one that has been dated to the eleventh century. It became a cathedral in 1914.

The cathedral has strong links with America, which goes back to the time of the Pilgrim Fathers. Thomas Hooker was the priest of the then parish church of St Mary's, but he held Puritan views and was being persecuted for them. Things came to a head but he refused to change his views and instead retired to Little Baddow. The harassment continued and so he decided to sail to Holland, which was more liberal. After a while he decided to emigrate to America, where he helped to found the state of Connecticut. To commemorate this fact a blue

Chelmsford Cathedral, 1903. (Copyright Chelmsford Cathedral)

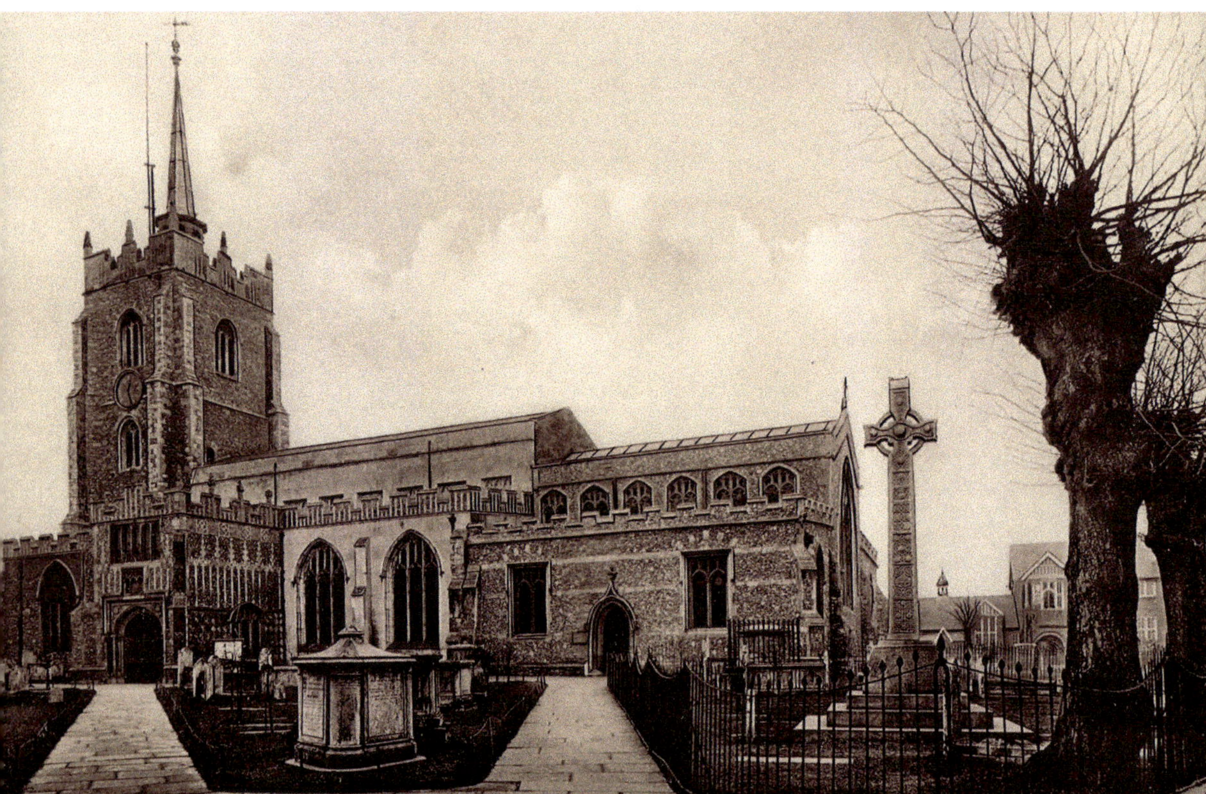

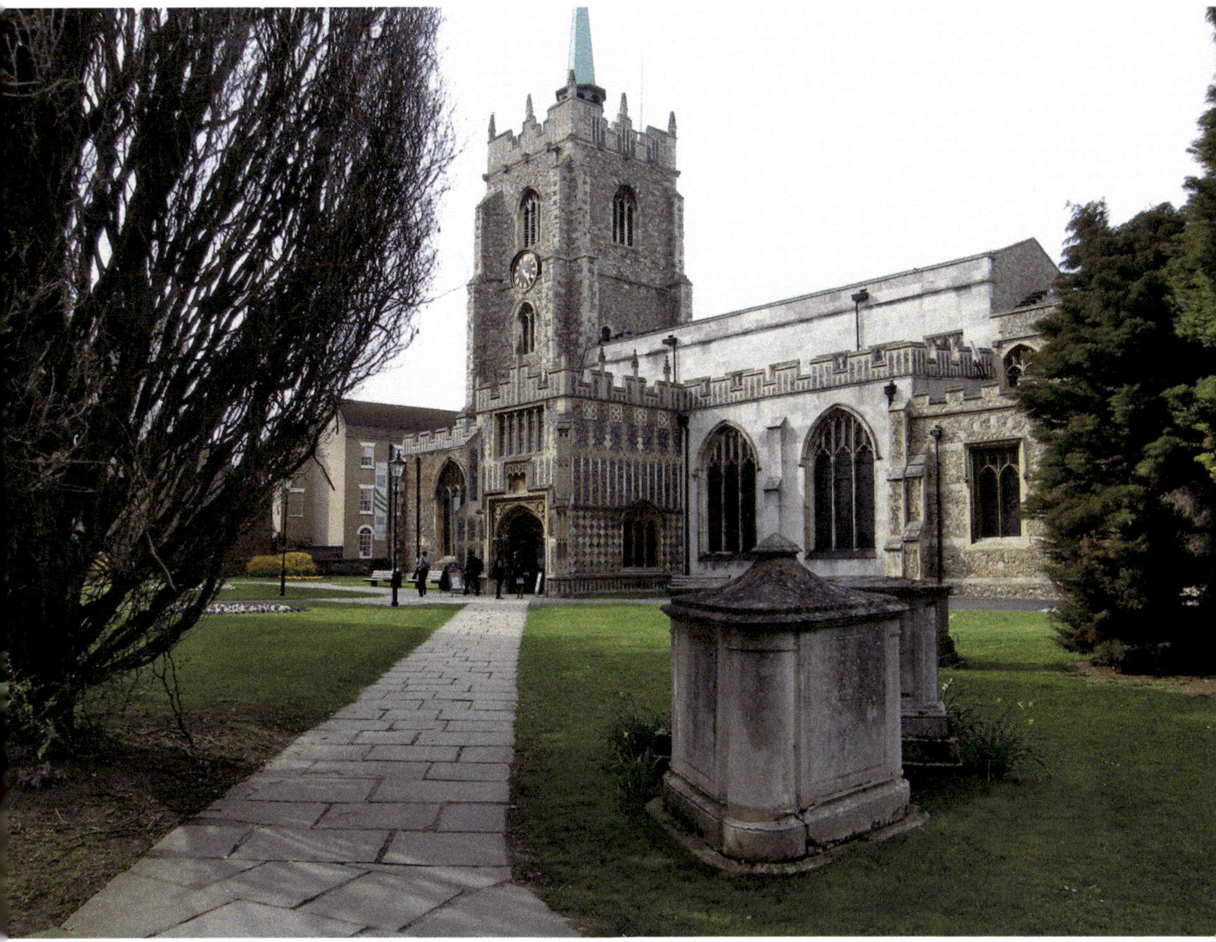

Chelmsford Cathedral, 2020.

plaque is fixed to the wall in the narrow alley opposite the south porch of the cathedral.

During the Second World War many of the airfields in Essex were manned by American airmen and many of these brave men gave their lives bombing Germany. To commemorate their sacrifice, a window was installed with the Stars and Stripes of America, the arms of their air force and of George Washington. The cathedral has many interesting features and is well worth a visit.

As night fell on 17 January 1800, some grave diggers had just finished excavating a grave near one of the pillars in the church which held up the roof and no doubt after a hard day's work they went into one of the local inns to slake their thirst. Suddenly, there was a tremendous crash and everybody rushed out to see a cloud of dust hanging in the air above the church. People wondered what had happened and gradually, as the dust cleared, they saw that the roof of the church had collapsed, because, unknowingly, the workmen had weakened the roof supports.

10. St Mary's Church, Great Baddow

One of the most picturesque churches in the Chelmsford area is St Mary's in Great Baddow. It stands majestically on a slight hill overlooking the White Horse public house in the High Road. It is understood that there was a church on the site before 1172 and that the Earl of Gloucester's daughter, Maud, had dealings in the building of the new church.

The Norman church originally had a nave and chancel and gradually, over the next 300 years, north and south aisles were added, as was the imposing tower and spire. It is thought that the De Badewe family probably financed many of the alterations, as they were one of the biggest landowners in the area. During the sixteenth century the roof decayed and had to be replaced and at the same time, two windows were added to improve the light. The north door was also blocked up to prevent the Devil returning, after he had been exorcised.

During the Peasants' Revolt of 1381, some of the men from Essex assembled in the churchyard and surrounding area while others met in Fobbing before marching on London. There were a number of reasons for the revolt but two of the main ones were that peasants were tied to the land under the feudal system and could not change jobs, although this had slightly improved since the Black Death of 1348, which had caused the deaths of 30–40 per cent of the population and therefore there was a shortage of labour. The other problem was the taxes imposed by Richard II to fight the war in France. It was the third tax in four years and it

St Mary's Church, Great Baddow, 1900.

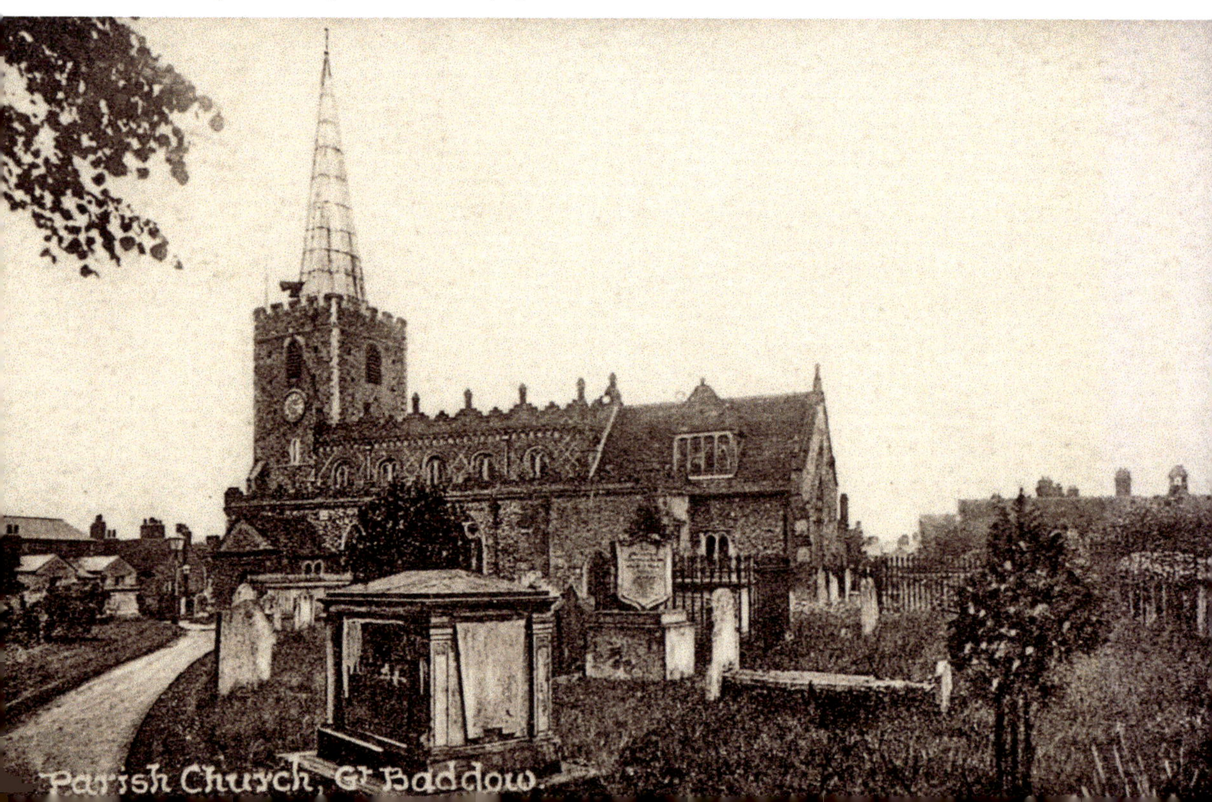

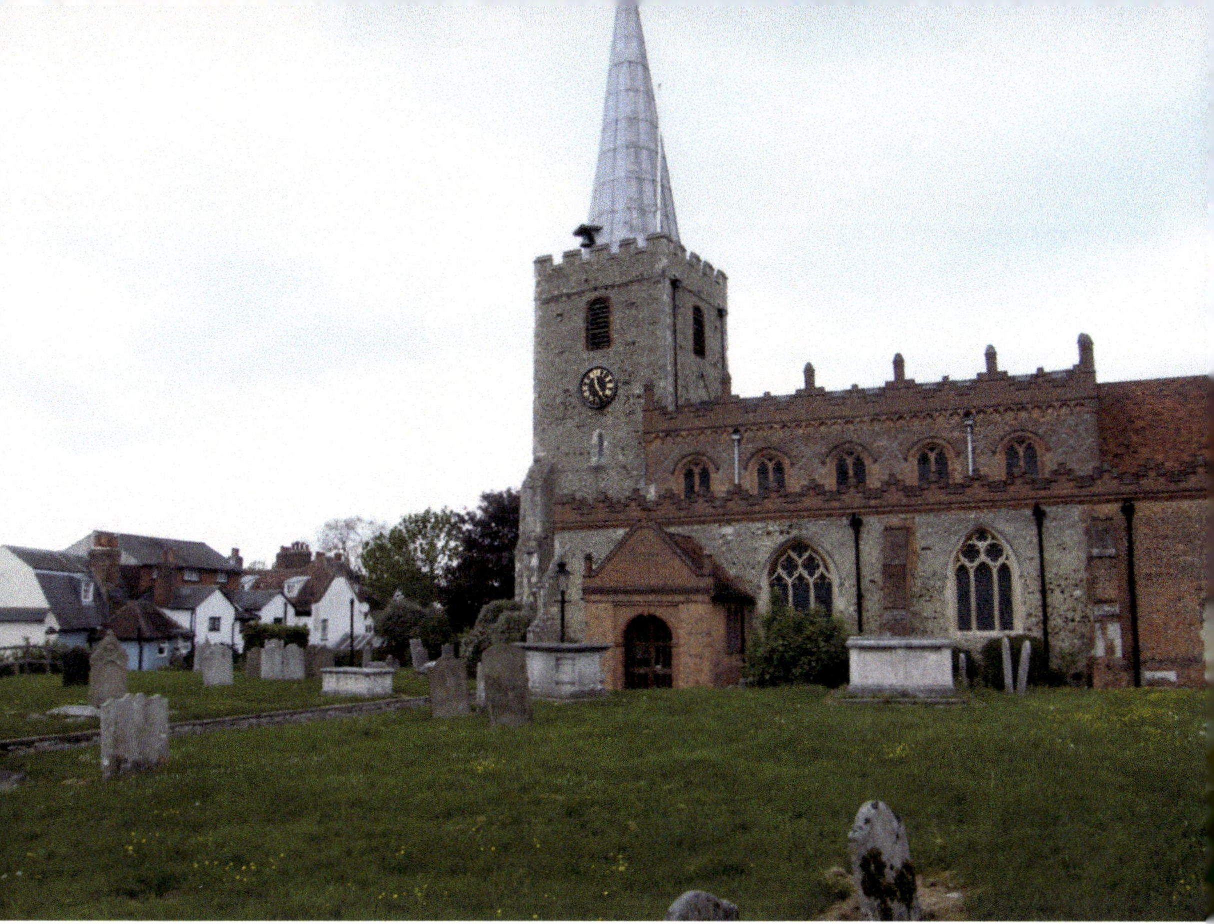

St Mary's Church, 2013.

amounted to one shilling, which many could not afford. When the royal official, John Bampton, rode into Essex to collect the money he was unceremoniously thrown out and the army received the same treatment when they were sent in.

The rebels, led by Wat Tyler, marched on London from Kent and a contingency set off from Essex via Chelmsford. On the way they broke into any government buildings they found and burnt the tax records. Bravely, the fourteen-year-old King Richard II rode out to meet the 60,000-strong crowd at Mile End on 14 June 1381 after the rebels had caused havoc in London. While the meeting was going on some of the rebels broke into the Tower of London, killing the Lord Chancellor and the Lord Treasurer, who they blamed for the tax. Richard agreed to meet some of the rebels' demands, just to get them out of the city. At that point some started for home but a substantial number stayed behind, wrecking property and getting drunk. The king agreed to meet them again the next day at Smithfield. The Lord Mayor became angry with Wat Tyler for the disrespectful way he was speaking to the king and slashed the rebel's throat – a wound that eventually killed him. The king made more promises he knew he could not keep and when the rebels left he went back on his word and hunted them down, executing many in Norsey Wood in Billericay.

No church would be complete without its ghosts and St Mary's is no exception. A ghostly monk appears and it has been claimed that he walks slowly between the pews and leaves by the west door. My favourite ghost story is that somebody said they saw a squad of Civil War soldiers parading outside the church.

11. West Hanningfield

For six centuries the timber tower has stood against the west wall of the south aisle of St Mary and St Edward Church in West Hanningfield. Historic England dated the tower somewhere between 1383 and 1395. The tower was built in the form of a cruciform. The church has a square bell tower with an octagonal spire and four bells that were cast in 1676. These hang on a frame with the name, Mary Gray, inscribed on it. At one time the belfry was constructed of wattle and daub. It is now weather-boarded.

As one approaches the beautiful arched porch, which was constructed during the fifteenth century, you are confronted by a massive oak door which is understood to be original. The nave is twelfth century and shows evidence of a Norman window. The outside of the north wall is built with Roman tiles, flint and rubble.

The Lady Chapel, it is believed, was built around 1330. Although the windows look as if they have modern frames, the rest are fourteenth century, when there

St Mary's and St Edward's, West Hanningfield.

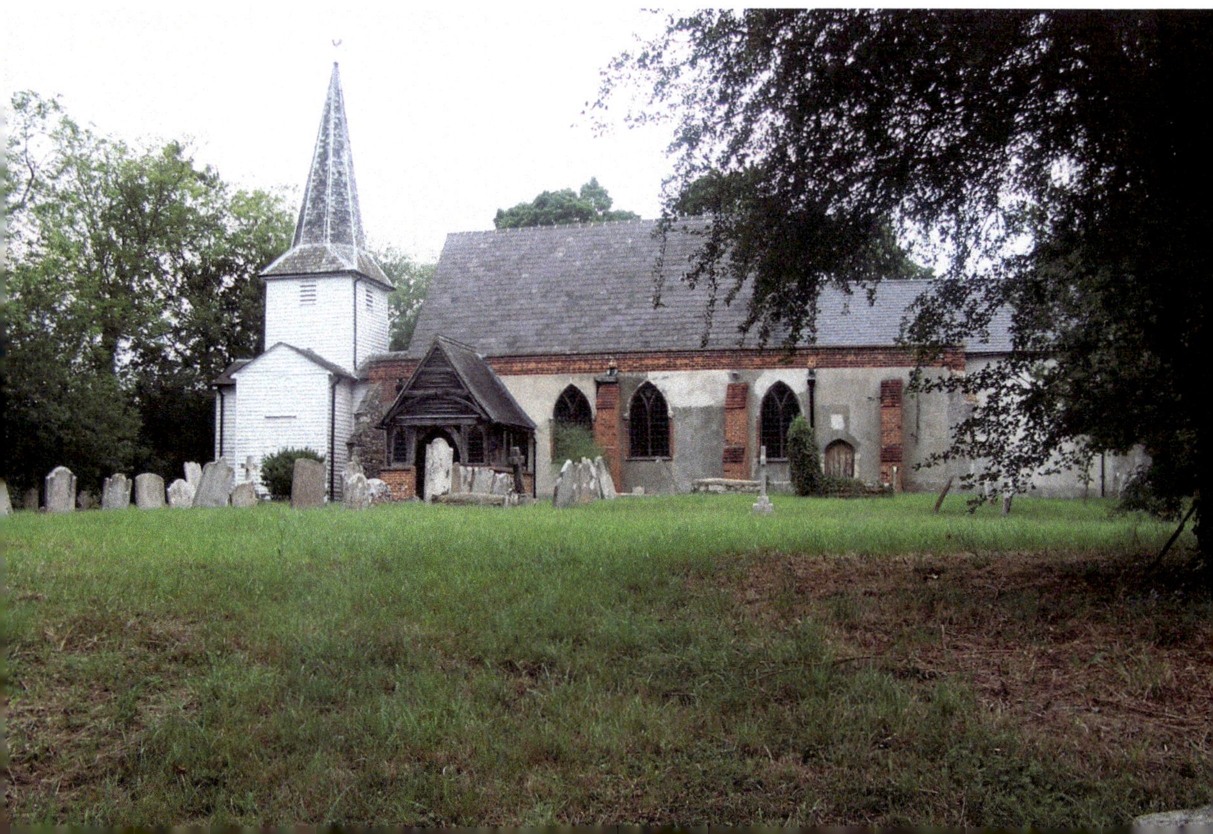

were a number of alterations to the church which were financed by the Clovilles, who were lords of the manor at that time.

One of the unique items in the church is the parish chest, which is 8 feet long and is the longest in the country. It is iron bound and has drop handles and a money slot. It is thought that it was constructed in the late thirteenth century. Like most churches it has an organ, which was installed in 1857 and was pumped by hand until an electric blower was installed. I can well remember, as a child, pumping the organ in Rawreth Church. It was hard work.

The church has many other features and is well worth a visit.

12. Chelmsford Museum

Chelmsford Museum is in Oaklands Park, off Moulsham Street. It is difficult to believe that the museum was started in 1835 by the Chelmsford Philosophical Society in the Governor's front room in the jail near the Stone Bridge. The Governor of the prison, Mr C. Neal, was a leading member of the society. By 1843 the exhibits of the museum had filled his parlour and no doubt, with a gentle nudge from his wife, the society moved the collection to a building in Museum Terrace and then to its present position in Oaklands House. The house is believed to have been called Oaklands because there was a great oak tree in the grounds,

Oaklands House, 1900.

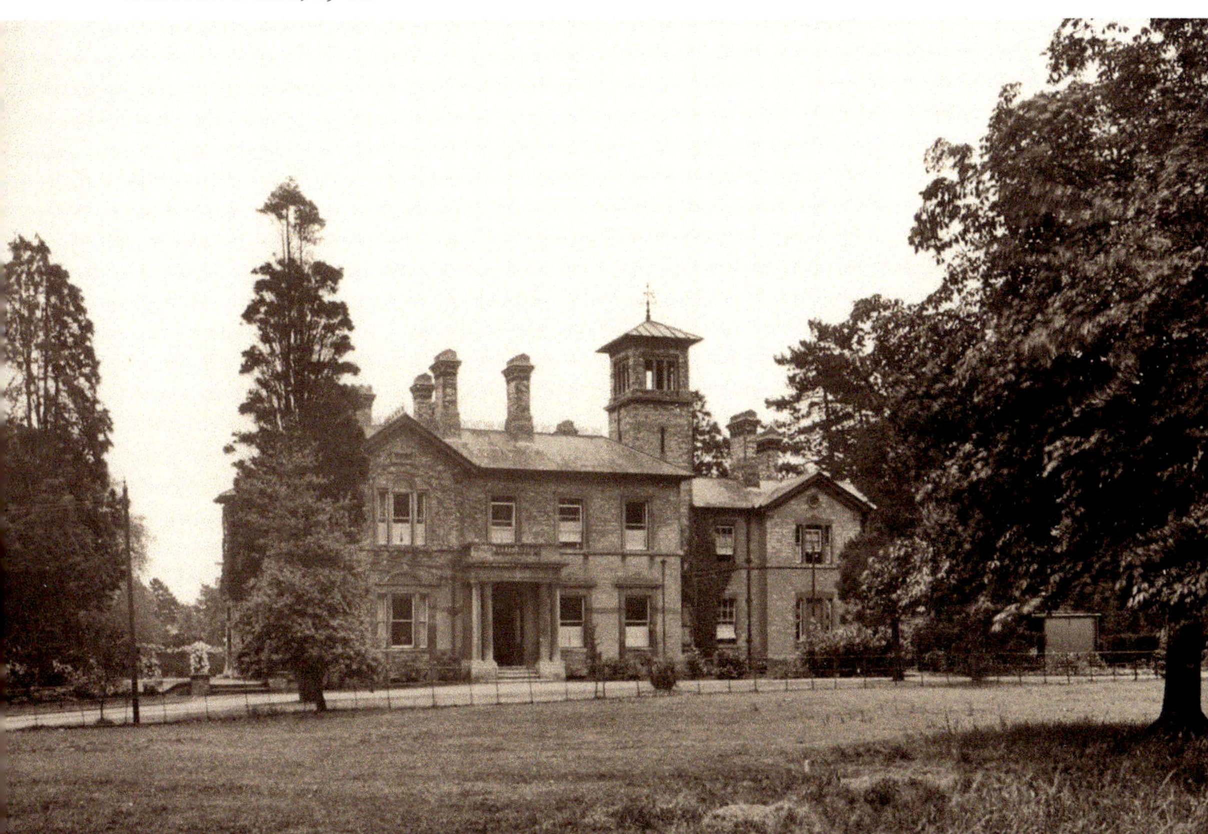

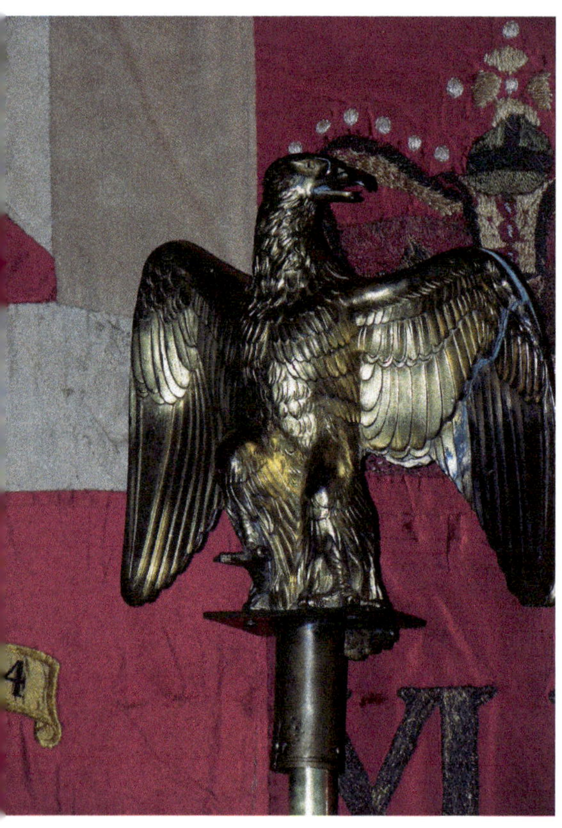

Left: French Eagle. (Courtesy of Chelmsford Museum)

Below: Chelmsford Museum, 2020.

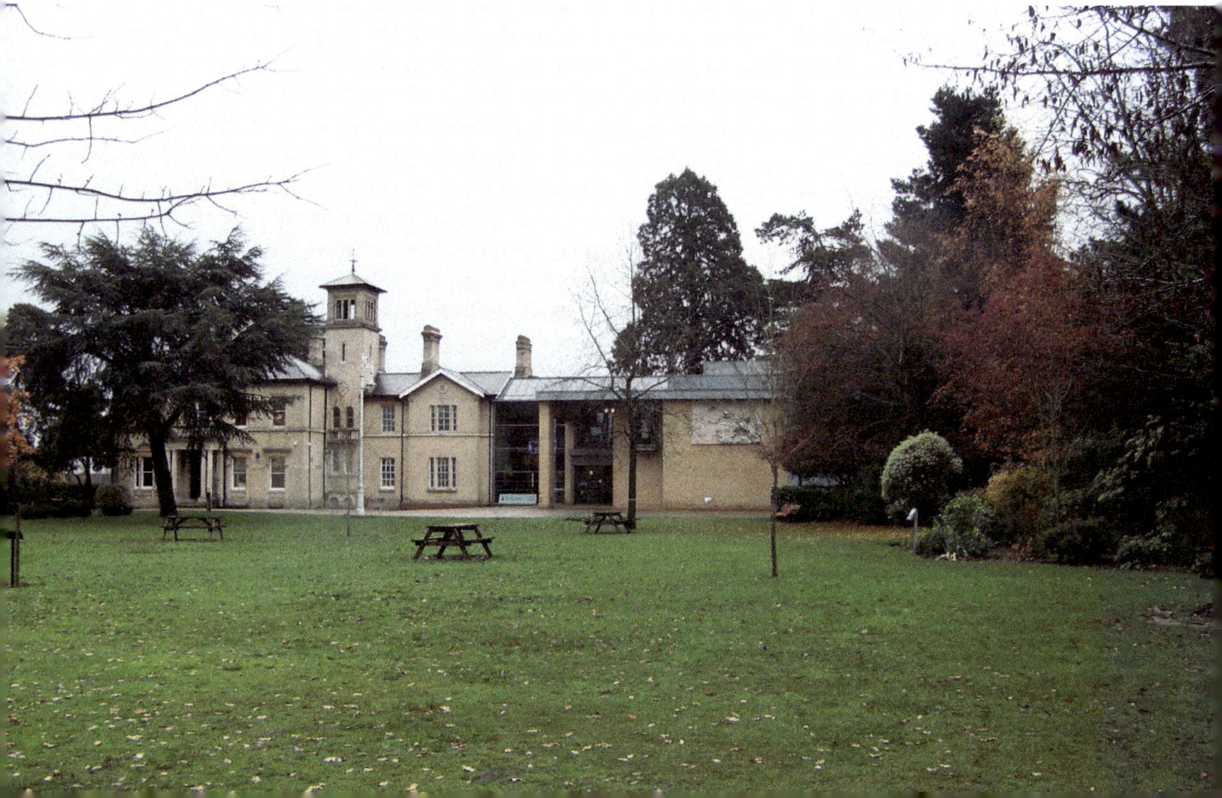

which had stood there for hundreds of years until the great storm of 1987 struck it down.

The original owner of Oaklands House was the Abbot of Westminster. In 1866 Alderman Frederick Wells bought it to accommodate his growing family. Alderman Wells appears to have been a very wealthy man, owning two businesses, a brewery and a coal merchants.

The house was purchased by the council in 1930 and they moved the museum in to it. Over the years the collection has been added to and then, in 1973, the Essex Regiment Museum moved its treasurers in. This new part of the museum was opened by the Duke of Gloucester and follows the history of the Essex Regiments, including one of its prized possessions, a French Eagle, which was captured at the Battle of Salamanca by Lt Pearce of the 44th Regiment during the wars with Napoleon in 1812. There were two Eagles captured at the battle, but one was snatched from the body of a Frenchman, who died clutching the flag, and therefore the deed did not receive the same accolade as that of the one captured by Lt Pearce. A Frenchman thrust his bayonet at him but just in time, Private Murray shot the enemy dead. Outside, in the grounds, stands a cannon which was captured at the Battle of Sevastopol during the Crimean War (1853–56). A number of them were captured and given to various towns and cities. Chelmsford's was first sited in front of Shire Hall but one night a group of youths fired it – but fortunately did not load it. Had they done so, the Saracen's Head public house opposite might not be with us today.

13. Cuckoo Farm

Cuckoo Farm in Church Road, Little Baddow, is a beautiful building believed to have been constructed during the reign of Elizabeth I, but who would think to associate the farm with the Fundamental Orders of Connecticut, which became the basis of America's democracy today.

Thomas Hooker lived on the farm after falling foul of the established church because of his religious views. He was a great orator and, in 1625, was invited to preach in St Mary's (now the cathedral), and people flocked to hear him. At that time Chelmsford was noted for its large number of inns and public houses and for its riotous living. Soon, he was made a curate, and for three years preached his doctrine to the congregation, but his views were controversial and were brought to the attention of the Bishop of Canterbury, who disagreed with what he was preaching and forced him out. He went to live in Cuckoo Farm, but the High Court Commissioners summoned him to appear before them. He refused to go and fled to Holland, where views were more liberal. Finally, he decided to start a new life in Newtown, America.

There he became a pastor, but soon fell out with the leaders of the church because only their members were allowed to vote in elections. In 1636 he and a friend, the

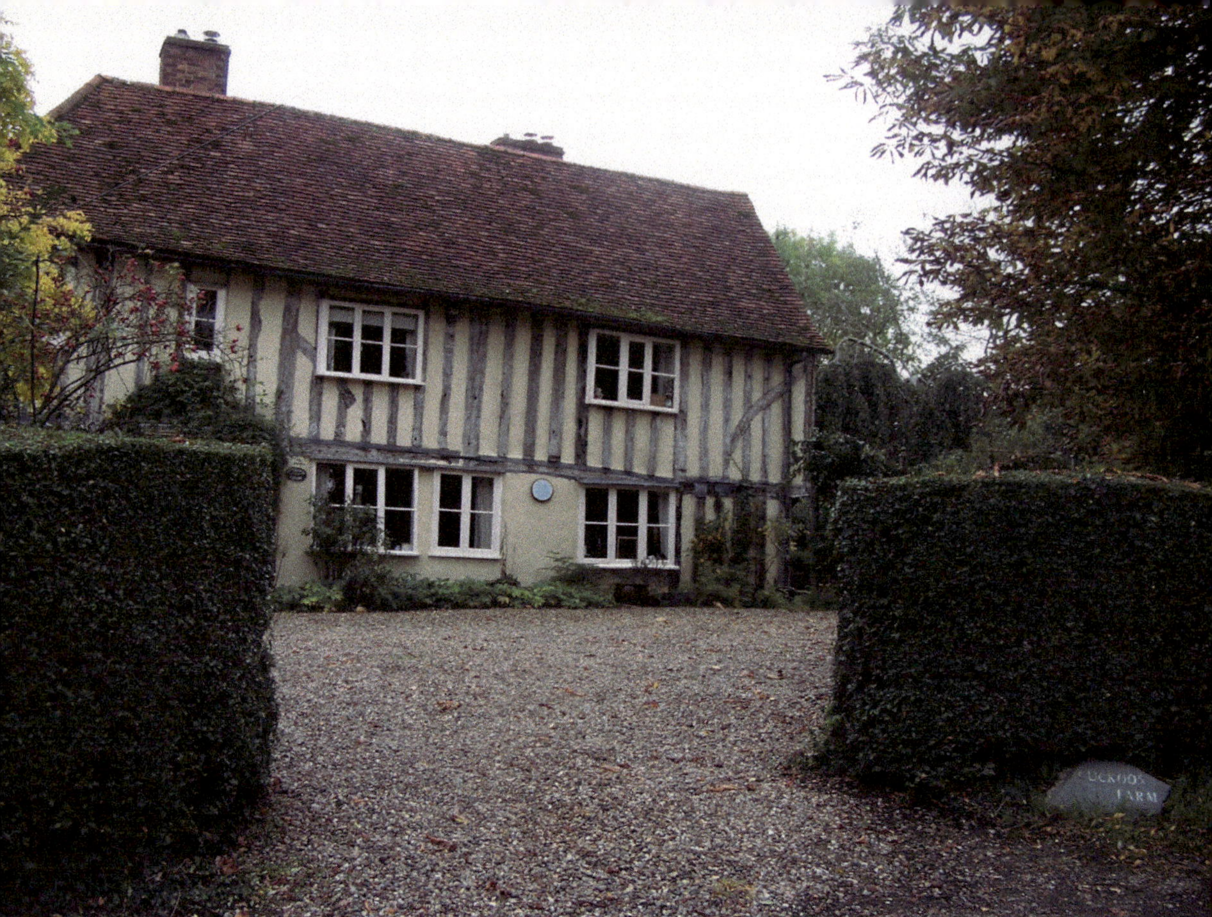

Cuckoo Farm.

Revd Stone, decided to make the trek to Hartford with 100 of their followers. It was here that he became a politician and was elected to represent Hartford and Windsor. He and Stone drew up a constitution for Connecticut, which became the basis of the American one. In 1647, at the age of sixty-one, he died, but no one knows where his grave is, nor does anyone know how he looked like.

14. Hylands House

It is worth taking an afternoon stroll through Hylands House's wonderful gardens or, if it rains, nip into the house and explore its secrets. The house was built in the Queen Anne style and was constructed around 1730 by Sir John Comyns and his nephew John Richard Comyns. Sir John was a well-known member of Lincoln's Inn and also the Member of Parliament for Maldon. He was appointed Baron of the Exchequer and was knighted in 1738. When he died in 1740 he had no children, so he left everything to John Richard Comyns.

In 1797 Cornelius Kortright, who was in the sugar trade, bought the house for £14,500 and immediately set about redesigning the gardens. He also planned to extend the house but never got round to it. His enjoyment of the estate was spoilt by the threat of an invasion by Napoleon. It was thought the French army would land at Harwich and march on London, passing through Chelmsford on the way. The country was in a panic and gun emplacements and earthworks were thrown up everywhere, including on the Hylands Estate. When Pierre Cesar Labouchere bought the house in 1814 he set about fulfilling the previous owner's dreams, but he had not taken into account the building of the railway, with its hundreds of navvies laying the tracks. He was so incensed that he sued the railway company and, after many civil actions in the courts, nearly bankrupted them. When he died, his son took it over and sold it to John Attwood, an ambitious man who was MP for Harwich. He had the house enlarged and added more land to the estate.

The next owner was Arthur Pryor, who was in the brewery business but he hardly touched the house during the forty-six years he owned it. Then, in 1905, the house was let to a Sir Daniel Gooch, who purchased it in 1907 and modernised it by installing electricity and telephones. He and his wife were renowned for entertaining and he loved exploring and went with Sir Ernest Shackleton to the South Pole but had to come home because of frostbite.

During the First World War the property was requisitioned by the government and turned into a military hospital, treating hundreds of servicemen. Sir Daniel ensured that the hospital wanted for nothing and bought many extras out of his own pocket.

In 1922 Mr and Mrs John Hanbury took over ownership of the estate but unfortunately, Mr Hanbury died a year later and his wife, Christine, inherited

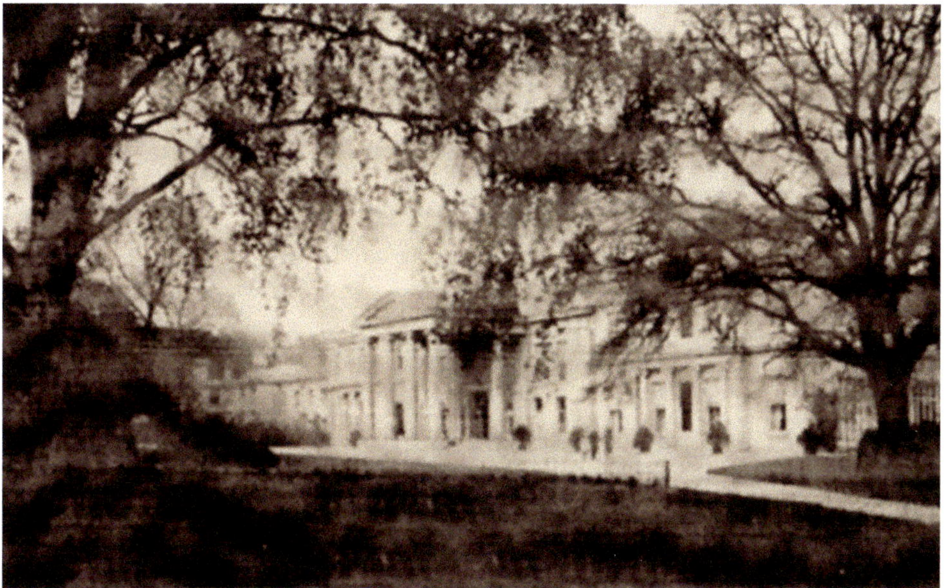

Hylands House, 1900. (Copyright Hylands House)

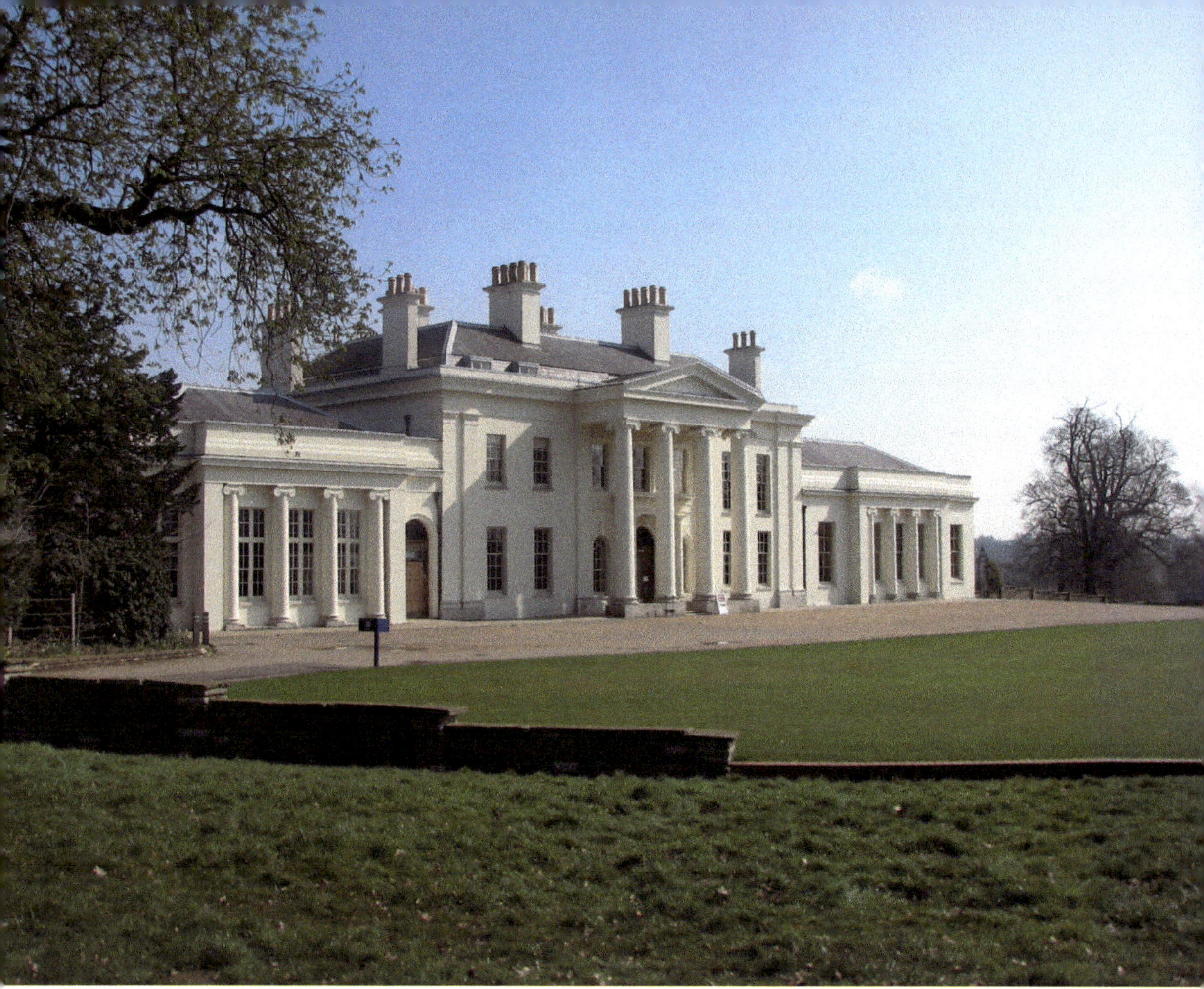

Hylands House, 2003.

the property. When the Second World War started in 1939, her son Jock was one of the first pilots to be killed and in the memory of both her husband and son, she created a private garden. During the war the estate was used as a prisoner of war camp and then, in 1944, the SAS took over the house and made it their headquarters, while Mrs Hanbury was still living in it. It is reported that one night, while the SAS were having a heavy drinking session, for a bet, Captain Paddy Blair Maine, the most decorated soldier in the Second World War, drove his jeep up the main staircase. Mrs Hanbury came out to see what the noise was and could not believe her eyes when she saw the jeep blocking the stairs. Staring at Paddy she remarked, 'Sir, I believe you have taken a wrong turning.' The SAS had to dismantle the jeep to get it down.

When the war ended in 1945, the unit was ordered to leave, but the problem was that they had more weapons than they had signed for. There was only one way out if they were not going to get into serious trouble: bury them in the garden. For years after the gardeners kept digging them up. Lady Christine Hanbury died in 1962 and the council took over the house in 1966.

15. Coval Hall

In 1701 the Marriage family lived in Coval Hall, Rainsford Road. They were Quakers and millers and two of them, Samuel and William Marriage, became trustees of the Quakers.

During the eighteenth century the famous Tindal family took over the property and most of the descendants made names for themselves in different fields. John Tindal became a rector in Chelmsford, James had an army career and one of his sons became a chaplain of the Tower of London – but unfortunately committed suicide.

The most famous of all was Judge Tindal, whose statue stands in Tindal Square today. He was born in 1776 in a building that was subsequently demolished and now houses Lloyds Bank at 199 Moulsham Street and has a blue plaque stating that Judge Tindal was born there. He was part of the defence team of Queen Caroline of Brunswick, who was charged with treason by her husband, George IV, for committing adultery with her Italian servant, Bartolomeo. The trial took place in 1820 in the House of Lords. One of her servants gave evidence against her and said she had seen Bartolomeo in the arms of the Queen and that one day she saw them bathing together. The defence maintained that the King wanted to get

Coval Hall.

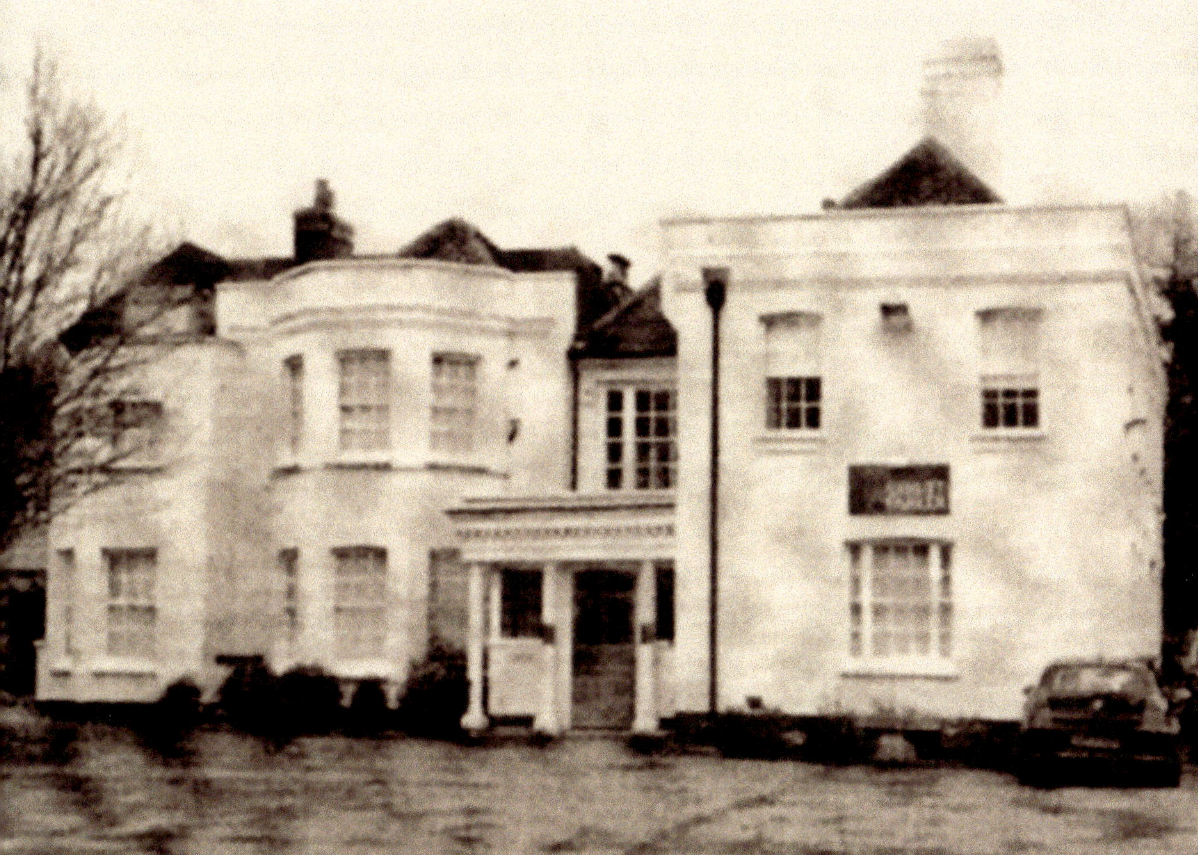

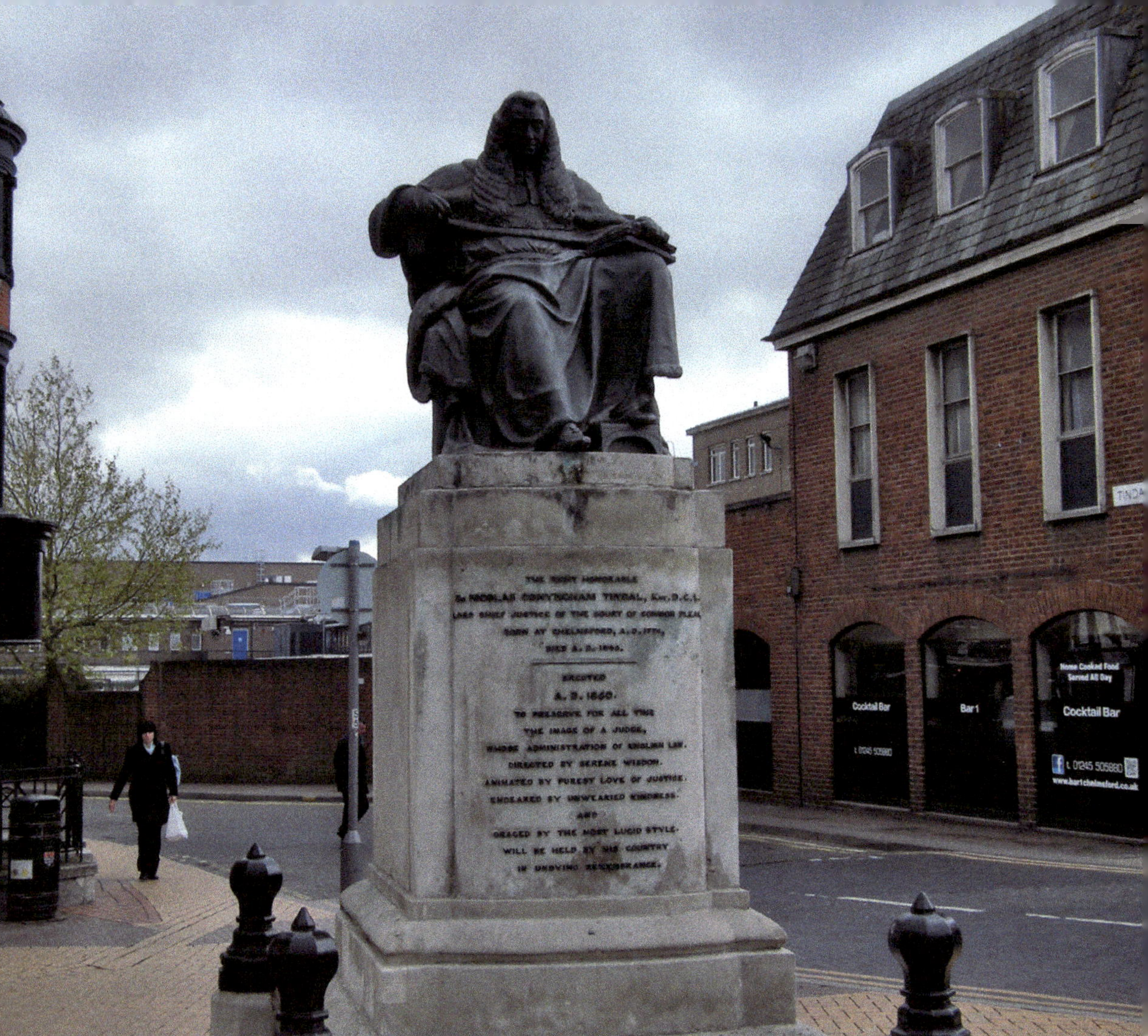

Statue of Judge Tindal.

rid of his wife so that he could marry his mistress. The Queen was very popular and every day crowds gathered outside the court. She was found not guilty and the crowds went wild and rioted, smashing windows of government buildings and hooting their approval.

Judge Tindal was involved with having the ancient law of trial by combat repealed when he defended Abraham Thornton for the murder of Mary Ashford. Apparently, the couple met at a dance and he had walked her part of the way home. Next morning, she was found drowned in a pit and Thornton was charged with her murder. He was found not guilty and Mary Ashford's brother, William, appealed. Thornton challenged him to trial by combat, which was still the law at that time. Ashford refused to fight him and the case was thrown out. In 1819 the ancient Act of Trial by Combat was repealed.

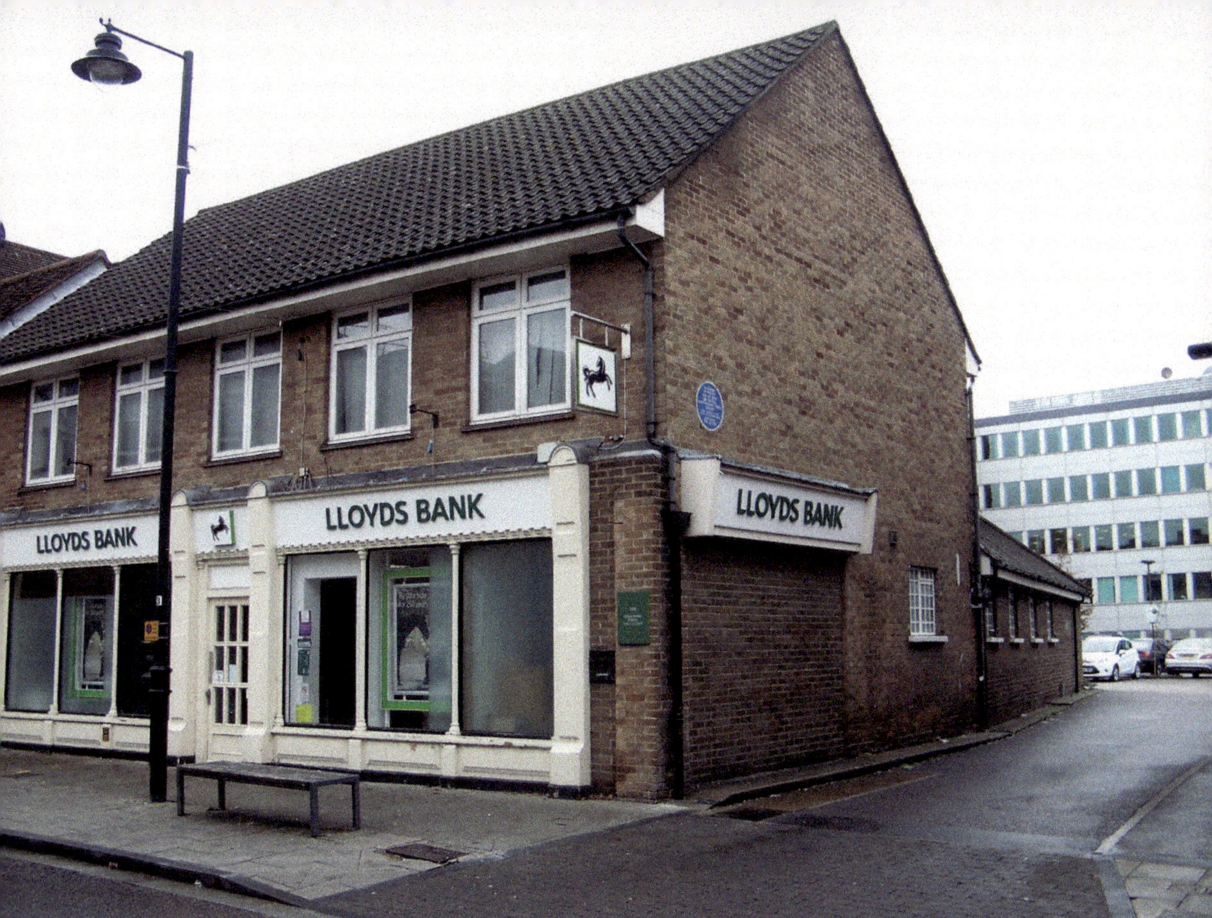

The site where Judge Tindal was born, now Lloyds Bank.

The hall remained in the hands of the Tindal family for three generations and today it is the head office of Strutt and Parker, a firm of estate agents who were established in 1885 by two friends, Edward Strutt and Charles Parker. Today, the firm has grown into one of the largest property partnerships in the United Kingdom.

16. King Edward VI Grammar School, Broomfield Road

The original school was set up in the friary in Moulsham Street by Edward VI in 1551.

It was financed by rents from farms and cottages in the surrounding area. Its objective was to educate boys of Chelmsford and Moulsham in the Anglican religion and classical languages. It was supervised by Sir Walter Mildmay, Sir Tyrrell and Sir William Petre. One of Sir William's descendants was imprisoned in the Tower of London.

For three years, from 1853 to 1856, the school was closed because of a dispute over what was taught. The school wanted to change the curriculum, but in order to do so they needed to ask parliament, which cost money – they could not afford it. They were forced to wait until the Endowed Schools Act of 1869 was passed, which enabled them to introduce modern subjects into the syllabus.

Until 1856, students had to pay something towards their education, as the income from the farms and cottages was insufficient to meet all the costs of running the school and only covered such subjects as classical and religious lessons. Gradually, the farms and cottages were sold, the last being in 1957. The 1944 Education Act abolished fees altogether.

The school moved to its present accommodation in 1892 and has always achieved outstanding results. It is ranked in the top fifty schools in the country in the National Examination League Tables. In 1981, *The Sunday Times* named it as the most successful state school as measured by Oxbridge open awards. The *Financial Times* rated it as the most successful state school at GCE advanced level for the years 1993–98. Further praises have deservedly been heaped upon the school by *The Sunday Times* who, in 2001, named it School of the Year. It came top in 2015 and was named in the Good School Guide, as well as being judged as outstanding by OFSTED. The school had always been a boys' school but, in 1976, the first girl walked through the gates to study Classics.

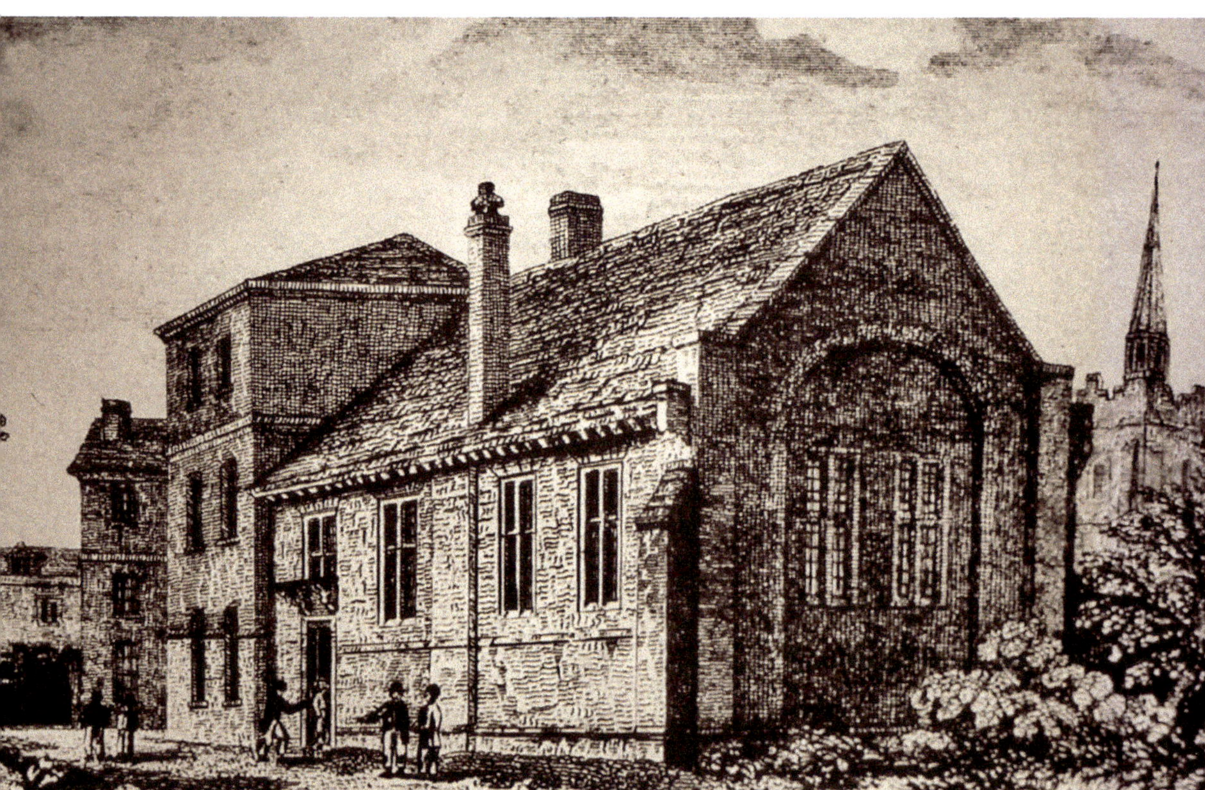

A Drawing of the original school in Moulsham Street, 1627. (Copyright)

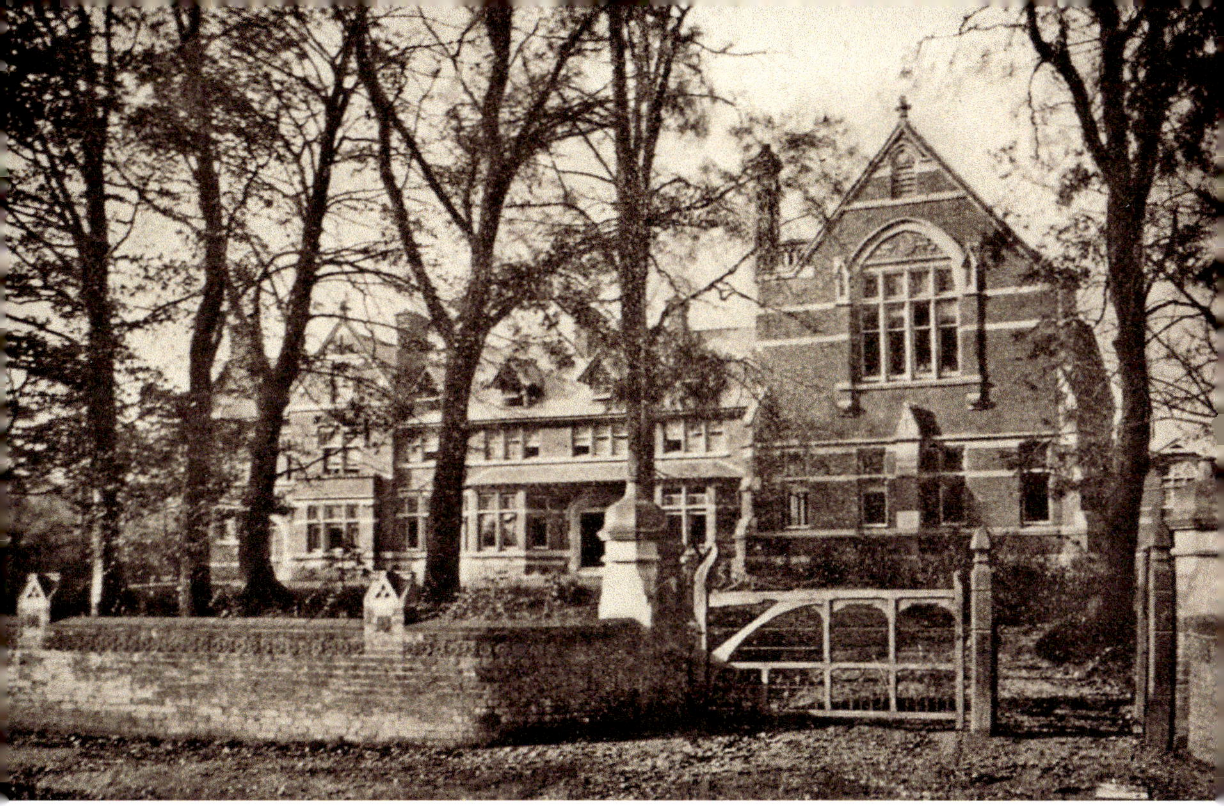

Above: The school in the 1900s. (Copyright KEGS)

Below: The school today.

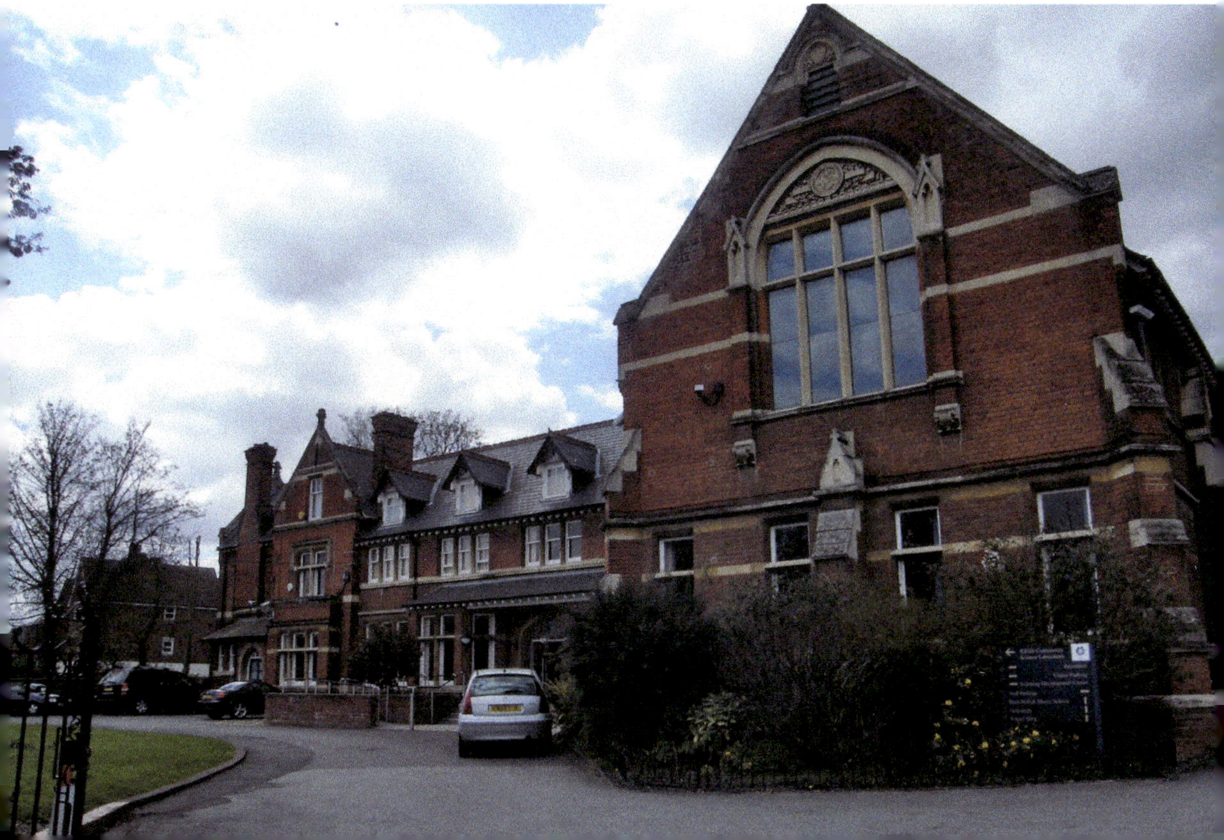

17. Chelmsford Girls' County High School

Chelmsford Girls' County High School in Broomfield Road was built in 1906 and the first seventy-six pupils streamed through the door in 1907. Today, the school has 930 students whose ages range from eleven to eighteen. Within a year the school had its own magazine and had set up an Old Girls' Society. In 1915, it was decided to set up a preparatory department to admit girls as young as eight. This department ran successfully for many years until just after the Second World War, in 1945, it was decided to close it. Competition to gain a place in the school has always been keen and its exam results are among the best in the country.

When the school first opened, public transport was very poor and many of the girls had to travel long distances, and so it was decided in 1910 to rent 39 Broomfield Road and board these students there during the week. Public transport gradually improved and in 1945 it was decided to discontinue this service. In the early days few girls went to university, but in 1916 Winifred Picking obtained a Natural Science degree at Girton College.

During the First World War the school played its part by acting as host to refugee students from Belgium. At that time there were Zeppelin and bomber raids but the school had no shelters and so the pupils were instructed to stay away from all windows and outside walls during raids. Luckily, they never had to carry out the instructions. It was different during the Second World War as the school was bombed a number of times and on one occasion all the windows were blown out, but luckily it was during the school holidays.

Chelmsford Girls' County High School, 1920. (Copyright Essex Record Office)

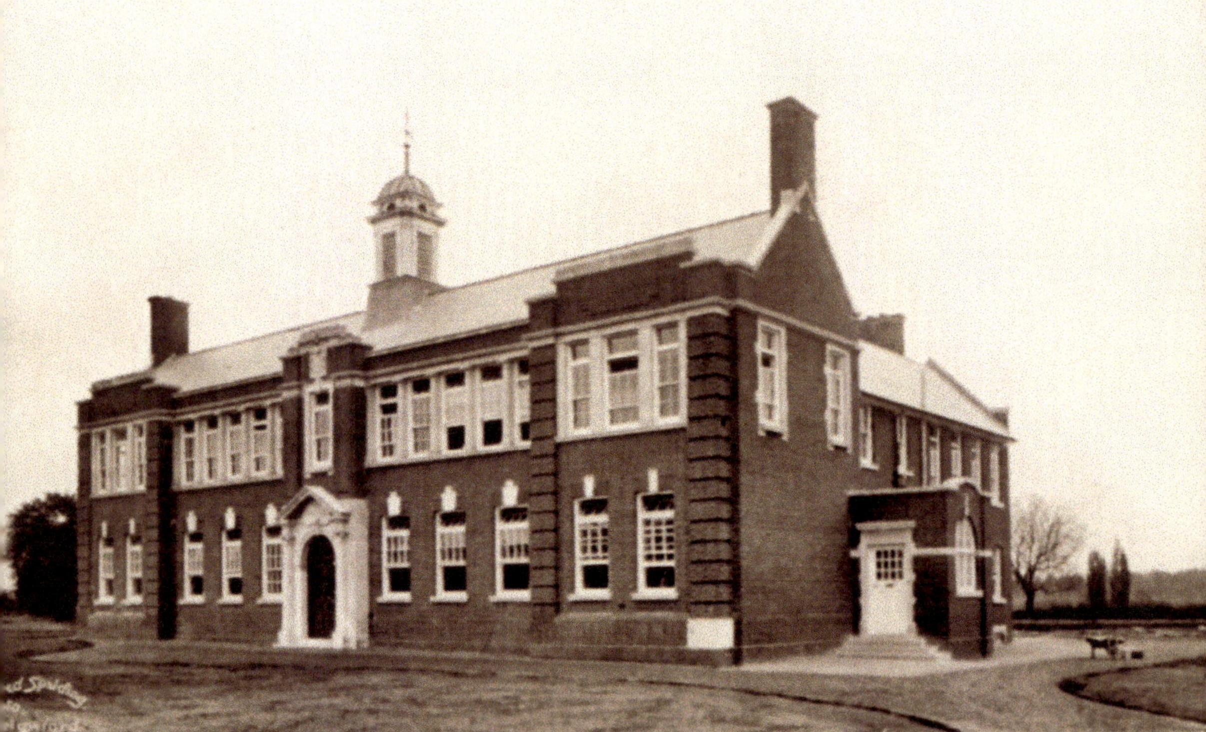

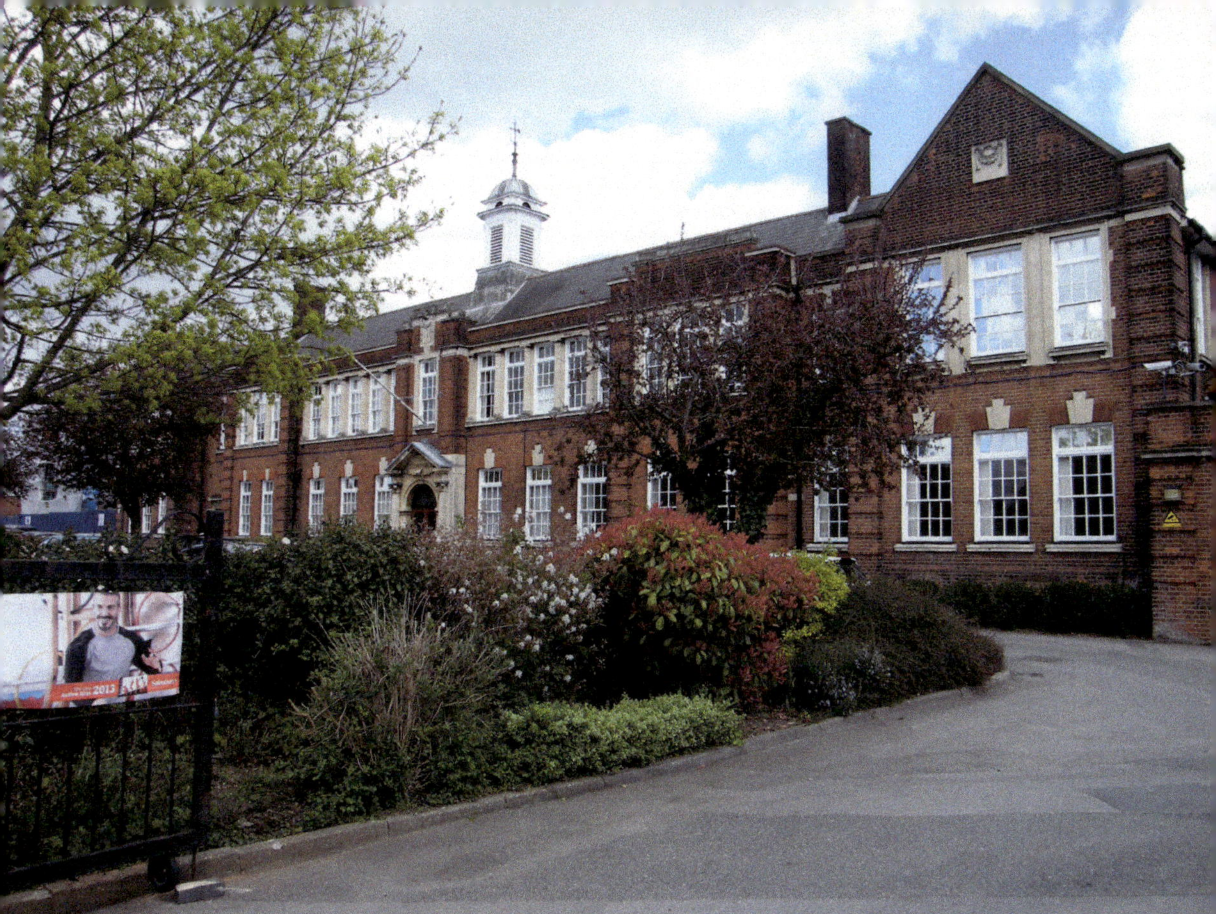

Chelmsford Girls' County High School, 2020.

There have been many changes over the years, one being that male teachers were employed in 1992 and a science block built. The school motto is 'We Carry the Torch of Life', and I am certain the school will flourish into the future.

18. New Hall School

New Hall Co-educational Independent Roman Catholic School is in one of the most beautiful buildings in Chelmsford. The estate on which it was built was granted to the canons of Waltham Abbey as far back as four years before the Battle of Hastings in 1066.

Over the centuries it has changed hands many times. In 1516 Henry VIII bought it and built a palace on it, naming it Beaulieu and in 1527 he held court there. Princess Mary, Henry's daughter by Catherine of Aragon, lived in the palace, but once Henry started divorce proceeding against her mother, he banned her from the palace. He later relented, making her Godmother to his son, Prince Edward.

During Henry's reign, a fire broke out which destroyed part of the palace which had to be rebuilt. When Mary died in 1558, and her half-sister Elizabeth inherited

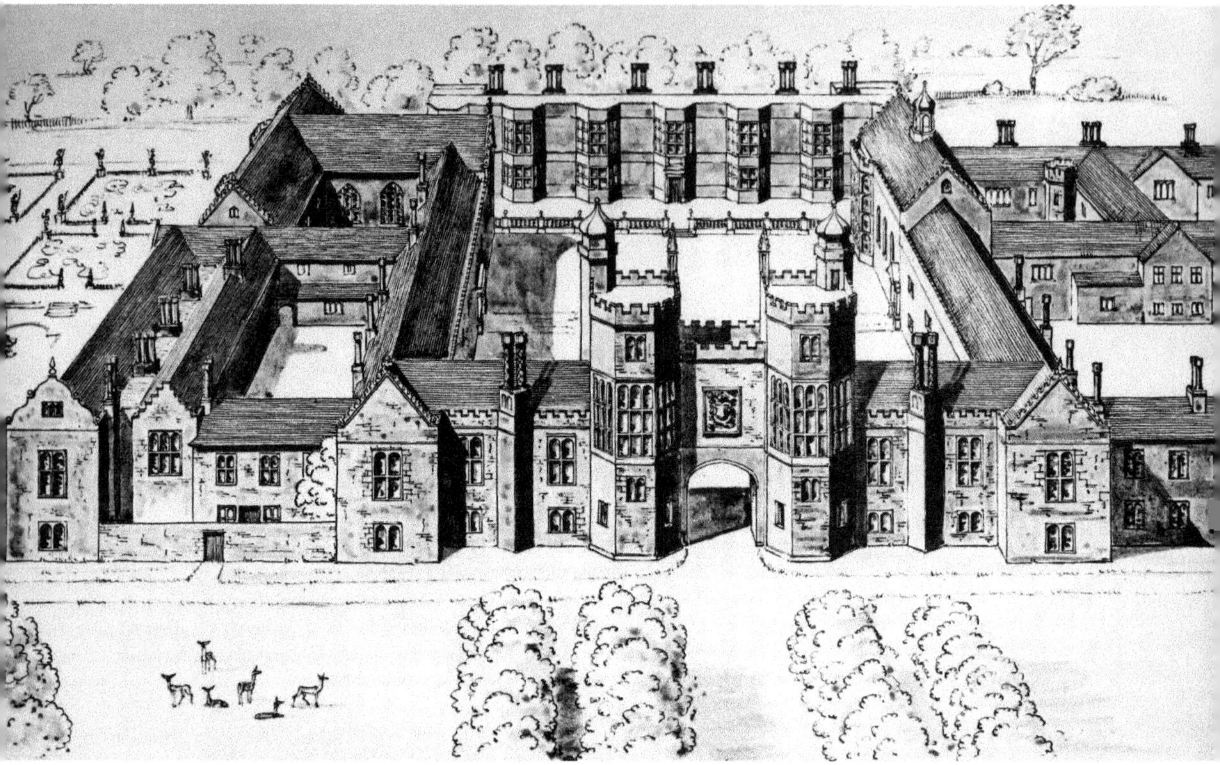

Above: Early drawing of Beaulieu/New Hall School. (Copyright New Hall School)

Below: New Hall School, 1900. (Copyright New Hall School)

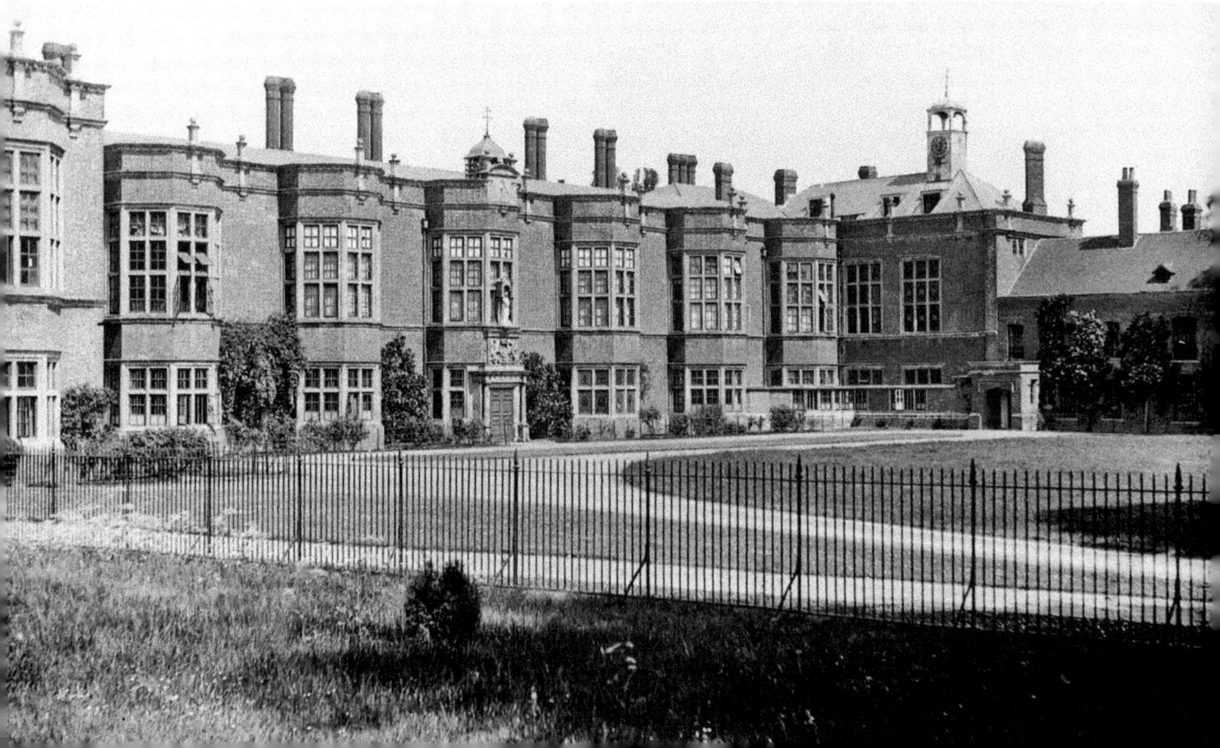

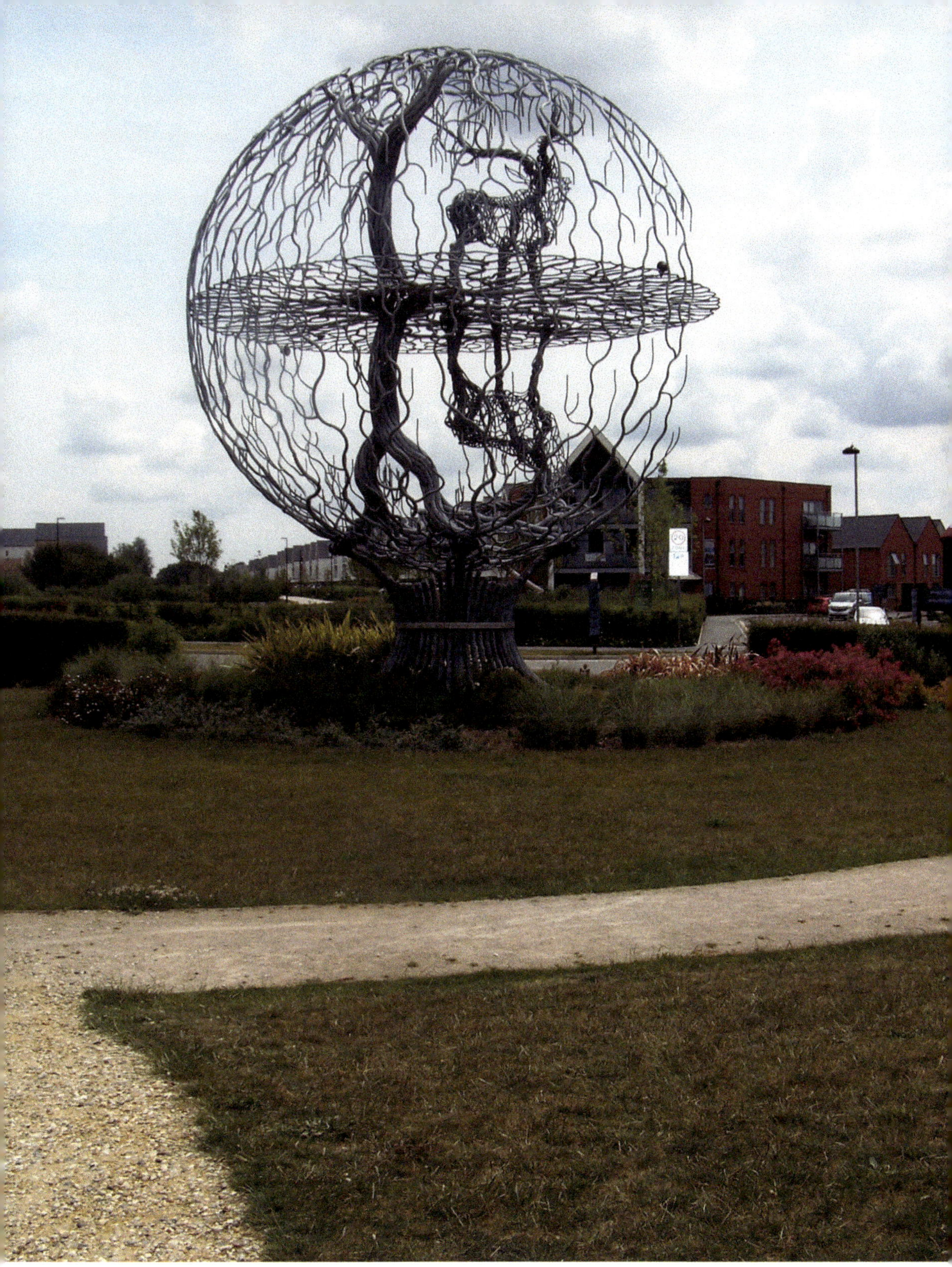

One of the beautiful sculptures.

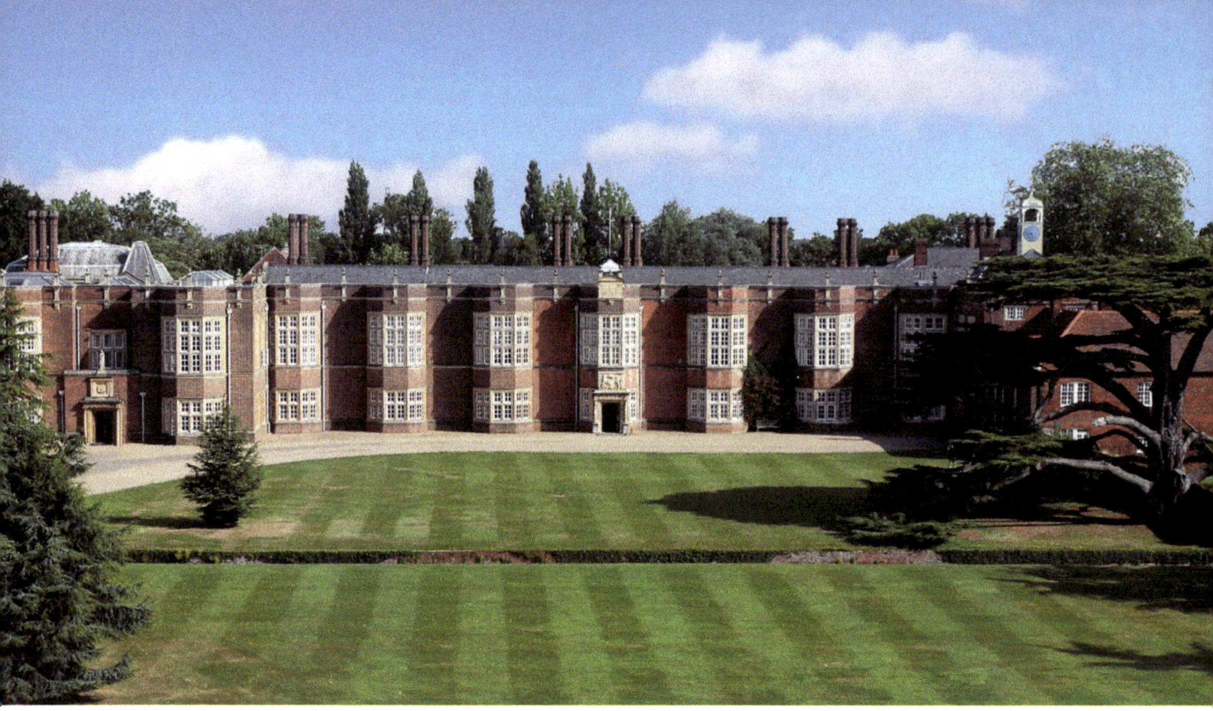

New Hall School, 2020.

the throne, she granted the estate to the 3rd Earl of Sussex, who carried out some building to the north wing and Elizabeth's coat of arms still hangs above the main entrance over the door.

During the Civil War (1642–52), Cromwell bought the estate and when he died, the Duke of Buckingham took it over and Charles II held court there. Unfortunately, the house became neglected and by 1737 parts had to be demolished and rebuilt.

Sixty-two years later, in 1799, the nuns of the Order of the Holy Sepulchre were driven out of Liege in Belgium and emigrated to England, establishing the school, which at first only educated girls but in 2005, admitted boys. Today the school has boarders of both sexes and is the only independent Catholic school in the area, and is one of the largest in the country. It has wonderful facilities such as a swimming pool, a national standard athletics track, football field and covers most sports. Recently some of their land was sold and a large housing development is taking place with many beautiful sculptures.

19. Anglia Ruskin University

The university in Bishop's Hall Lane was built on part of the old Hoffmann's factory and is close to the site of Bishop's Hall Mill, which was owned by the Bishop of London, who also owned the Manor of Chelmsford. He was Bishop for twenty-four years from 1051 to 1075. Bishop's Hall was recorded in the Domesday Book of 1086.

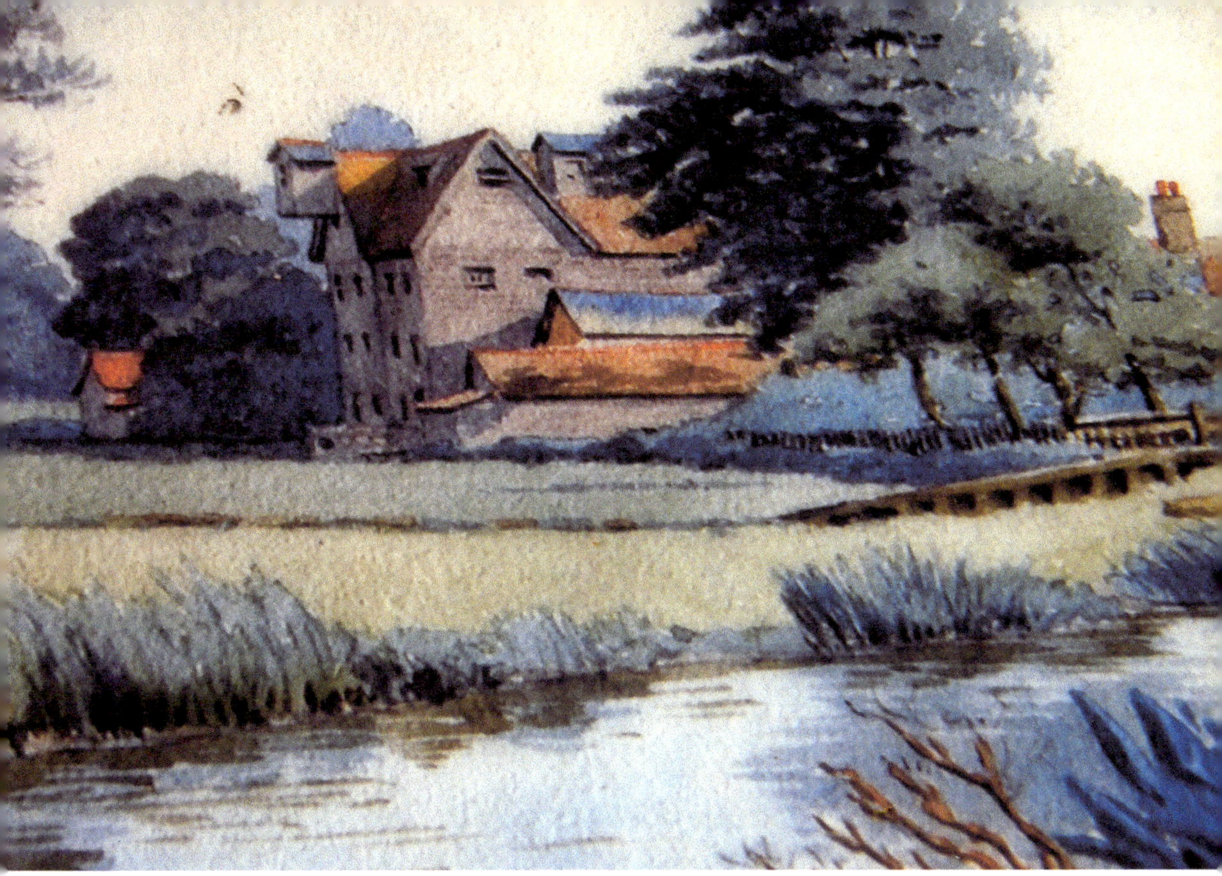

Above: A painting of Mill House. (Copyright Chelmsford City Council)

Below: Anglia Ruskin University, 2013.

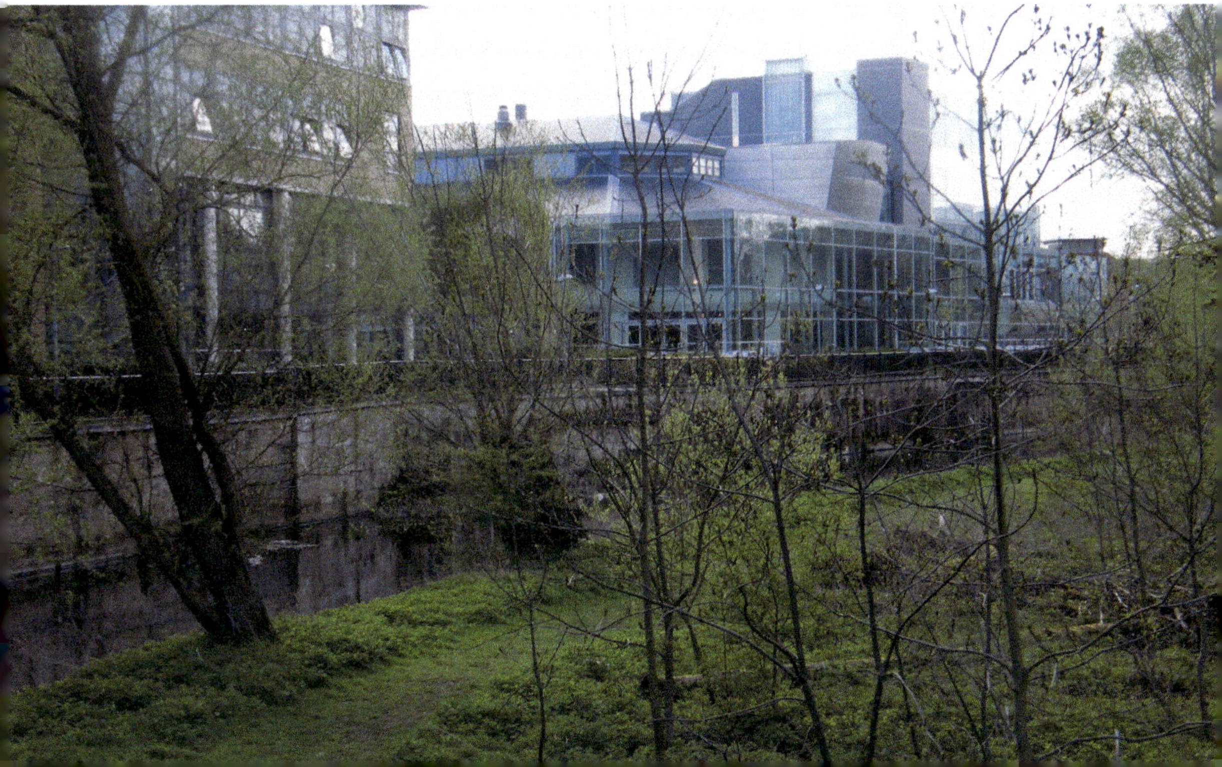

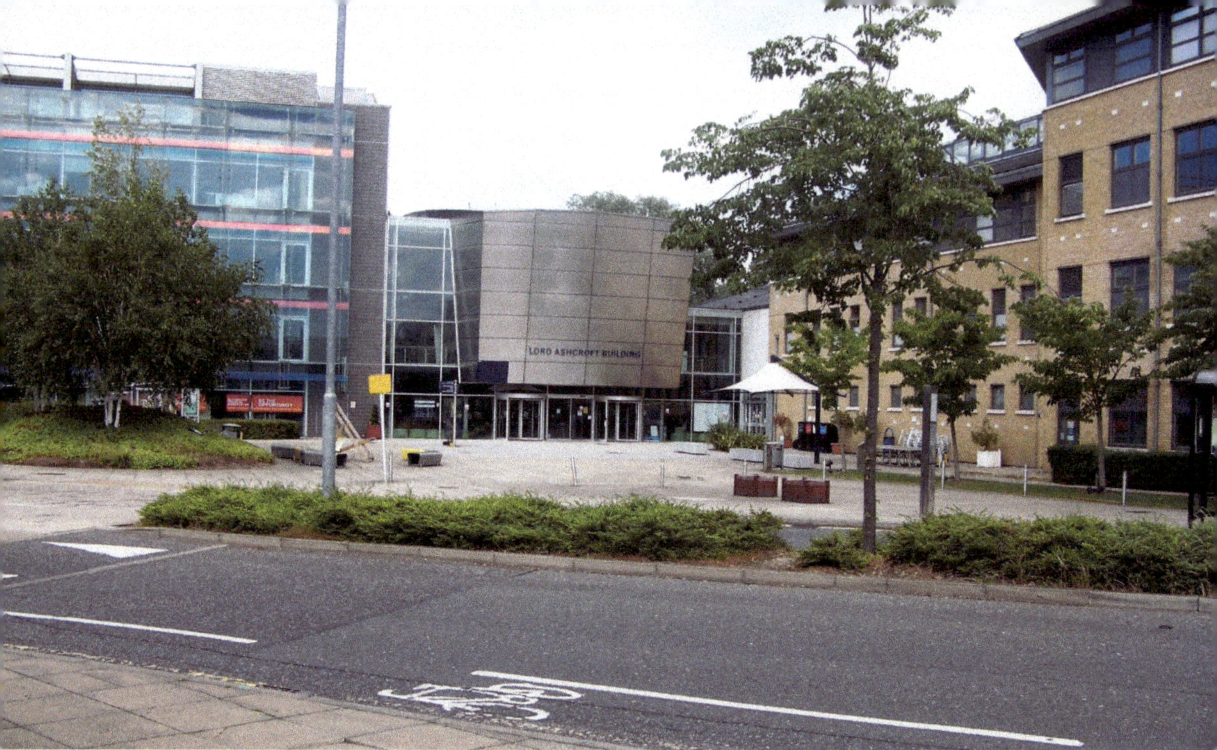

Part of the university, 2020.

Henry VIII acquired the properties during the Dissolution of the Monasteries and when he died, Queen Elizabeth I's auditor, Thomas Mildmay, purchased the Manor of Chelmsford in 1563. Amazingly, it was kept in the family until 1917 when they sold it to Hoffmann's, who built the famous ball bearing factory on it and exported their product all over the world. In 1990 the factory was demolished and the university built on it.

The university originated in Cambridge School of Art. It was set up by William Beamont in 1858 and it became a university in 1992. It changed its name to Ruskin in 2002. It has campuses not only in Chelmsford but in Cambridge, Peterborough and London and together the four campuses have over 39,000 students. Chelmsford runs sixty-nine courses, ranging from accountancy to acute care.

Anne Knight, whose father was a greengrocer and Quaker, lived in the area in 1787. She was instrumental in women's suffrage and published leaflets on the subject and on anti-slavery. She formed the women's branch of the anti-slavery campaign and in recognition of her work she had a village named after her in Jamaica and has had a blue plaque erected in Duke Street.

20. Chelmsford & Essex Hospital

Chelmsford & Essex Hospital in New London Road was originally a dispensary to treat the poor and was set up by local doctors and surgeons in 1818 at their own expense. There was such a demand that in 1870, an infirmary was set up in

Moulsham Street, next to a public house, which proved to be very unsatisfactory. The infirmary had very little room and at one time, when there was an outbreak of cholera, a tent had to be erected in the garden to accommodate the flood of patients.

The demand for the infirmary's services had grown to such an extent that ten years later the committee decided to build a hospital. The Lord Lieutenant of Essex, Thomas Trevor, opened an appeal fund and the money came pouring in. Soon £4,680 had been raised, which was just enough to start building. Frederic Chancellor and Charles Pertwee were responsible for the planning and liaised with Dr James Nicholls and Dr Edward Hunt, to ensure that the hospital had all the facilities that were required to run it efficiently.

The site they chose for the new hospital was in London Road and it was opened by the Countess of Warwick in 1883. Unfortunately, the hospital ran into financial difficulties and had overspent by £1,000 (around £121,089 today). The committee rose to the occasion and arranged fetes, carnivals and concerts and soon raised the much-needed additional money. The hospital was two storeys high and was free for the poor, but it did have two wards for private patients. The ground floor had

Chelmsford & Essex Hospital, 1900s.

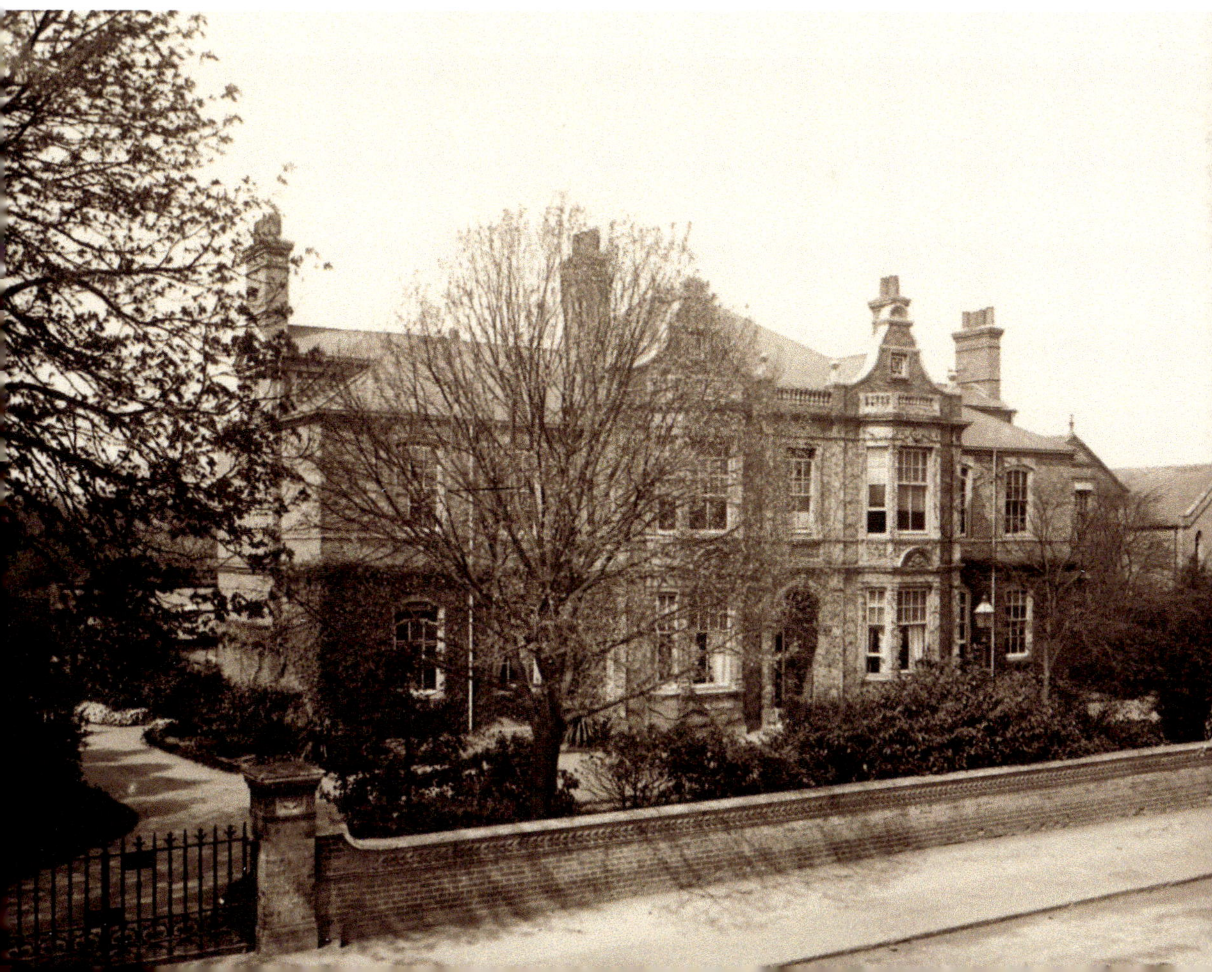

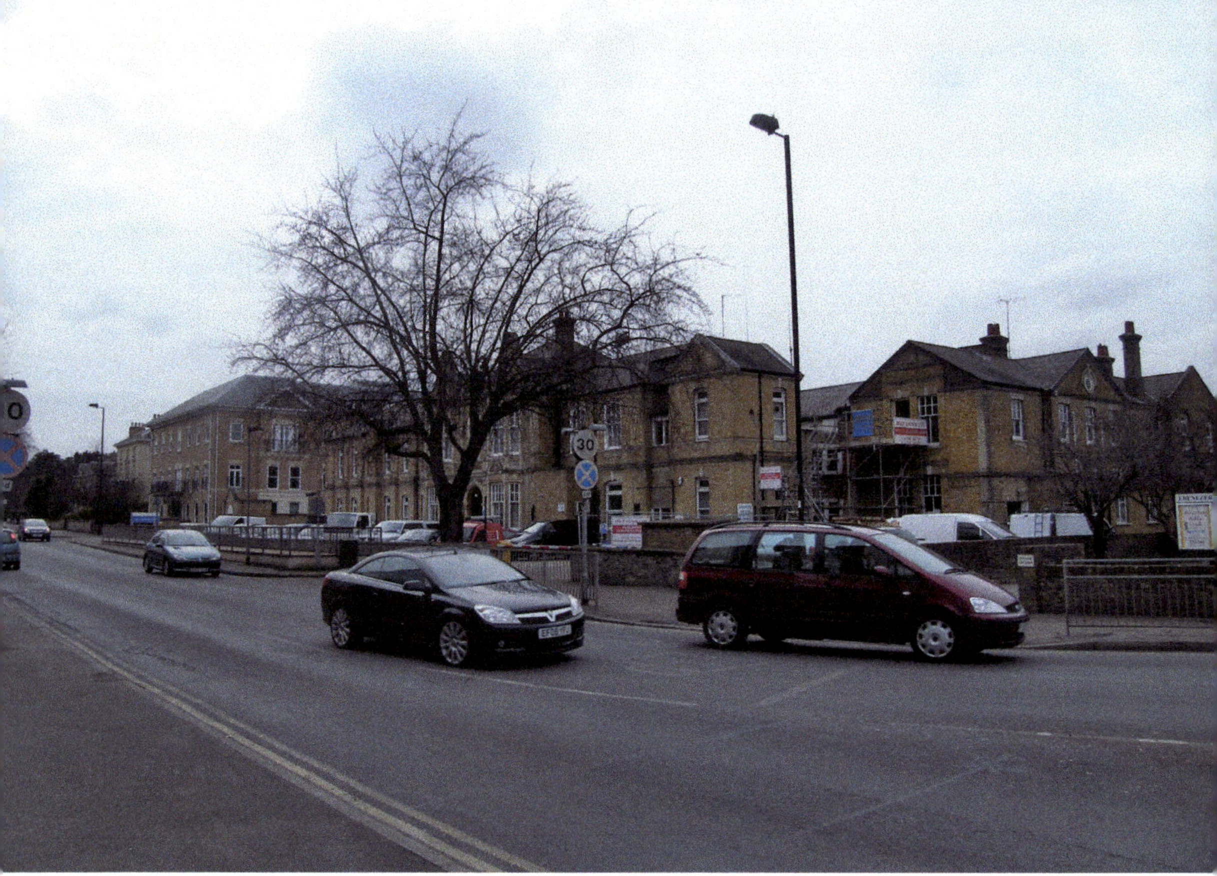

Chelmsford & Essex Hospital, 2013.

an accident ward and two wards with four beds for men and two for women. They also had two more wards with six beds each on the second floor.

In 1946 the hospital came under the umbrella of the National Health Service and became a general hospital. Then, as Broomfield Hospital expanded, Chelmsford Hospital gradually became a day clinic, providing an excellent breast-screening service, and saved the lives of many women, including my wife's. I understand that the hospital is to close after 130 years' service to the community.

21. Broomfield Hospital, Court Road, Chelmsford

Essex is very lucky to have such a fine hospital as Broomfield; it has saved thousands of lives over the years, including mine. The Edwardian family Radcliffe owned an estate called Little Dumplings and built a mansion house on it in 1904. They lived in the house until finally it was passed down to the daughter, Constance, who sold it to Essex County Council. They decided to build a hospital on the land for the treatment of tuberculosis, which during the 1930s and 1940s was creating havoc. Submissions were put out and Staverton won the contract and agreed to build the sanatorium for £22,993. They started work in 1937 and finished it three years later in May 1940, which was a year into the Second World War. During the war, half of the 312 beds were allocated to wounded servicemen but the hospital was exclusively for men.

The cure for tuberculosis in those days was plenty of sunshine, fresh air and good food. Patients were put on the south-facing balconies, even in the depth of winter, to take full advantage of any sun. It helped that vegetables were grown in the hospital grounds. It took between six months and four years to cure a patient of the disease. Obviously being shut up for that length of time, the men became bored because radio and television were both in their infancy and unavailable. To relieve the monotony the hospital came up with the idea of showing films on Friday nights, which quickly became the highlight of the week. Porters would race down the corridors pushing beds loaded with patients in order to obtain the best places in the room where the films were showing.

To care for the needs of the patients, there were 100 staff and the first manager, Dr William Yell, created a family atmosphere. With the introduction of streptomycin, which cured tuberculosis, the call for specialist treatment declined and gradually the hospital turned to general medical care.

The biggest change was when the National Health Service was introduced in July 1948 but the hospital still stuck to its policy of only admitting men and it was not until 1959 that women were admitted and six babies were born. By the 1960s, Broomfield became a general hospital, but it still had one ward for the treatment of chest infections.

Broomfield Hospital, 1940. (Copyright Broomfield Hospital)

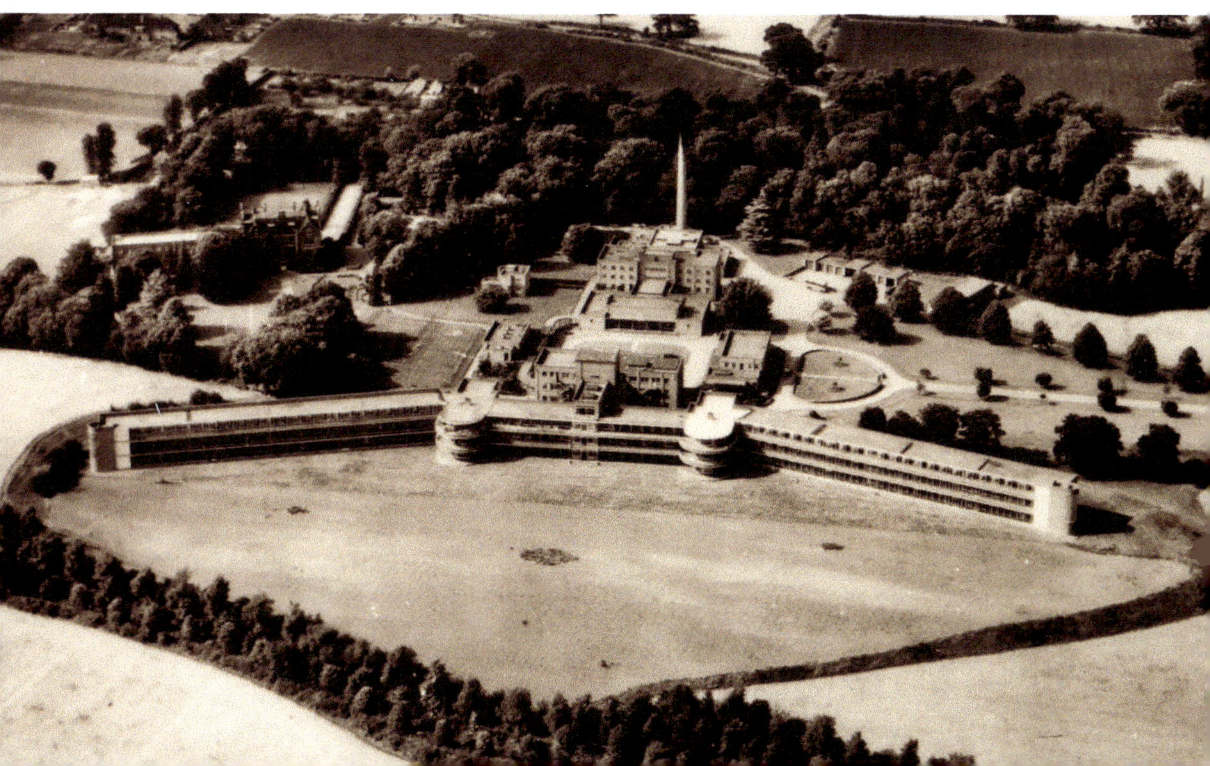

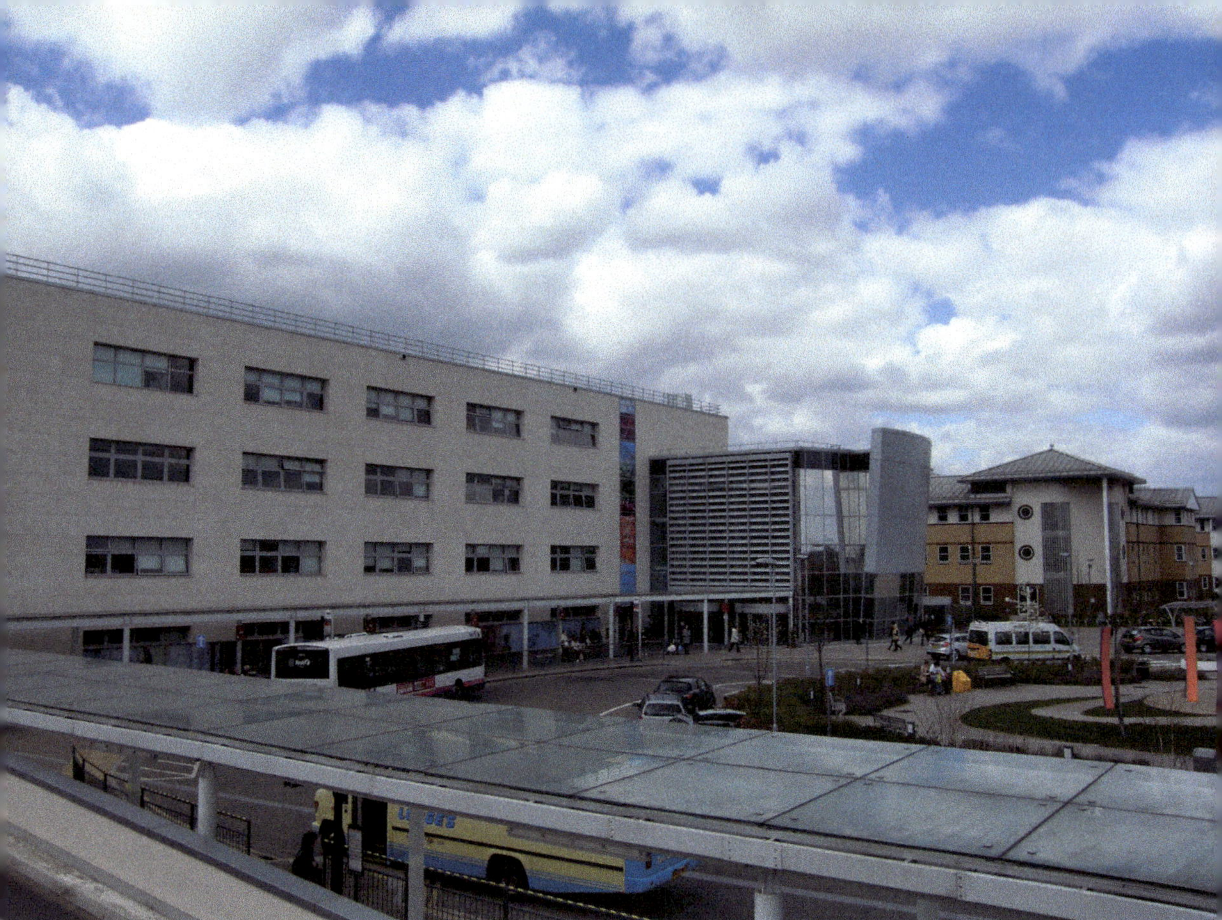

Broomfield Hospital, 2013.

In 1984 major improvements were made and an Accident and Emergency department was opened, plus a rehabilitation centre and more operating theatres. This is a great hospital and we are lucky to have it.

22. Workhouse/St John's Hospital

St John's Hospital was built on the site of an old army barracks that went back to the Napoleonic Wars of 1798–1815. It was used to accommodate troops, who were marching the 45 miles to Harwich in order to embark for France. At times, during this period, there were more troops in Chelmsford than citizens.

After the Battle of Waterloo in 1815 and the French defeat, there was no need to keep a large army, so the government reduced the regiments to a size that was compatible with peacetime and dispensed with barracks like St John's. Following the introduction of the Poor Law Act of 1834, St John's was converted into a workhouse for the destitute in 1837, and in 1877 an infectious unit was built.

The inhabitants of the workhouse hated it, because the regime was extremely strict and families were separated. In order to be admitted, a family had to be

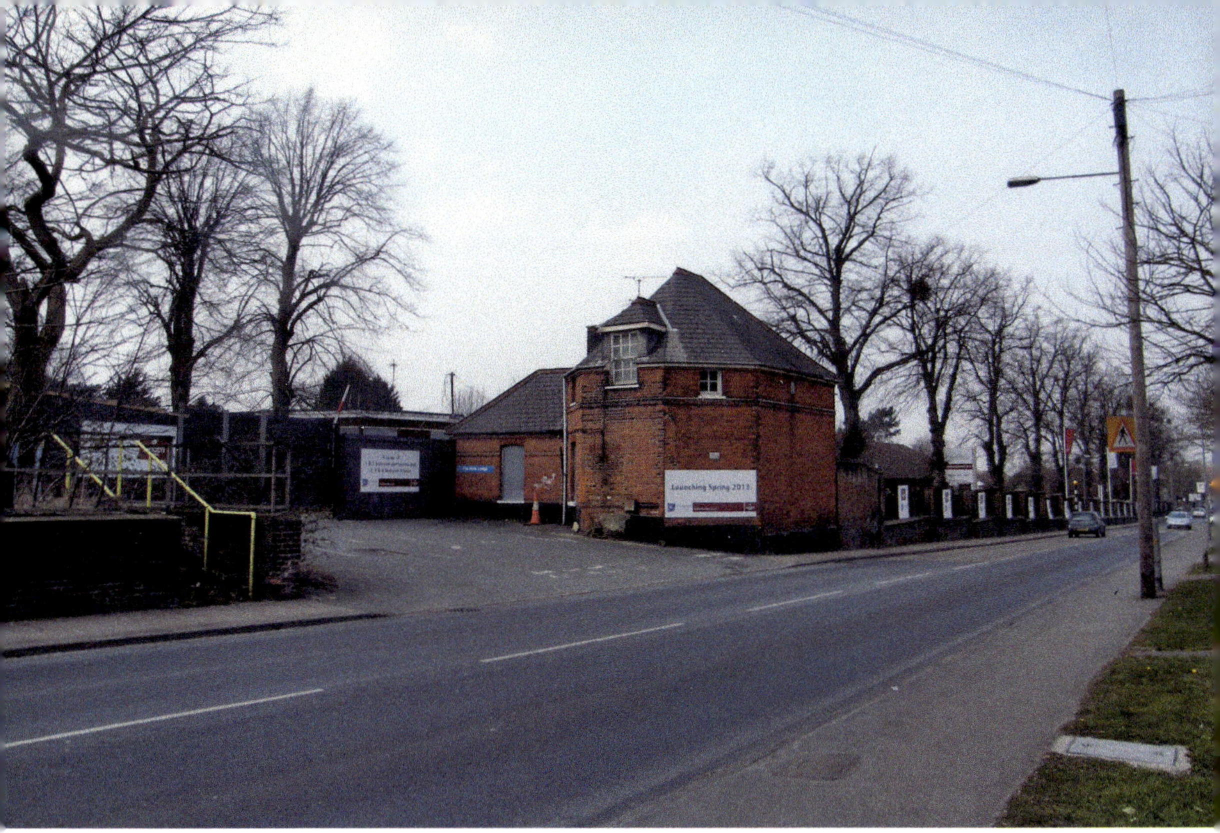

Above: The old workhouse gate, which has not changed over the years.

Below: The hospital being demolished in 2013.

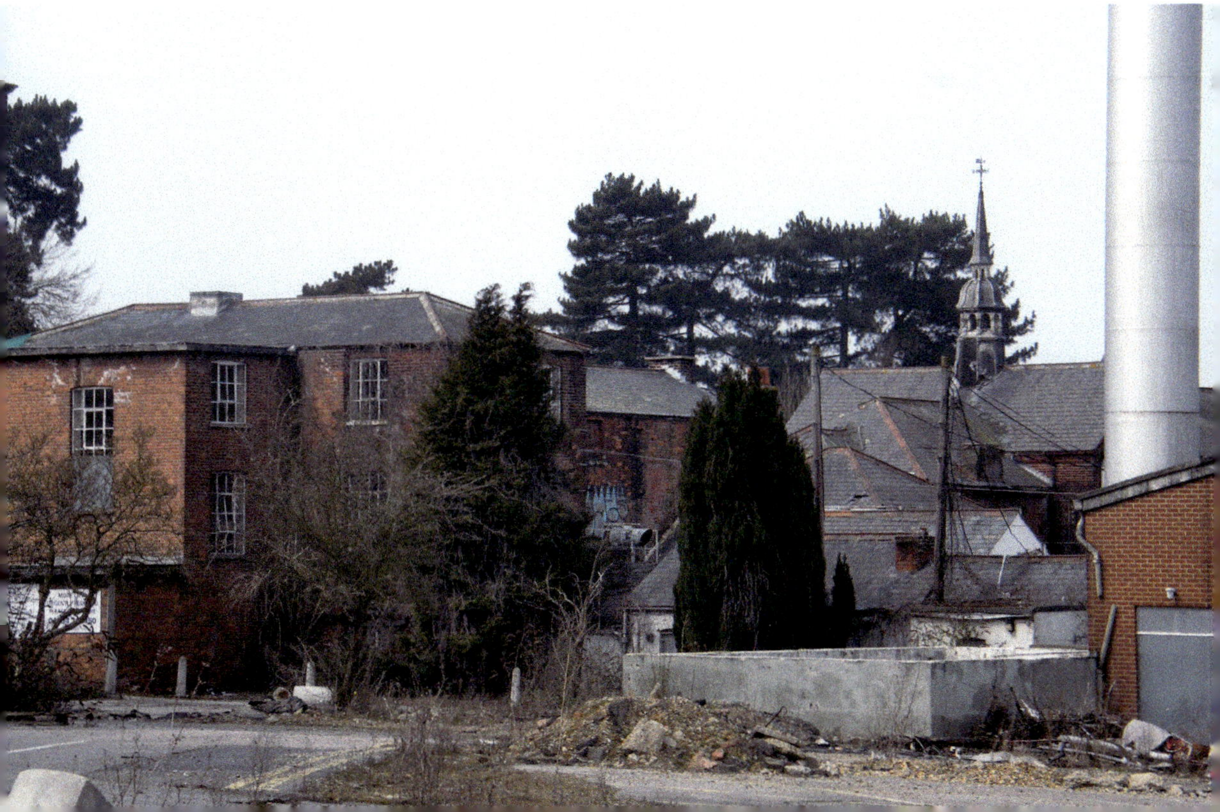

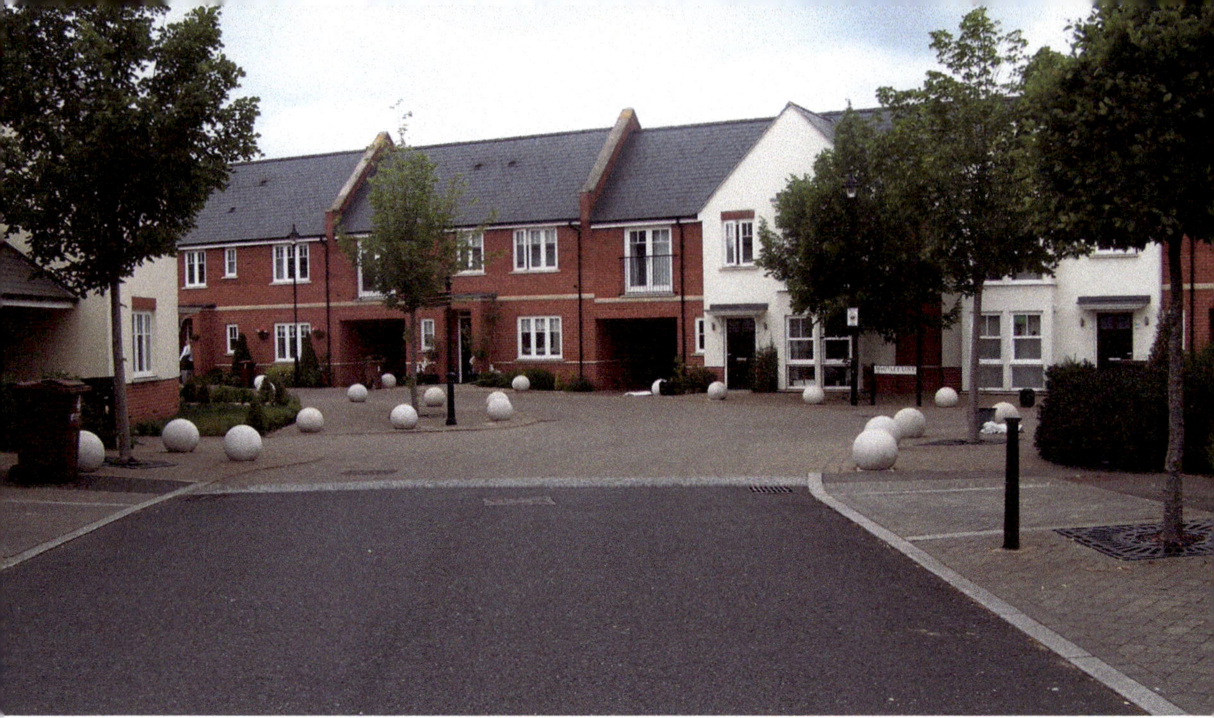

The housing development on the site today.

desperate. They had to have lived in the parish for two years, be homeless, an orphan or old. On entering the gates, the sexes were immediately separated. Those who were fit had to work, including children if they were old enough. Men were made to break stones while women were made to do household chores, such as cooking, sewing and weaving. They were only paid between a 1d and 5d, according to their skills.

They were given three meals a day consisting of oats, made with water, for breakfast, broth for lunch, made from the water that the meat for the evening meal had been boiled in with a few onions thrown in, if they were lucky. They were given beer to drink, as it was safer than water. There was a scheme to try to keep families out of the workhouse. If a working family man fell ill and could not work, the authorities might have made him a payment of a shilling to tide him and his family over.

In 1915 the workhouse was closed and converted into a hospital and in 1926, a maternity unit was opened. Over the years hundreds of babies were born there but the last two were born in November 2010, when the hospital closed. The hospital specialised in nose and throat operations and had a unit for blood tests. The land was sold and today the site has a housing estate on it.

23. Ingatestone Hall

Right on the border of Chelmsford is Ingatestone Hall, which is such a beautiful building in outstanding red brick and with such history that I had to include it in this book. During Henry VIII's Dissolution of the Monasteries (1536–41) one of

Cromwell's assistants, William Petre, was given the task of inspecting monastic houses in the south of England. His role was to establish how much they were worth and persuade the abbots, by various means, to give up their land and possessions to the King. He visited a number of abbeys but when he inspected Ynge-atte-Stone (now known as Ingatestone Hall), he was so impressed that he decided to take out a lease on the estate.

In 1539 the land and property were surrendered to the King and William Petre bought it from him for under £900. Pope Paul IV took the view that Henry had acted illegally by confiscating the Church properties and excommunicated him. Ironically, although William Petre was involved, the Pope excluded him from the Interdict on proviso that he set up almshouses for the poor. The original almshouses were demolished and rebuilt in Ingatestone High Street. William Petre demolished an old servant's cottage on the estate and built a manor house on the site, which remains almost the same today. The house forms a hollow square and for its day was very modern. Most houses at that time had to obtain their water from wells and used buckets for their human functions, but Ingatestone Hall had running water and flush toilets. The water came from springs which were still being used until recently.

When William Petre died he was survived by his widow who continued to live in the house. Their son bought a property in Brentwood and the family lived there for over 300 years but they still owned Ingatestone Hall and used it from time to time. The 9th Lord Petre did use the property in 1764, while alterations were

The gate, Ingatestone Hall.

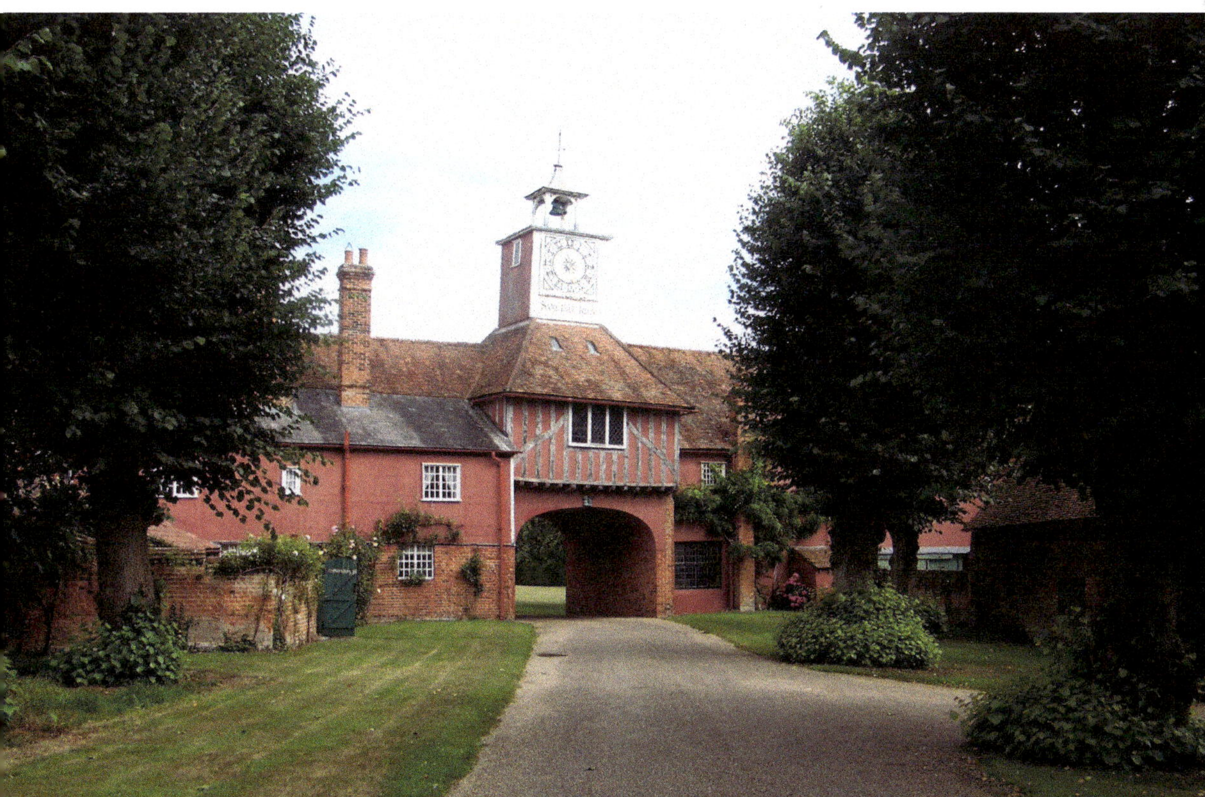

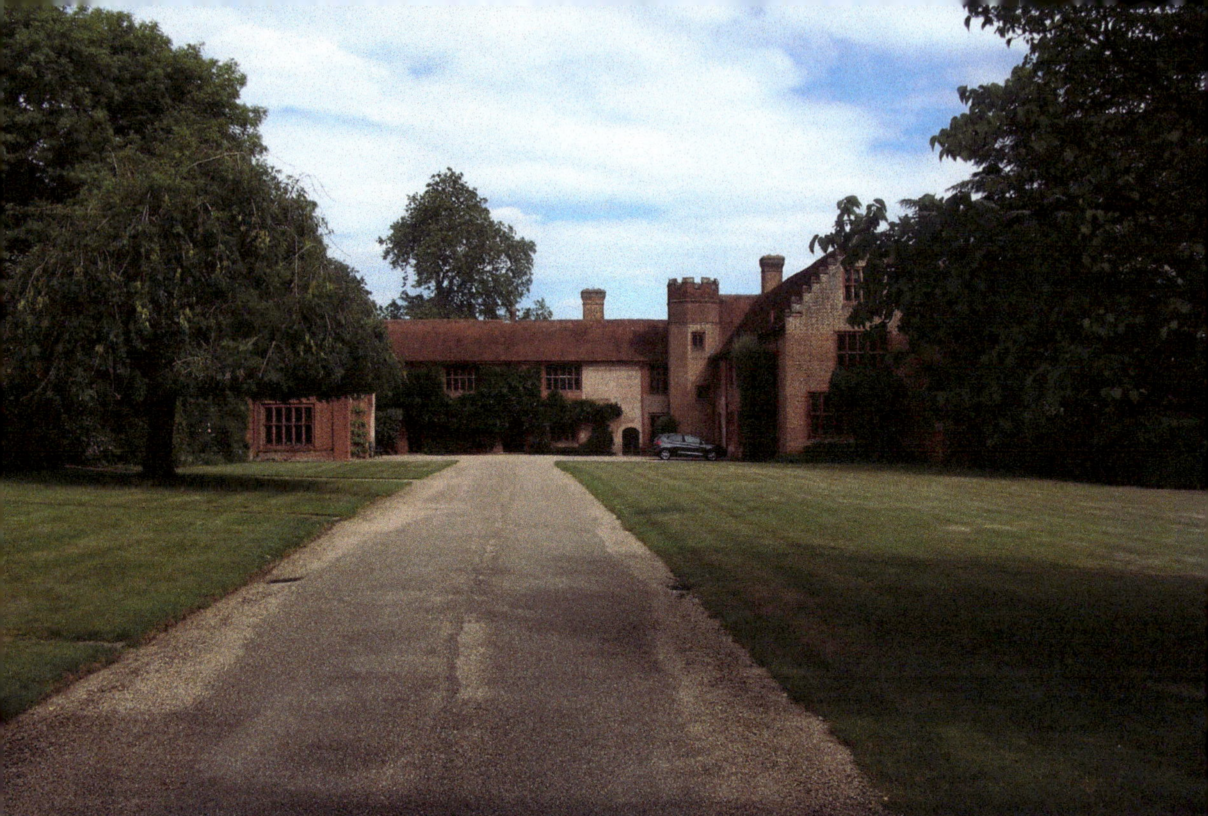

The Hall today.

being carried out to Thorndon Hall, the Brentwood property. When he moved back he carried out some major alterations to Ingatestone Hall by demolishing the west wing and modernising it by removing walls and making passageways. Most houses in those days did not have passages but one room led into another. Unfortunately, the way the work was carried out did cause problems in later years.

The 16th Earl died in the First World War, and the family moved back to Ingatestone Hall and his wife, Lady Rasch, began restoring the house. During the Second World War part of the house was used by Wanstead Girls' School, who were evacuated there to escape the bombing. After the war the north wing was let out to the Essex Record Office, who remained in occupation until 1970.

24. Hoffmann's Ball Bearing Factory

In 1898 Britain's first ball bearing factory was set up in New Street and Rectory Road, Chelmsford. It was an offshoot of an American company that was owned by Gustav Hoffmann, but managed in Britain by two cousins, Charles and Geoffrey Barrett. It became famous for the accuracy of its products, which were exported all over the world. The factory employed both men and women and it made a major contribution to winning both the First and Second World Wars, as ball bearings were used in every moving part of aircraft, tanks and ships.

During both wars the Germans targeted the factory. I can find no record of the factory having been hit during the First World War but in the Second World War, on 19 December 1944, a V2 rocket caught the western edge of the factory, where the workers had just finished a tea break and were returning to their benches, full of the joys of Christmas after listening to the Salvation Army, who had just entertained them. The V2s gave no warning but just fell silently out of the sky and the first anyone knew was when they exploded. Sadly, the rocket killed thirty employees, as well as killing nine other people in adjacent roads, and there were also 138 civilians injured. One body was never claimed and is buried in Chelmsford Cemetery with the employees of Hoffmann's. It was the worst loss of life in Chelmsford during the Second World War. The rocket not only destroyed part of the factory but wrecked many houses in the surrounding area, making dozens of people homeless. In the factory a fuel tank exploded and a major fire started. The firm's firefighters rang the fire brigade and then bravely fought the fire, but found they had no water as the rocket had burst the mains. Then someone came up with the bright idea of using the river. When the fire brigade arrived they used a hydrant in Rectory Road. Everyone tried to help, including the American airmen at Boreham who rushed into Chelmsford to help dig out the bodies and treat the injured, taking many of the homeless back to their camp. Thirteen of those who were killed lay side by side in Chelmsford Crematorium.

For years, Hoffmann's were the best in their field of engineering but by 1969, other companies had caught up with the technology and Hoffmann's amalgamated

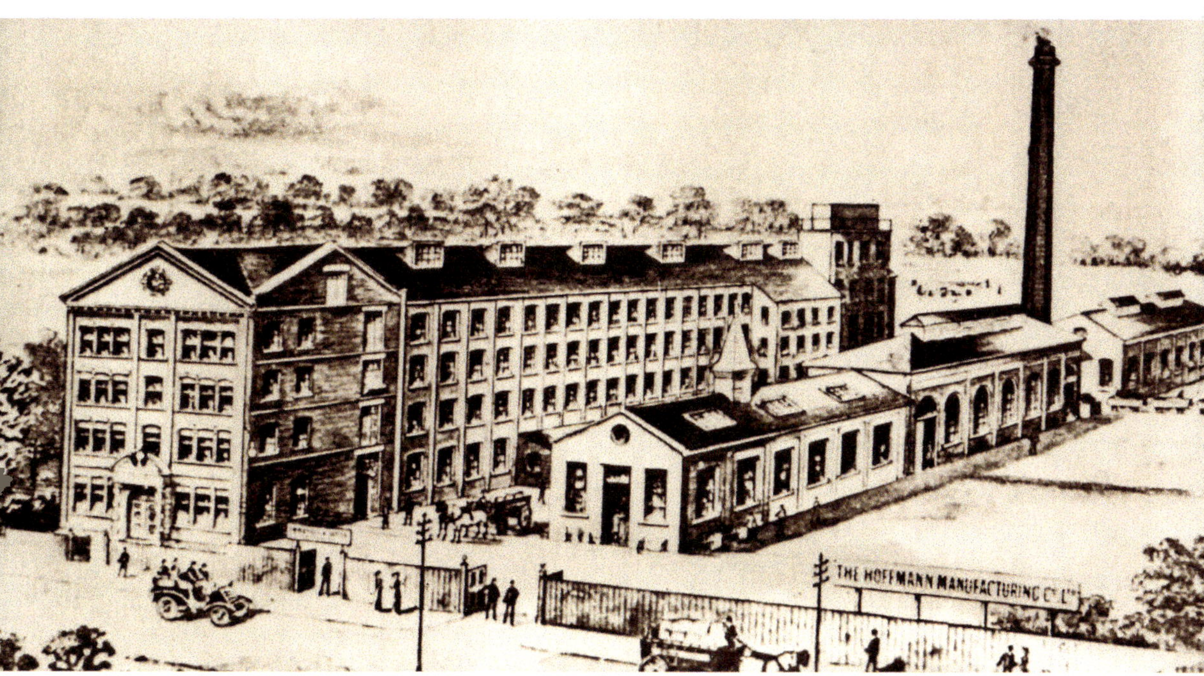

Hoffmann's factory around 1900.

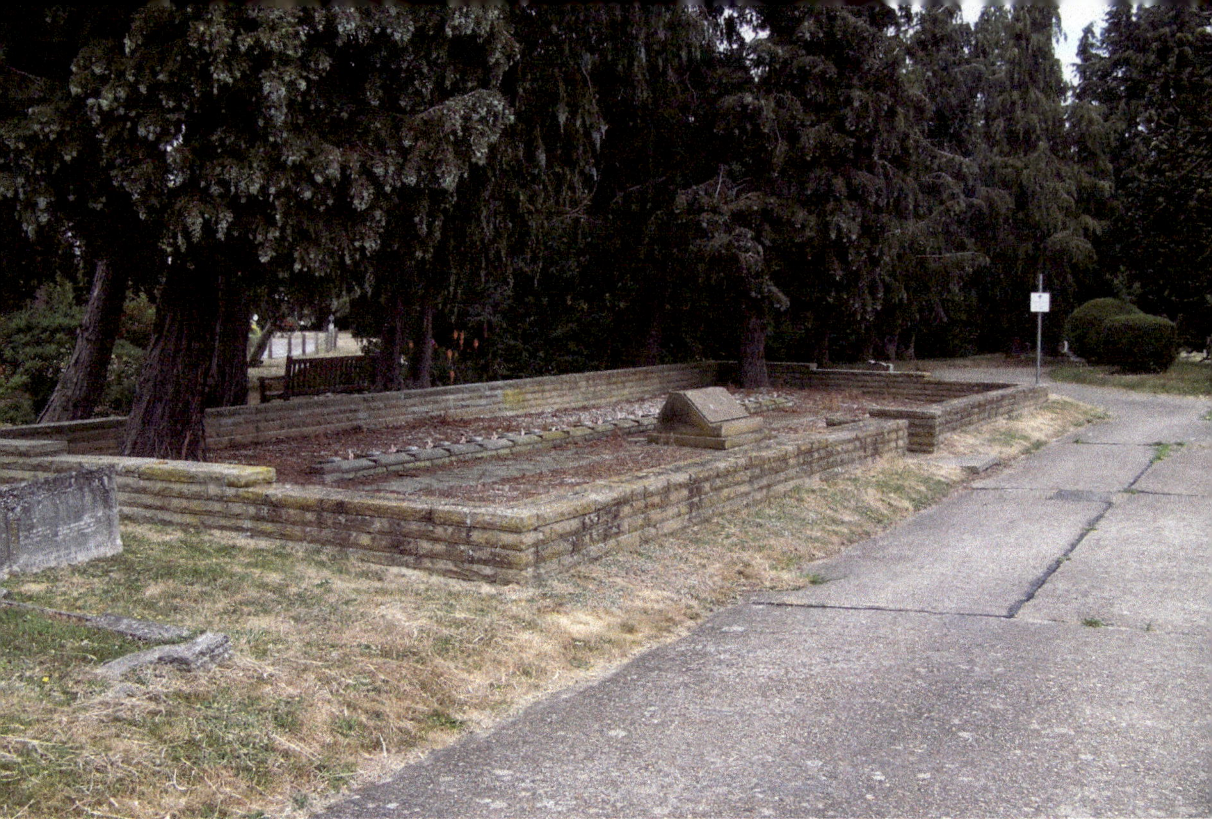

A memorial in Chelmsford churchyard to thirteen of the people killed in the bombing raid.

with Ransome and Males Ball Bearing Company. Finally, the firm was taken over by NSK, a Japanese company, and moved the factory to Newark-on-Trent. The company that had been one of the major employers in Chelmsford since 1898 disappeared. Most of the factory was demolished in 1990 and became part of the Anglia Ruskin University.

25. Marconi's

Chelmsford is famous for being the birthplace of radio but at the time Marconi was experimenting with radio, there were a number of other inventors who were doing the same thing. Two of these were Heinrich Hertz and Nikola Tesla, but Marconi improved on the invention. Marconi was born in 1874 in Bologna, Italy, and moved to Britain when he was twenty-two years old. He submitted a patent on his version of the invention and then set up a factory in Hall Street, Chelmsford, employing fifty staff. Taking the initiative and seeing the potential of his invention, he started giving demonstrations to the Post office and Army and Navy on Salisbury Plain.

He was determined to show what his invention was capable of, but at that time radio was not vocal but in Morse code, which was a series of dots and dashes, each representing a letter. He was the first person to send a wireless signal over the open sea, from Holm Island to Lavernock Point in Penarth. The message was very simple: 'Are you ready?'

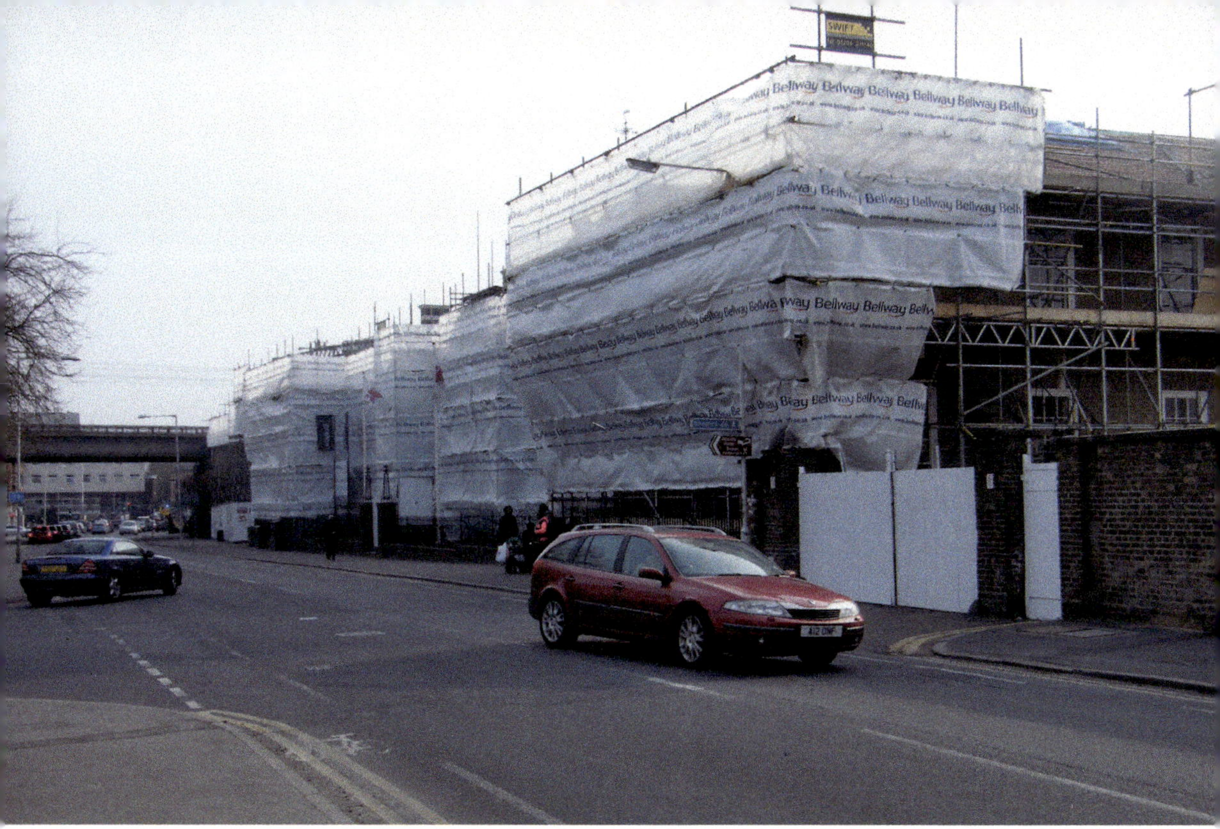

Above: The site of Marconi's premises before recent restoration.

Below: Marconi's after modernisation, 2020.

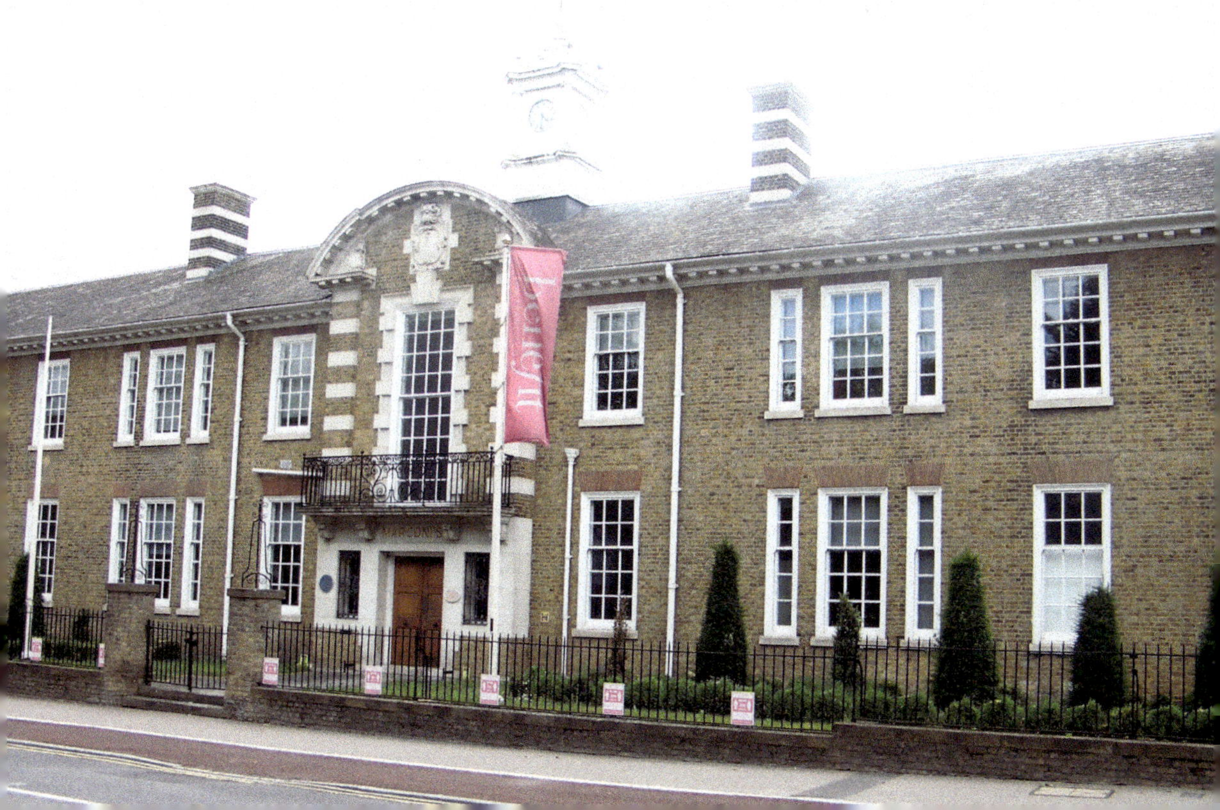

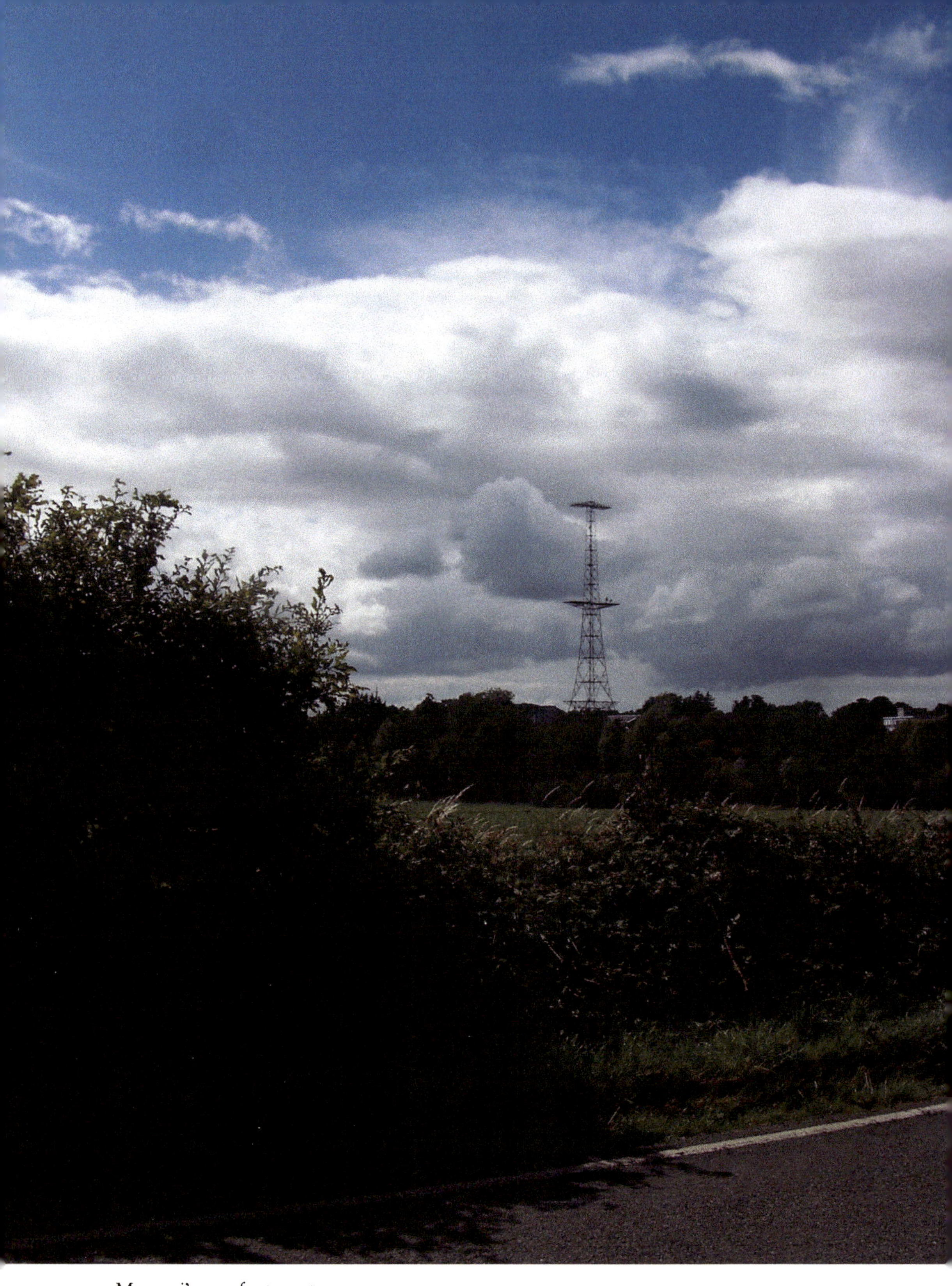

Marconi's 450-foot mast.

There were many sceptics who said that his signal would not travel more than 200 miles because of the curvature of the Earth, but he proved them wrong by transmitting across the Atlantic in Morse code. Up to that time, communication had been only by cables under the sea, the first one being in 1858 from Ireland to Newfoundland. With the new invention, ships were able to communicate with one another at sea, rather than using flags or semaphore. The first human voice broadcast was by Canadian Reginald Fessenden on 24 December 1906 from Brant Rock, near Boston.

After sixteen years Marconi's business outgrew its premises and larger ones had to be found, so he built a factory in New Street. His first voice broadcast was made by Dame Nellie Melba in June 1929. The equipment he used to broadcast was a bit 'Heath Robinson' – the microphone was a telephone mouthpiece and a cigar box. Soon, Marconi was broadcasting for just half an hour a week. He still continued to experiment and gradually made improvements at his plant. The site covered 25,000 square yards and had a mast 450 feet high.

Unfortunately, during the Second World War the factory was targeted by German aircraft and one night, in 1941, it was hit, killing seventeen people and injuring twenty-nine. In 1999, the defence division was taken over by British Aerospace but they still kept control of the Military and Secure Communications, which was based in New Street but in 2008 was transferred to Basildon.

26. Britvic Westway

Britvic was one of the worldwide companies that Chelmsford gave birth to. It is difficult to believe that this international company started off in a small chemist shop in Tindal Street during the nineteenth century, yet at one time it employed over 200 people. It originally commenced trading as British Vitamin World Company, making water-based soft drinks.

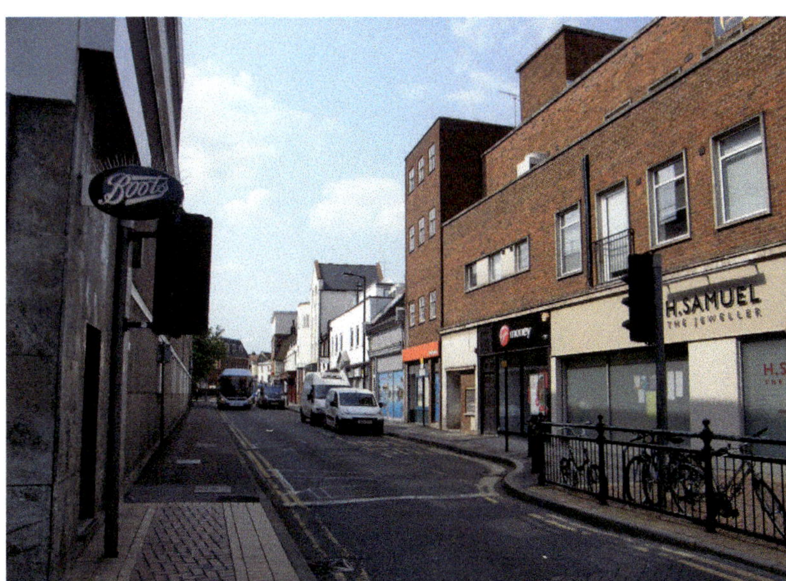

The small chemist in Tindal Street where Britvic started.

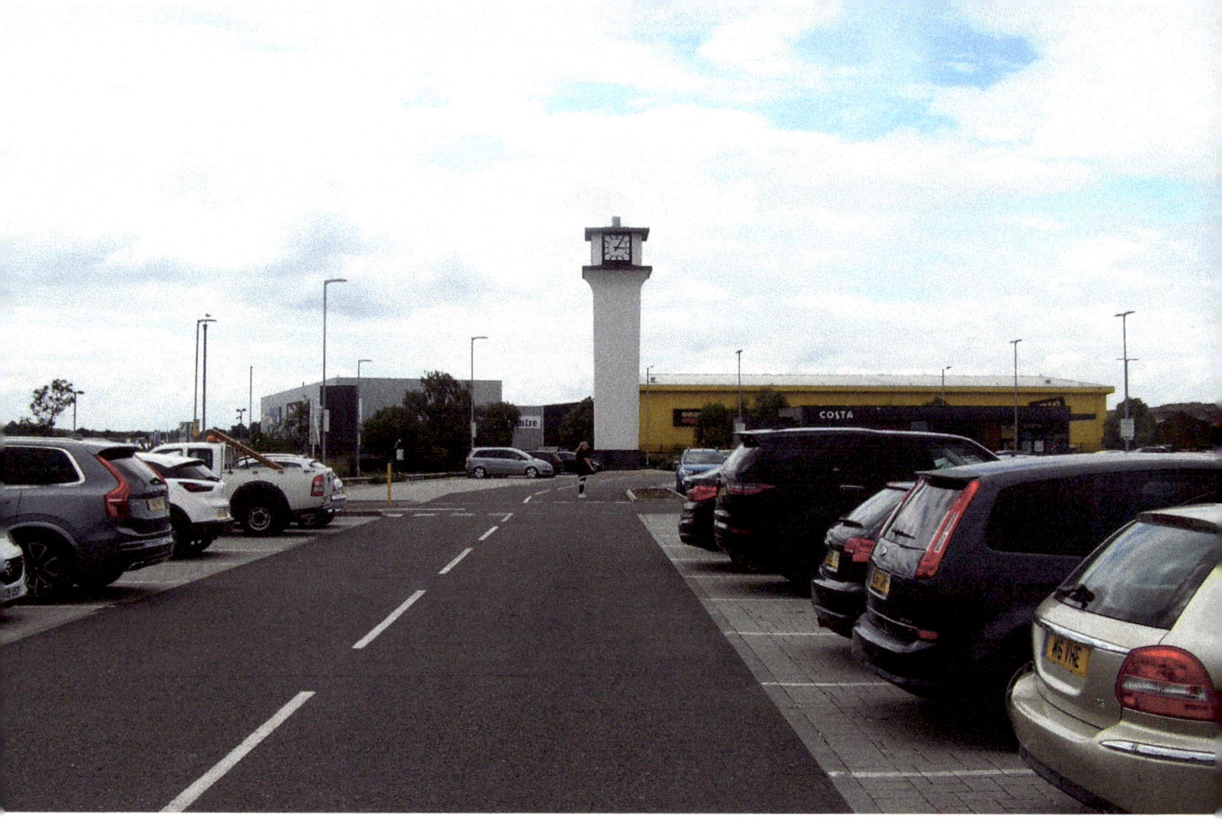

Above: The Britvic clock, left as a memorial in the retail park.

Below: The Britvic offices, 2013.

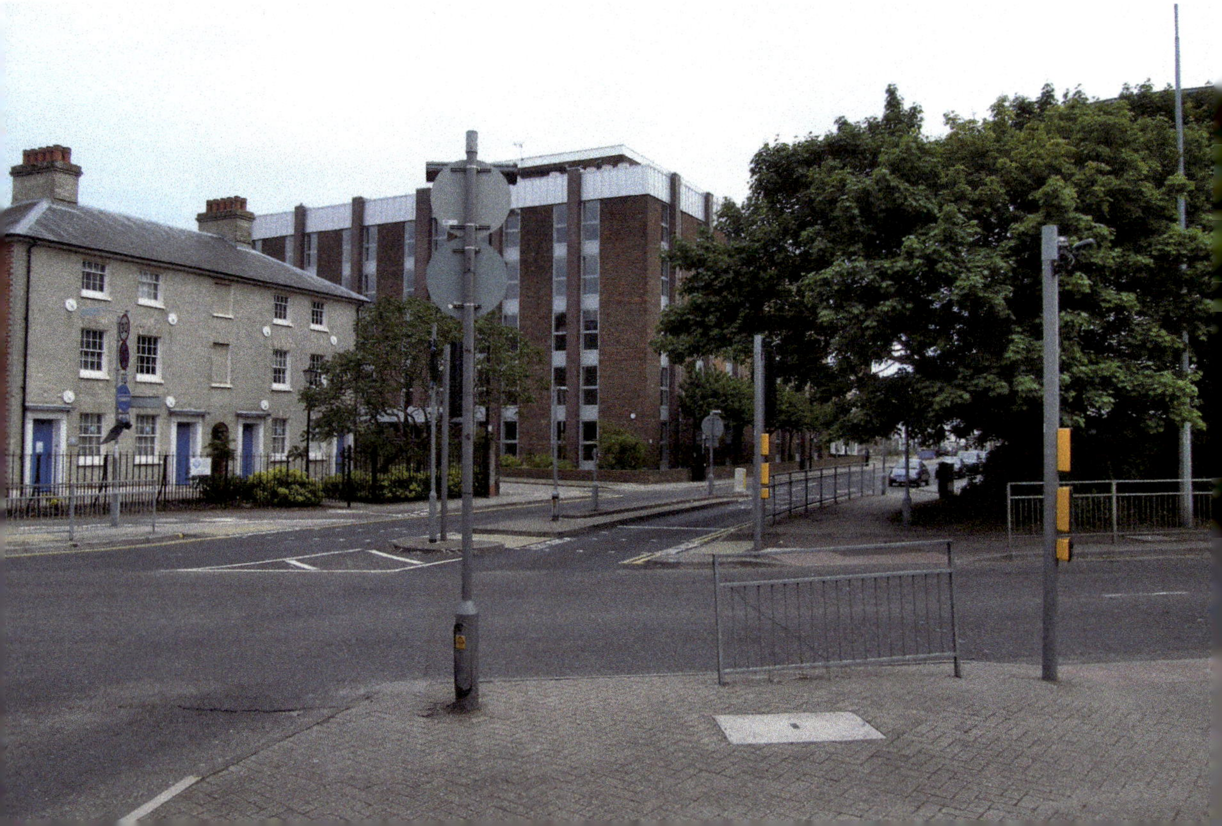

It was not until 1938 that the business began to expand under the direction of James MacPherson, who set up his headquarters in Broomfield Road. The company started exporting their products to over fifty countries all over the world. In 1971, the company changed its name to Britvic, and in 2005 bought out another soft drinks company called Cantrell and Cochrane. In 2012, the firm moved its headquarters to Hemel Hempstead but retained its factory on the Widford Industrial Estate. Then, in 2012, it merged and set up regional offices in France and Dublin. It was acquired by a company called Showerings of Shepton Mallet and subsequently became part of Allied Breweries. This is a business that from its humble beginnings has gone from strength to strength. Sadly, it moved out of Chelmsford, making its 200 staff redundant. As a memento of the company they left their clock, which stands tall and proud in Westway.

27. Old Moulsham and Chelmer Mills

A mill has stood on the site in Parkway for centuries and was mentioned in William the Conqueror's Domesday Book of 1086. It has been in the Marriage family since the seventeenth century. Surprisingly it was taken over by seventeen-year-old twins named William and Henry after the death of their father.

Chelmer mill in 2013.

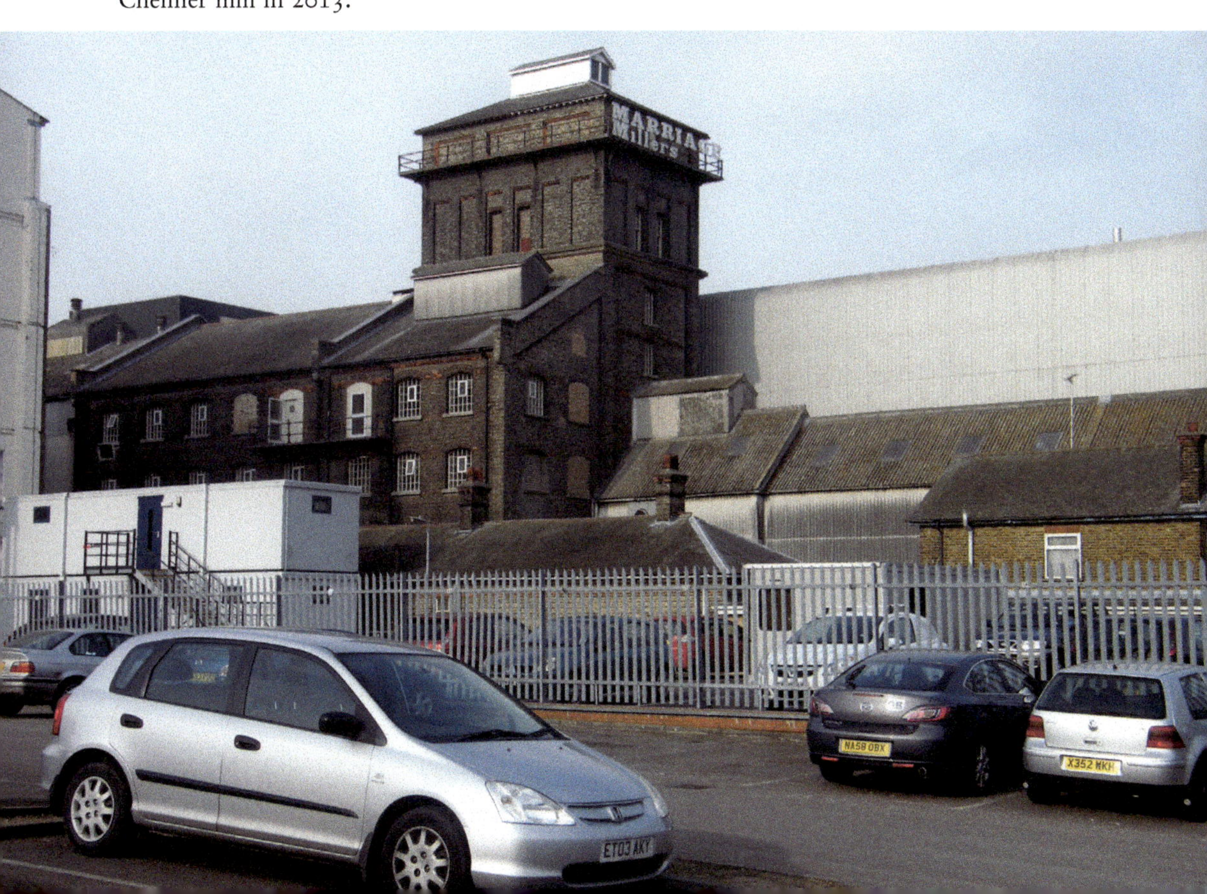

Before the twins took over the mill the price of corn rose to such an extent that many poor families were starving, so much so, that in April 1772 a crowd of over a hundred gathered and armed themselves. They marched on the mill, broke in and stole sacks of flour and carried them down to the marketplace and sold them. They then bought some much-needed food. The authorities became so frightened that they called in the army to quell the riots, but the army sympathized with the crowd and refused to take action.

The present mill was built in 1819 and was originally powered by water and wind. The twins must have heard about steam engines, which were first

The Old Moulsham Mill, Parkway, late 1800. (Copyright Marriages)

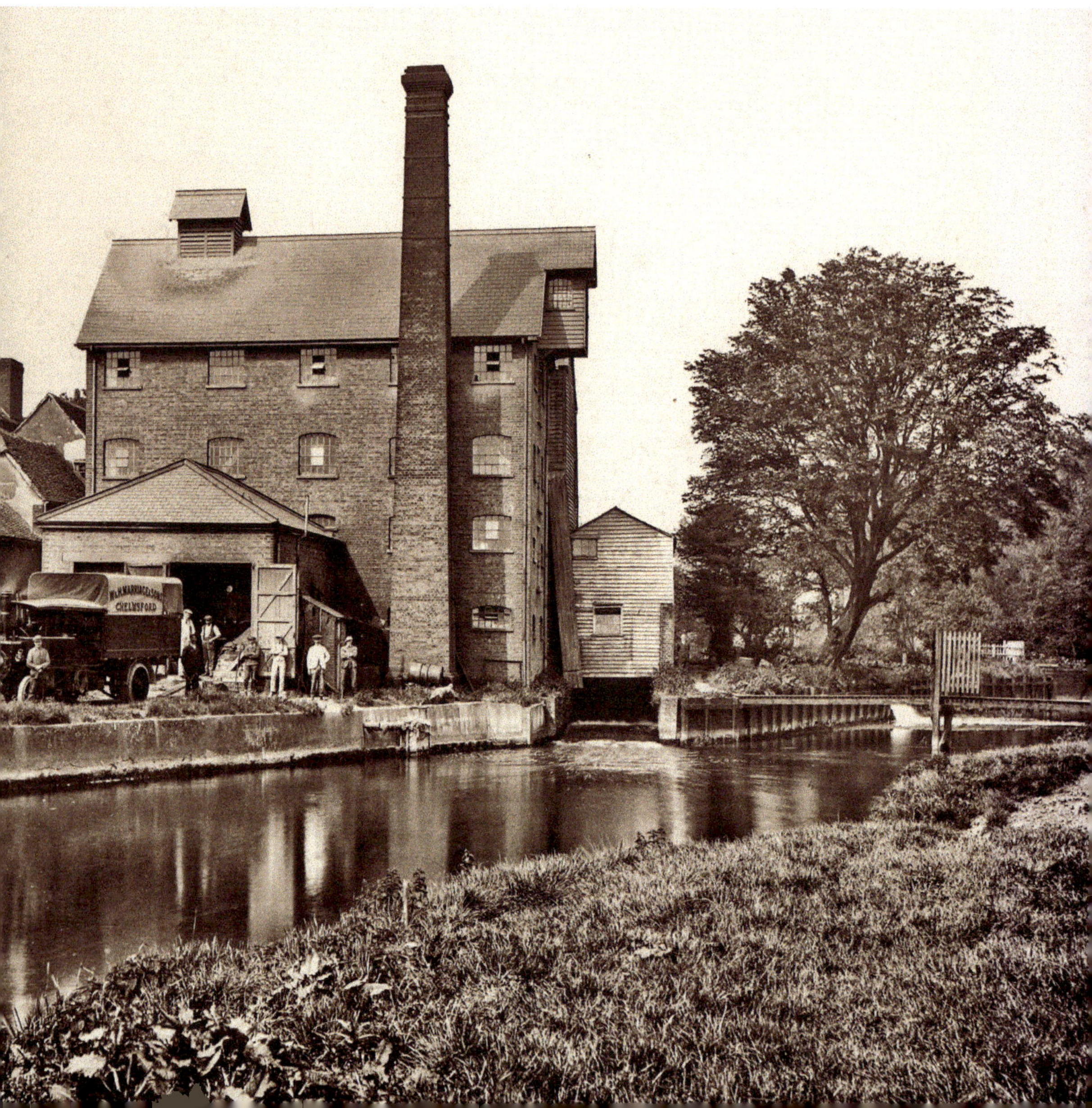

commercially used by Thomas Newcomen in 1712 and being an enterprising pair, in 1836 William and Henry converted the mill to steam power, so that they did not have to rely on the English weather. At that time corn was brought from Maldon on barges pulled by horses up the Blackwater and the Chelmer canal. During 1860 and 1890 extensive repairs were carried out to improve the mill's efficiency.

In 1891 it would seem that their sons were as adventurous as their fathers as they installed a mechanized rolling system. The new equipment was a great success, so much so, that they decided to expand and build Chelmer Mill in New Street. It was built in 1899 and again they showed good business sense by choosing a site by the railway so that they could take advantage of coal deliveries to power their machinery and distribute the flour to London. As time went on the family used to buy wheat from Chelmsford Corn Exchange and this continued until 1950 when they started dealing directly with local farmers. In 1972 they closed the Moulsham Mill but still used their Chelmer Mill. In 1983, after major reconstruction, the Moulsham Mill was opened as a business and craft centre, with over fifty licences, and is well worth a visit.

W & H Marriage is one of the oldest milling companies in the country. It has been in business since 1824 and is still run as a family business.

Up-to-date image of Old Moulsham Mill, 2013.

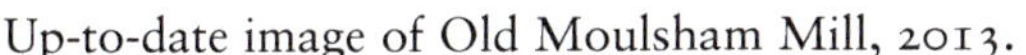

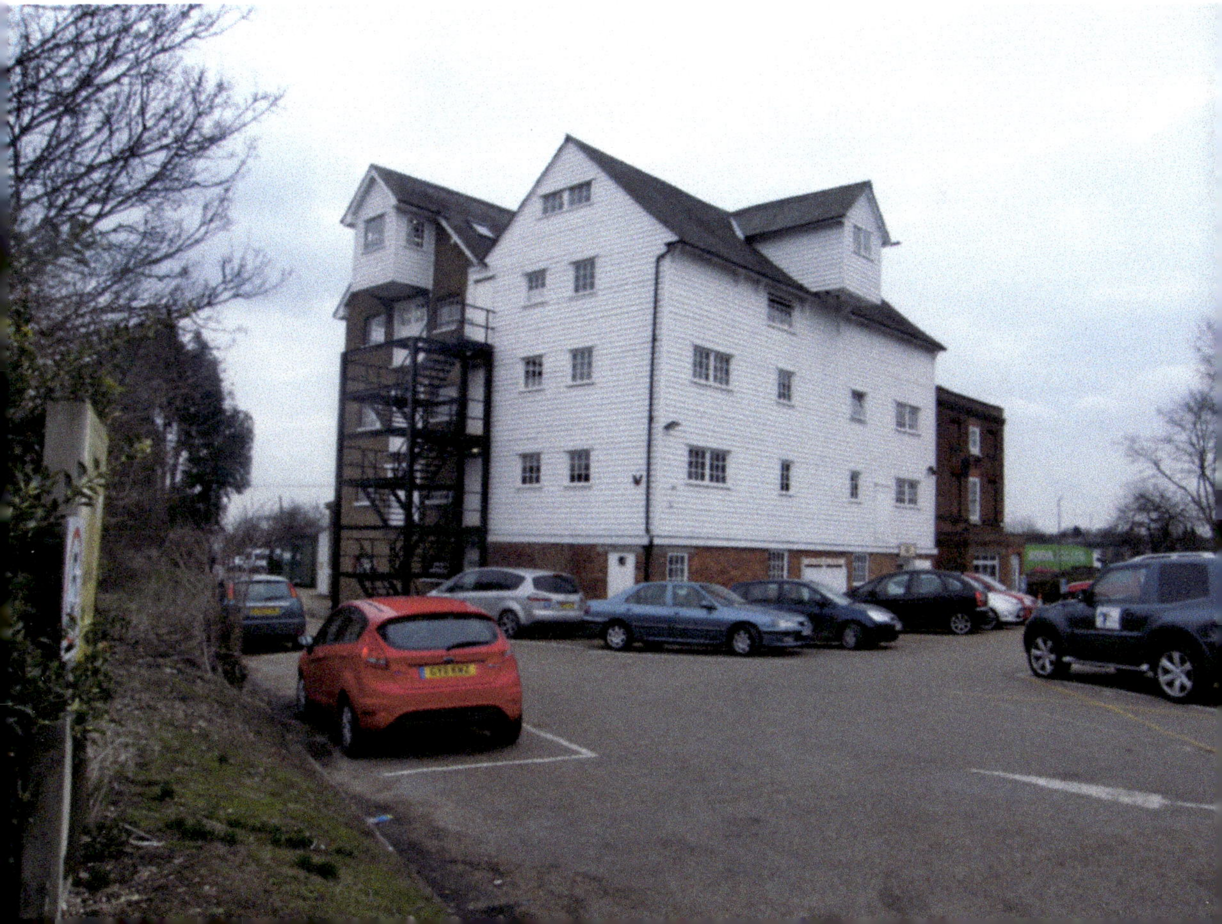

                    Chelmsford in 50 Buildings

28. Stock Windmill

The windmill, situated in Mill Lane, was constructed in 1816 near an adjoining post mill and was owned by William Moss and later taken over by his son, John, in 1838. The last miller to own the mill was Frank Semmens, in 1929. There were a number of types of windmill, from a post mill to hollow post mills. The post mill was a post sunk into the ground with sails attached, the machinery being placed behind the spinning wheel on the floor. They were fairly unstable, especially in storms. There were at one time two post mills on the Stock site, but these were demolished in 1890. With the invention of the steam engine in 1698, the face of engineering began to change and this transformation included windmills that before steam had to rely on the unpredictable British weather. It was not until 1902 that a steam engine was installed in the mill, but sadly it produced its last sack of flour in 1929.

In 1945, just after the Second World War, Essex County Council bought the mill and unfortunately it began to deteriorate through lack of maintenance. By 1977 it had lost its fantail, and only had one pair of sails. In 1991, it was decided to restore the mill and major repairs were carried out, helped by a grant from English Heritage.

The mill has five storeys and is over 40 feet high. It has four sails with a six-bladed fantail. It is open on the second Sunday of the month between April and September and is well worth a trip out.

Stock Windmill.

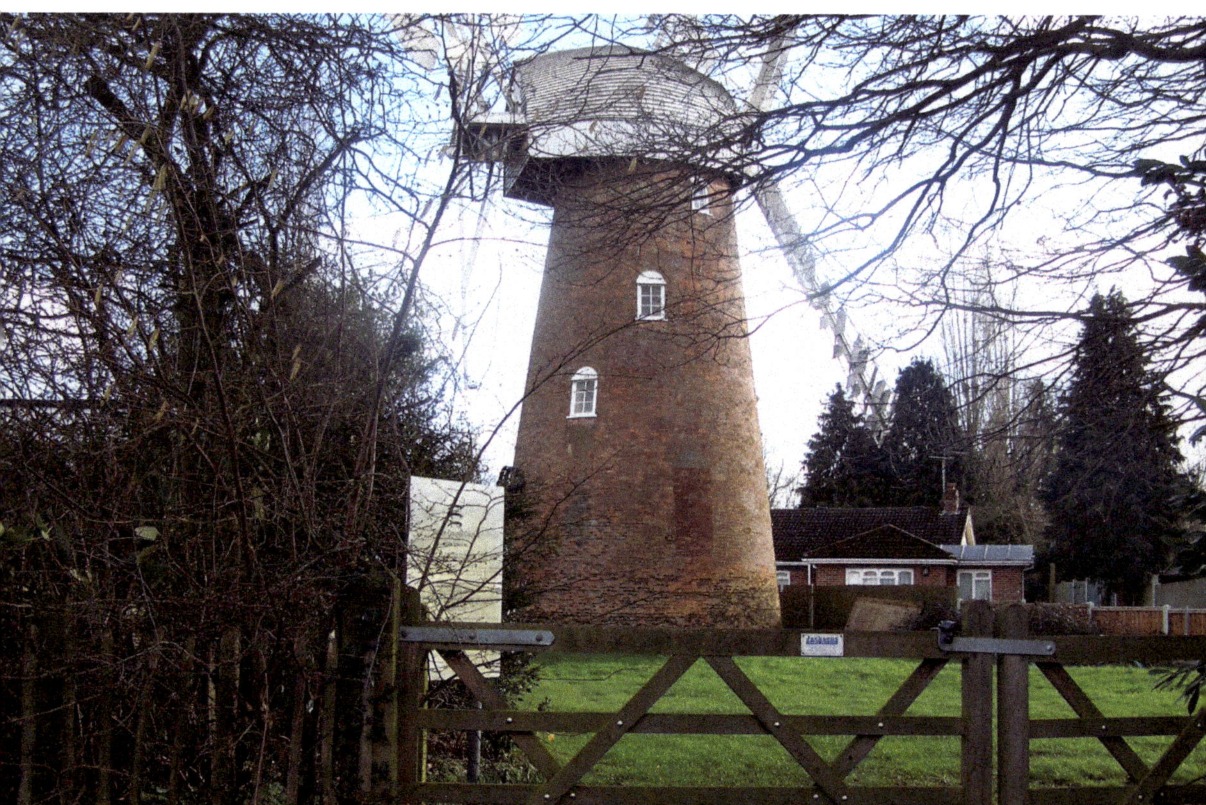

29. Coleman and Moreton

Today, a private medical centre stands on the site where once stood a firm that manufactured agricultural equipment, steam engines, manhole cover and parts for iron bridges. Coleman and Moreton started manufacturing in 1843. The factory was situated on the left-hand side of New London Road, opposite the Chelmsford and Essex Hospital.

At first it was managed by Richard Coleman, then leased to him and finally he bought it.

For their time, they were a very progressive company, bringing in a nine-hour day for their workers. This was such an unusual event that they threw a party for the employees and their wives. The cutting of the hours and the party caused such a stir that it was reported in the *Essex Weekly News* on 6 November 1874.

The firm allowed the workers to set up the Chemsford Star Co-operative Society and later, also to link up with the silk workers of Braintree, who had been in existence since 1864. The society grew and by 1868 it had 275 members and became the Chelmsford Star, which is still in existence today. The Rochdale Society was the original organisation and came into being in 1844. It was £1 to join then and it is still the same today.

On the left of the photograph can be seen County Ice Rink, which was built on the site of Coleman and Moreton. (Copyright Chelmsford Museum)

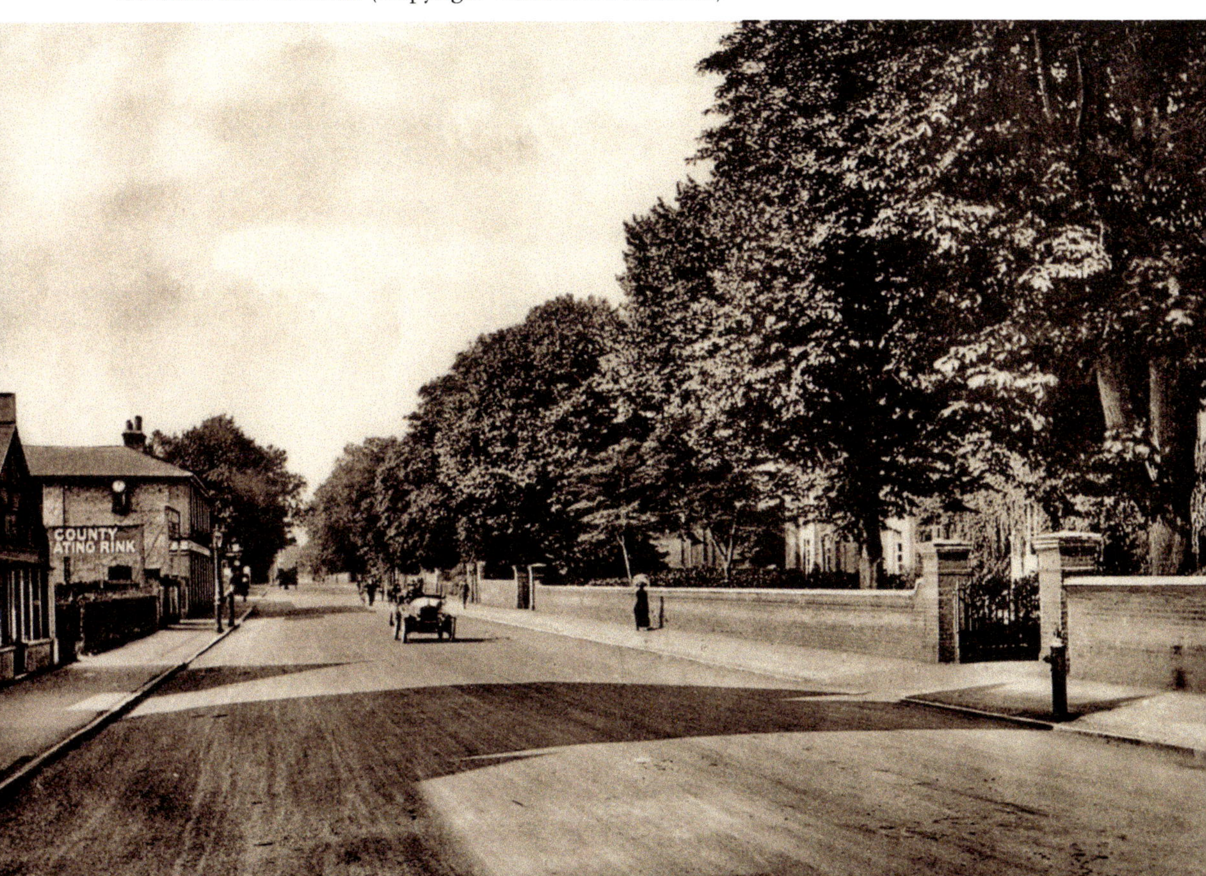

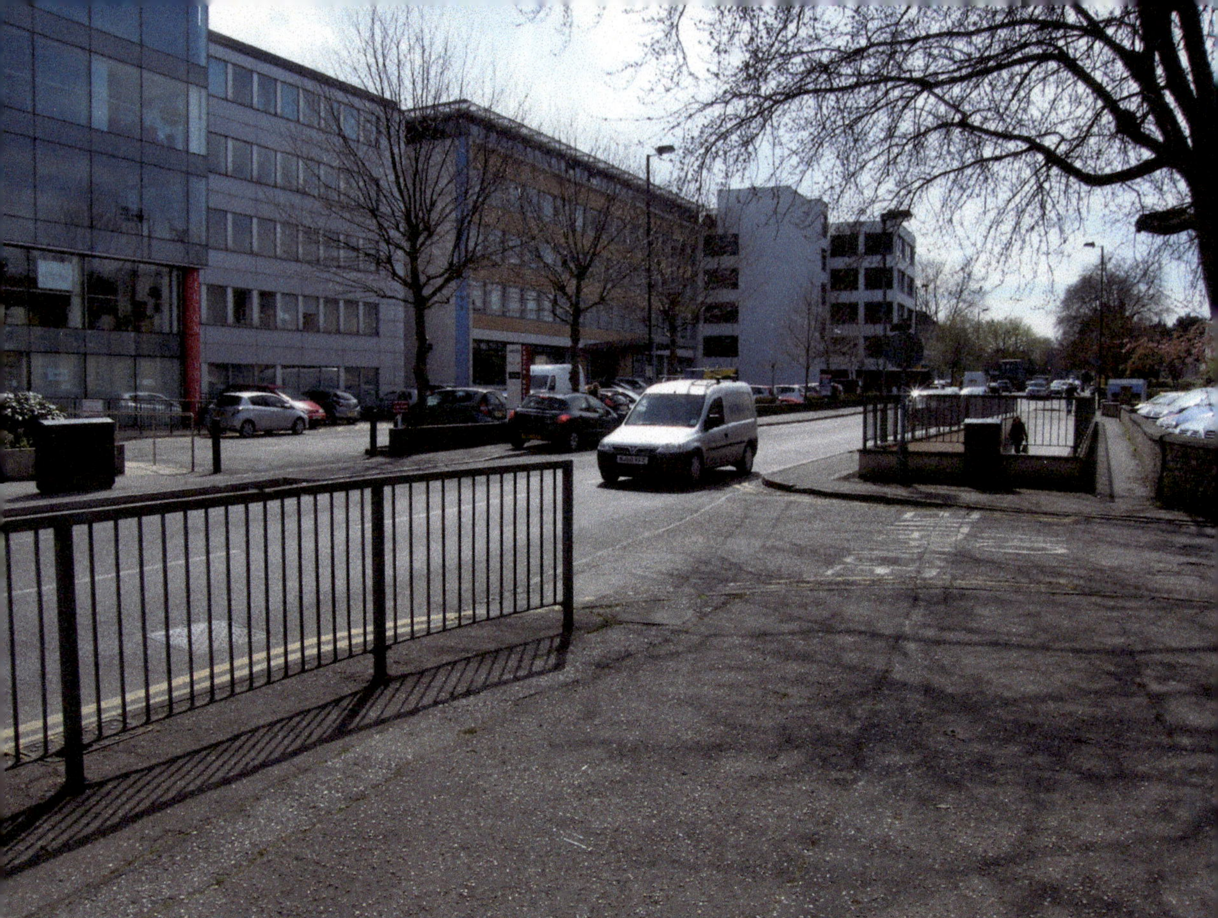

Private medical centre on the site where both the factory and ice rink were.

Cheap corn was imported from America and Canada during the latter part of the nineteenth century and flooded the home market, causing it to shrink. This affected the sale of farm machinery. The firm was sold in 1907 and a skating rink was built on the site just after the First World War.

30. *Essex Chronicle*

The *Essex Chronicle* appeared on the streets twenty-four years before *The Times* and has reported on every major event since its inauguration in 1764. It kept its readers informed of such historical happenings as the American War of Independence (1775–83) and the Battle of Waterloo in 1815 and of course the First and Second World Wars.

Its original works stood in Chelmsford, near where Marks & Spencer stands today. The business was started by William Strupar, who took over a printing works. He sold magazines, bibles and anything to do with writing. He even sold quills and writing paper. He was a very forward-thinking man and soon realized that Essex did not have its own paper, and so he took a chance and tentatively

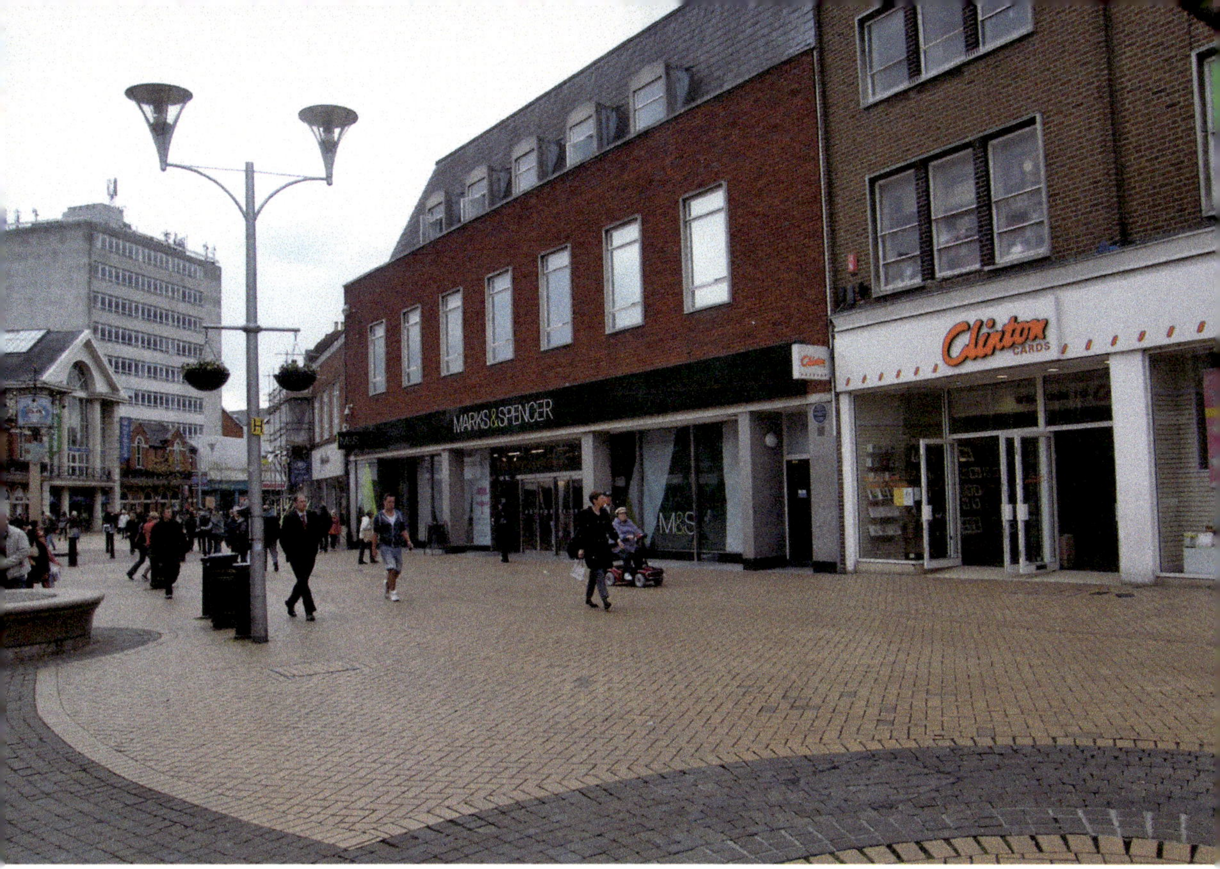

Above: Marks and Spencer showing the spot where the *Essex Chronicle's* first edition was printed in 1764.

Below: The *Essex Chronicle's* building.

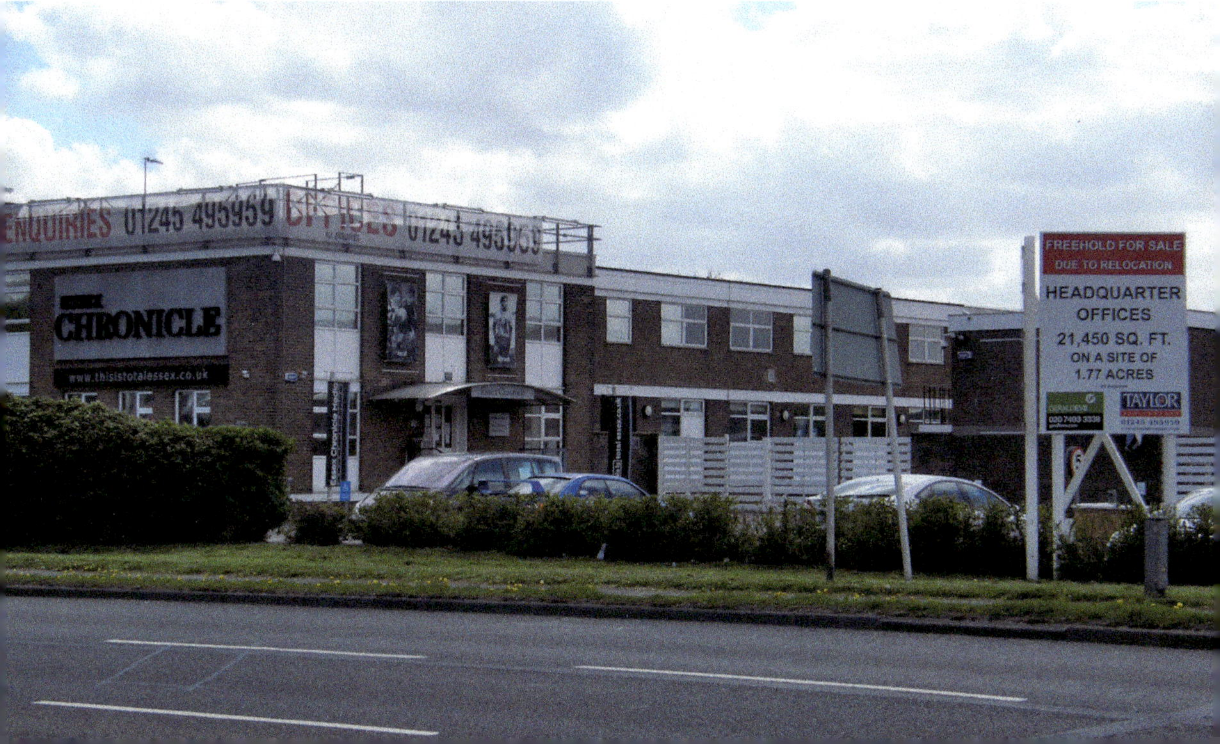

printed one. It became a roaring success and he started not only reporting events that would interest the Essex man, but ones that would catch the readership of all.

William Strupar realized that not only could he earn money by selling his papers but that he could sell space for advertising as well. Over the years the papers have featured all the major historical events that have affected our country. They recorded Napoleon's capture and imprisonment on Elba in 1814 and his escape on the sailing ship the *Swift* and his 100 days of power until his final defeat on the battlefield at Waterloo in 1815, which was equivalent to winning the Second World War.

The paper is still very popular and despite the relatively modern technology of television, email and other means of communication, the paper is still going strong. It has changed its name a number of times over the years. In 1963 it started printing in colour and although it has had a number of moves since its days in the High Street, it is still going strong at its base at Westway.

31. Stow Maries

Just outside Chelmsford, hidden away in Hackmans Lane, is Stow Maries, a First World War aerodrome with many of its original buildings that have stood the test of time. It is run today by an army of volunteers and is open to the public on Saturdays and Sundays from Easter onwards. During the course of the summer they hold special days, with First World War planes giving aerial displays.

During the First World War, Stow Maries was one of four aerodromes in Essex. At the start of the war, Britain had only eleven pilots in the army and very few aircraft and the navy had eight. The French and Germans had many more. The Germans, in particular, were well advanced before the war and had built up a number of bombers and fighter planes in addition to their Zeppelins. As early as 1912 they had drawn up plans to raze London to the ground. The first German air attack was in spring 1915, and it caused chaos as Britain was totally unprepared. In fear, civilians rioted and demanded action. As a result, the government set up the Home Defence Squadrons, whose role was to protect London's approach from the east.

In 1916, 37 Squadron, who had BE1s, was moved to Stow Maries from France. The BE1 aircraft were very flimsy and made of wood and paper and could not match the German aircraft's manoeuvrability nor reach the heights of the Zeppelins. The British pilots soon learnt to be patient and wait until the Zeppelins were returning to their hangars and were losing height, then the British aircraft would swoop down, firing as they went.

Stow Maries' first Commanding Officer was nineteen-year-old Lt Ridley, who was promoted to Captain when he took over the station. One of his roles was to drop spies behind enemy lines in France. If he had been captured, he would have been shot. In March 1916, seven Zeppelins were sighted over the English

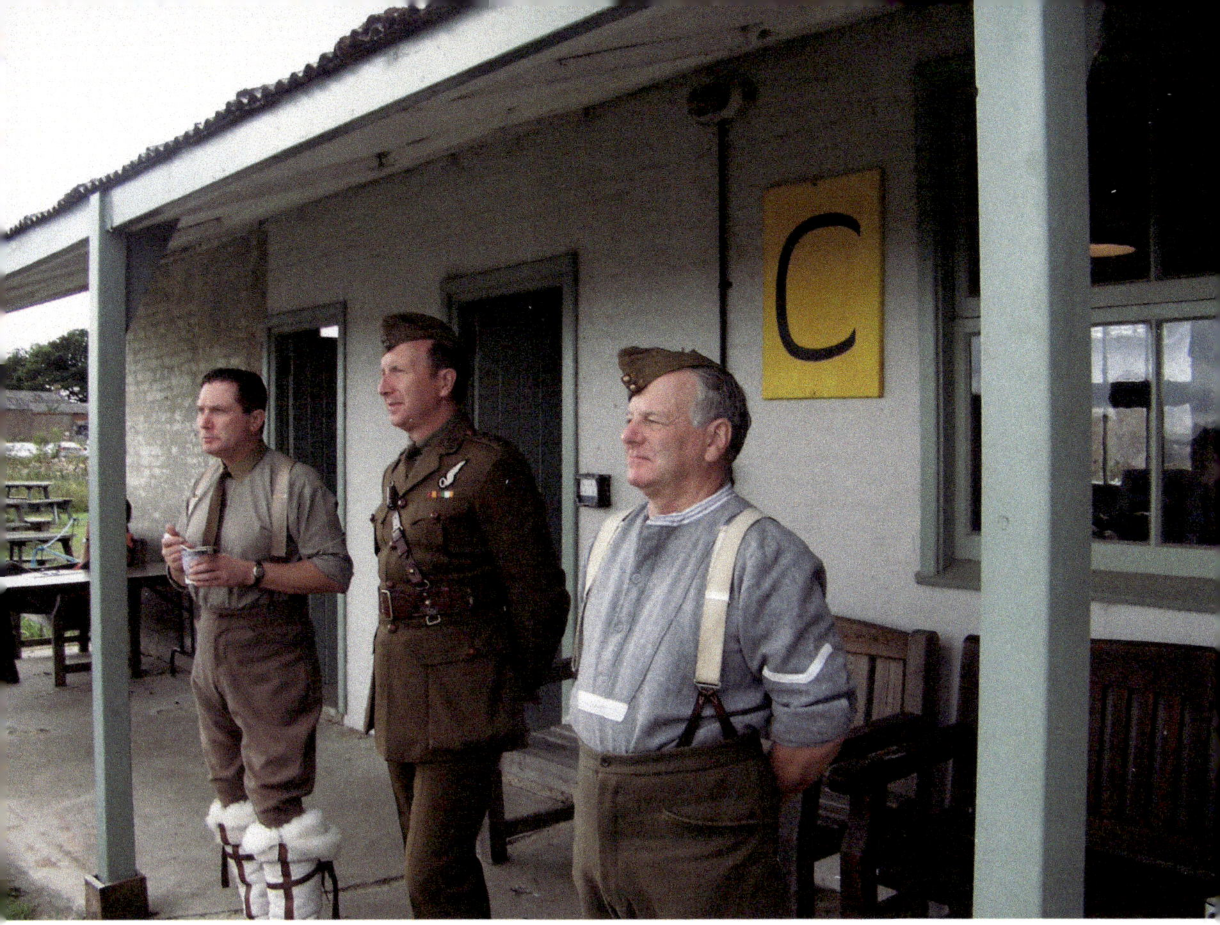

Above: The Airmen's building with volunteers dressed in First World War uniforms.

Below: A replica of a B1 First World War plane.

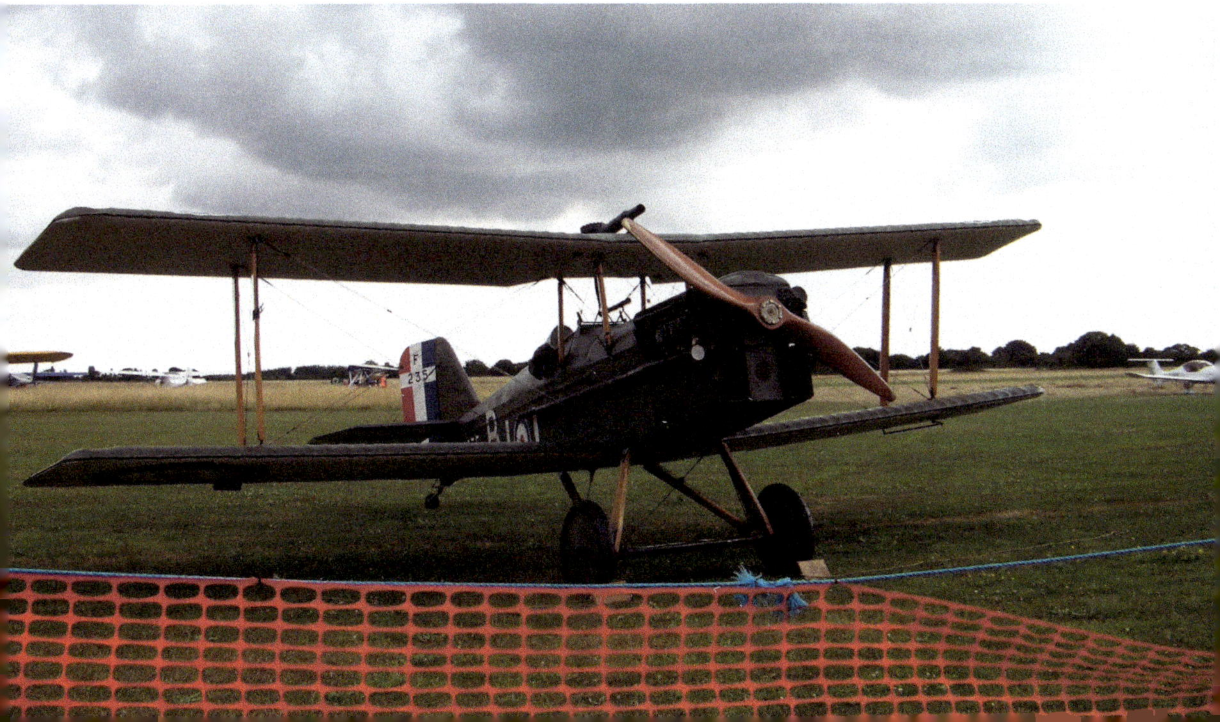

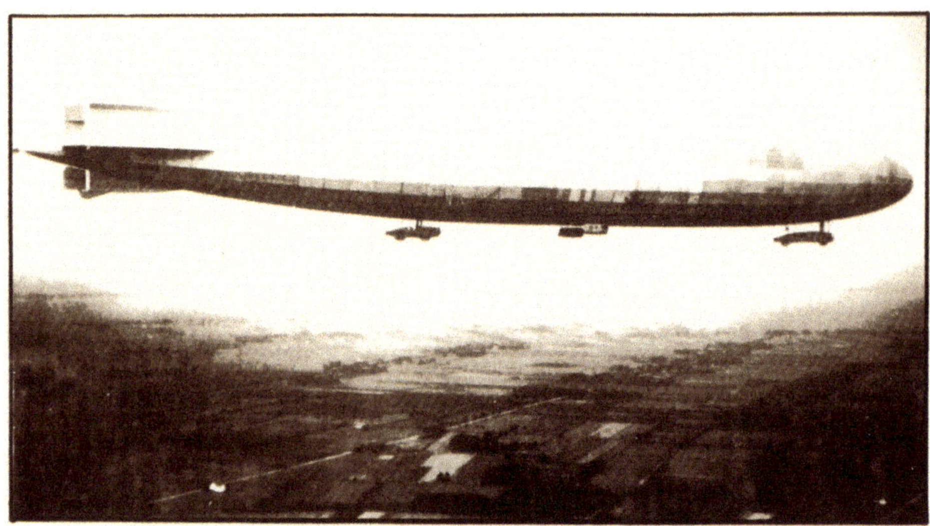

German Naval Airship Service Zeppelin L 32 in flight over Germany.

German Zeppelin of the First World War.

Channel and 37 Squadron was scrambled to intercept them. One of the enemy was caught in the searchlights and Captain Ridley shot at it. Then the anti-aircraft guns opened up and the Zeppelin burst into flames, crashing near Margate. As the war progressed, Stow Maries received better planes. Sadly, the squadron lost ten airmen but none of them were shot down by enemy aircraft. Two were killed by friendly fire and the others lost their lives in flying accidents.

32. Gray & Sons, Chelmsford Brewers Ltd

It is nice to know that Gray & Sons Brewery, set up in 1828 by Charles Stanton Gray, is still going strong today, although not in the same building. The original buildings are still standing at the junction of Springfield Road and the High Street, now Zizzi. I am given to understand that there is evidence to show that the beer was brewed at the rear of one of the oldest inns in Chelmsford, The Black Boy Inn, which has been demolished. Gray's business began to expand to such an extent that it was necessary to find additional premises to take advantage of the increased trade. They found suitable premises in Gate Street, Maldon, and moved there in 1870 and continued brewing in both places and supplying Essex public houses until 1974 when Greene King, a brewing business since 1799, became the main beer suppliers. Gray & Sons moved to their present place of trading in Rignals Lane.

Interestingly, outside their premises in Rignals Lane stands a phoenix, which was inherited from the Phoenix Insurance Company who rented part of the brewery in Springfield Road. They were a company set up in 1782 by the sugar

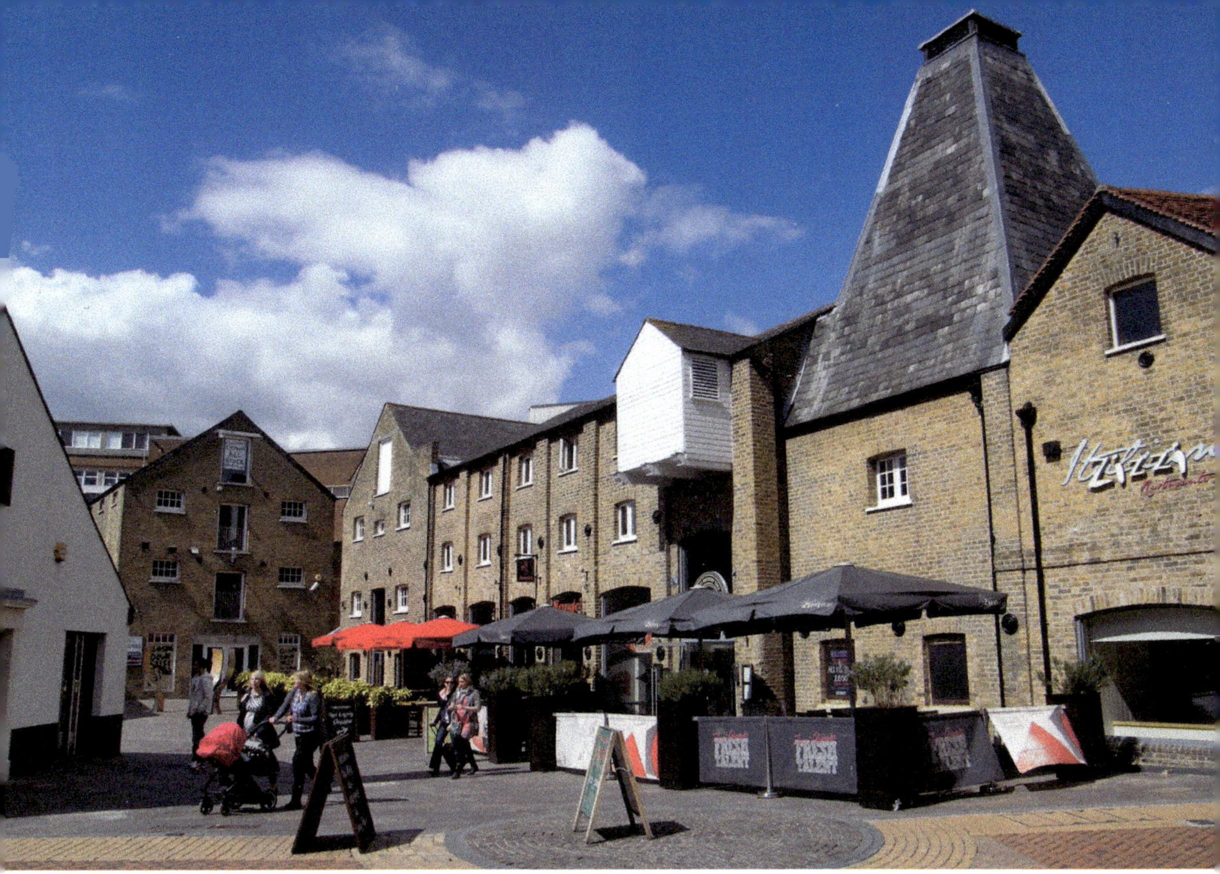

Above: The Brewery buildings 2020, now Zizzi Restaurant.

Below: The ordinal brewery. (Copyright Gray's Brewery)

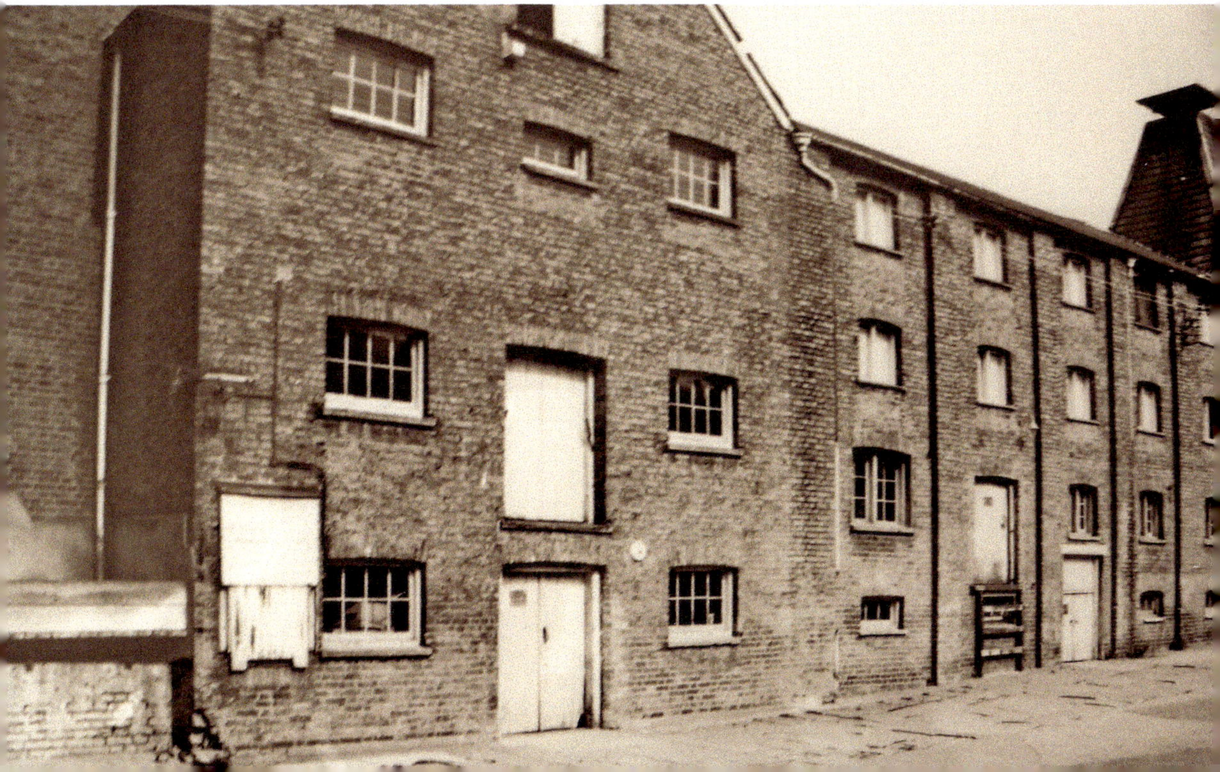

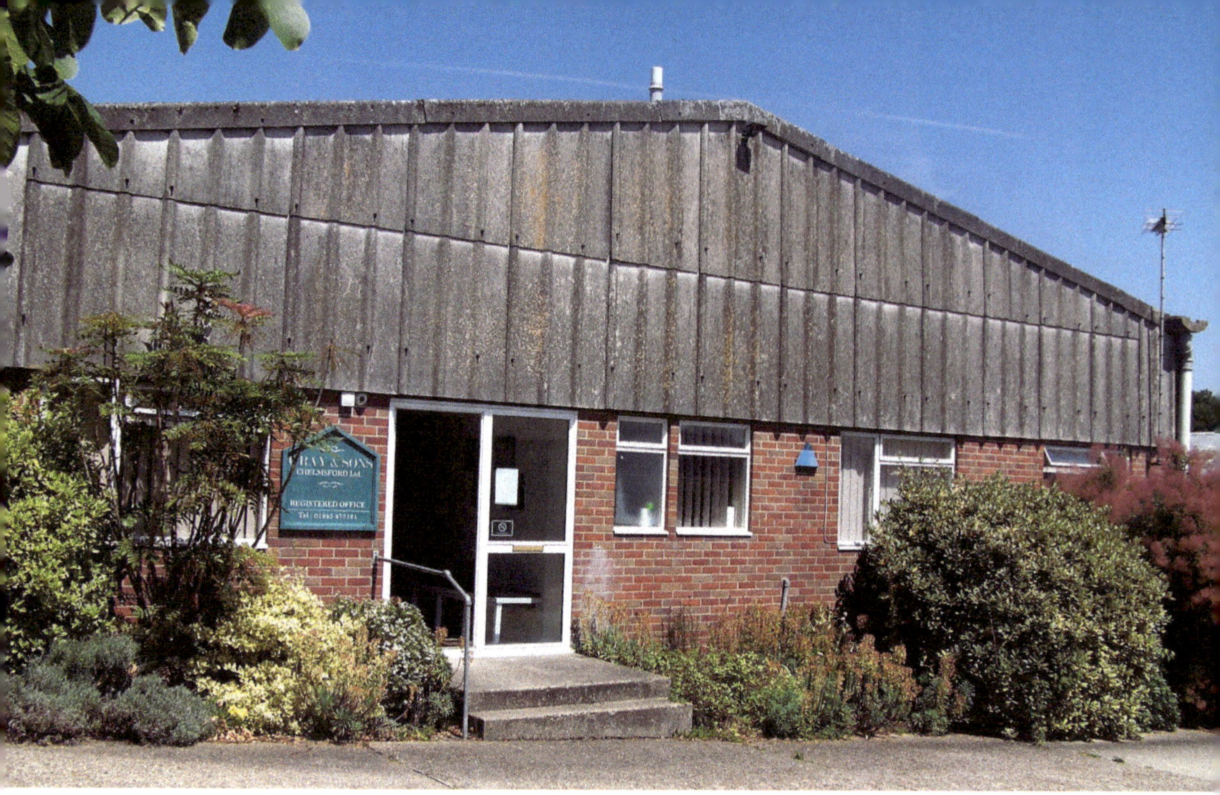

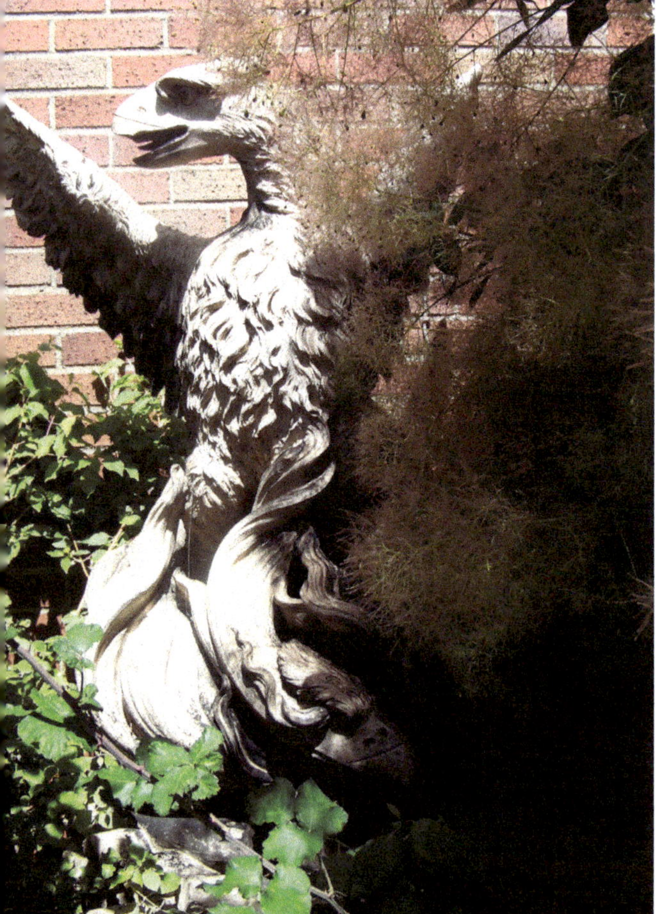

Above: Gray's Brewery, 2020.

Left: A statue of the phoenix outside the brewery.

refiners because they were tired of paying exorbitant premiums to the insurance companies for fire protection. They later expanded into other forms of insurance. At that time there was not a national fire brigade, so they formed their own and dressed their crews in red. If you had a fire and you had one of their phoenixes outside your premises, you were safe, and they would put out the fire. But if you did not, they stood by whilst your premises burned.

33. Pillboxes

A remnant of the Second World War are the pillboxes that were positioned along the routes it was thought the Germans would use when they invaded Britain. There are a few remaining in Essex and two have survived the ravages of time on the old A130, and are now listed as Grade II buildings.

They are constructed of concrete with slots through which small arms can be fired. Often, they had a tank ditch dug round the outside, although they were not able to withstand tank or artillery fire. They were camouflaged, to give them an element of surprise. During the war, 28,000 were built, but today only around 6,000 remain.

Pillbox.

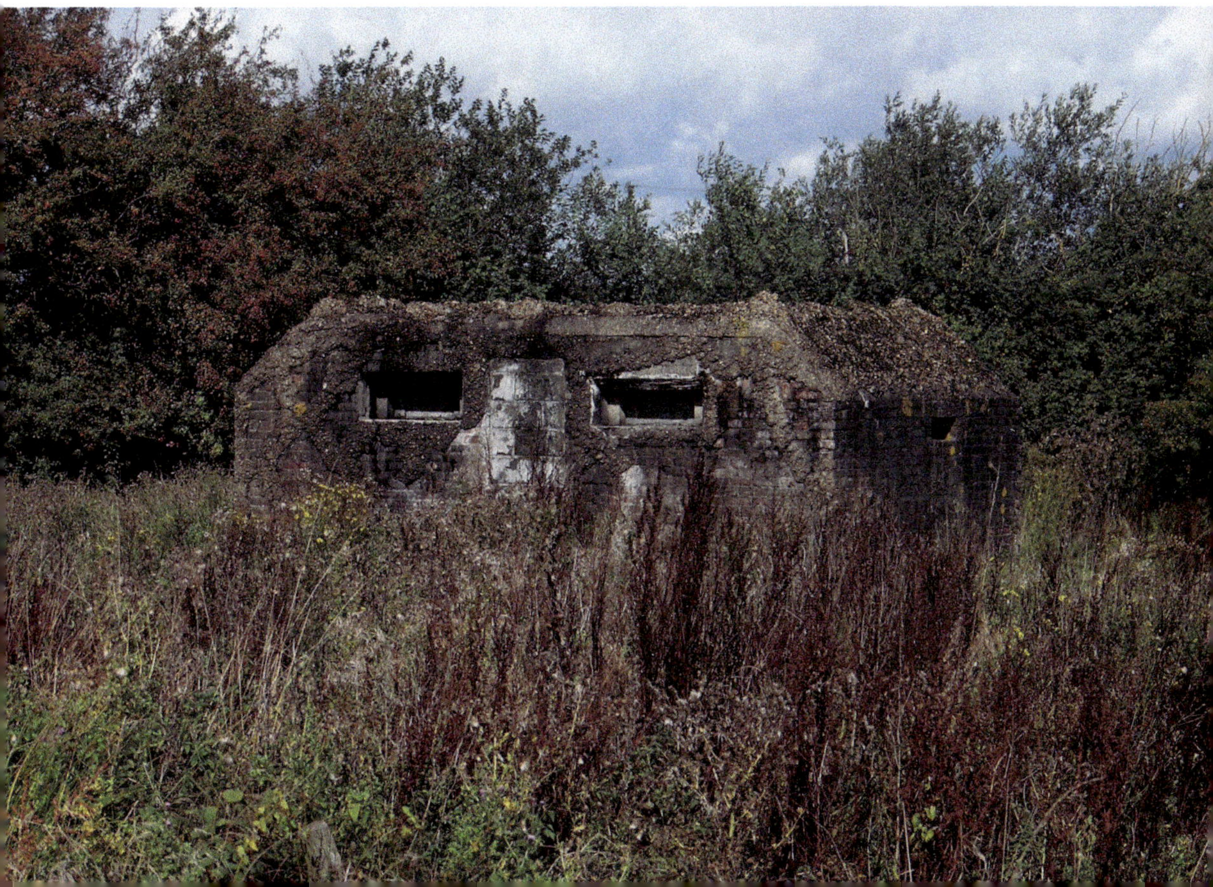

It is thought they were called pillboxes because their shape resembled medical boxes. The first German pillboxes, during the First World War, were so light that when an explosion went off near them they flipped over. There were a number of different shapes of pillboxes but they were designed to have all-round vision. Sir Ernest Moir invented one which was easy to erect and had interlocking concrete blocks with a steel roof and was suitable for the use of machine guns.

34. The White Horse, Great Baddow

There were two White Horse public houses in the Chelmsford area. One is located at 78 High Street, Great Baddow, and the other was in Townfield Street and has now been demolished. One of them was, or is, haunted by the ghost of Thomas Kidderminster, who was murdered. The White Horse in Great Baddow was built, it is believed, in the sixteenth century. Thomas Kidderminster had just sold his properties in Ely and was travelling to London to join his wife and had a considerable amount of money on him.

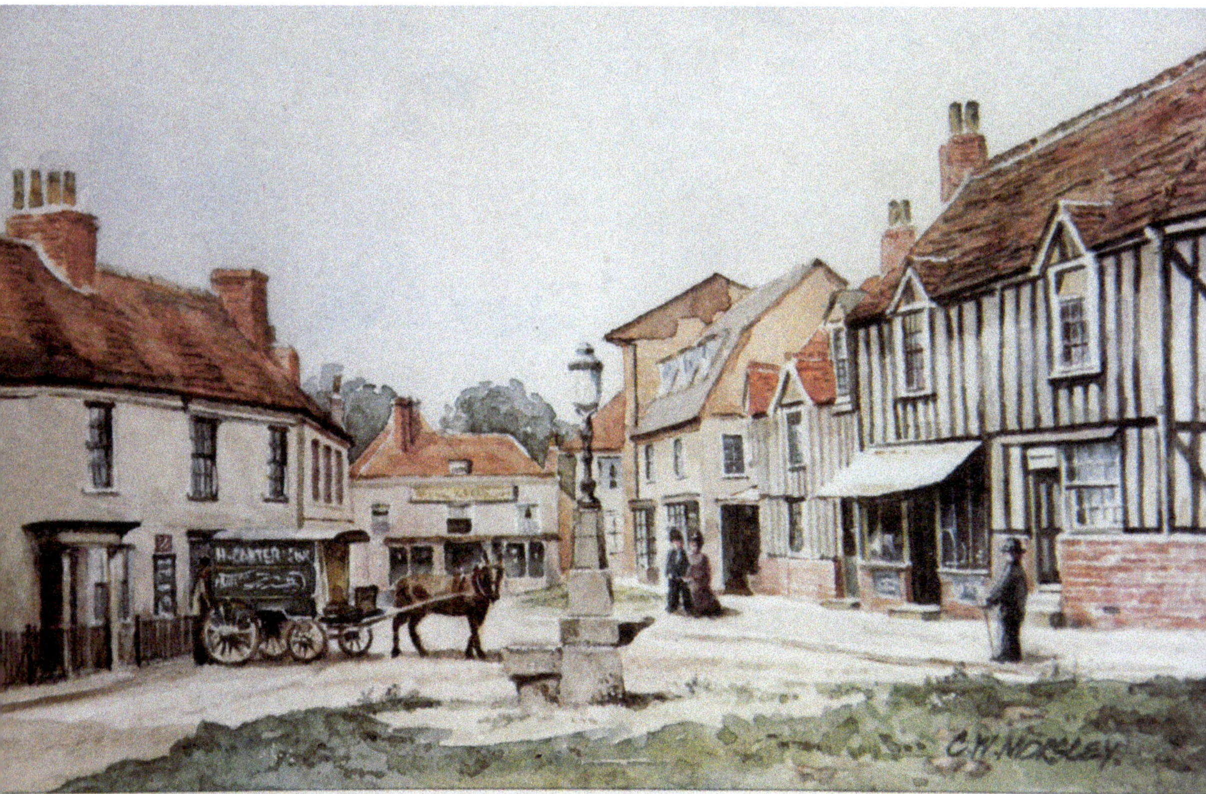

The White Horse, 1890.

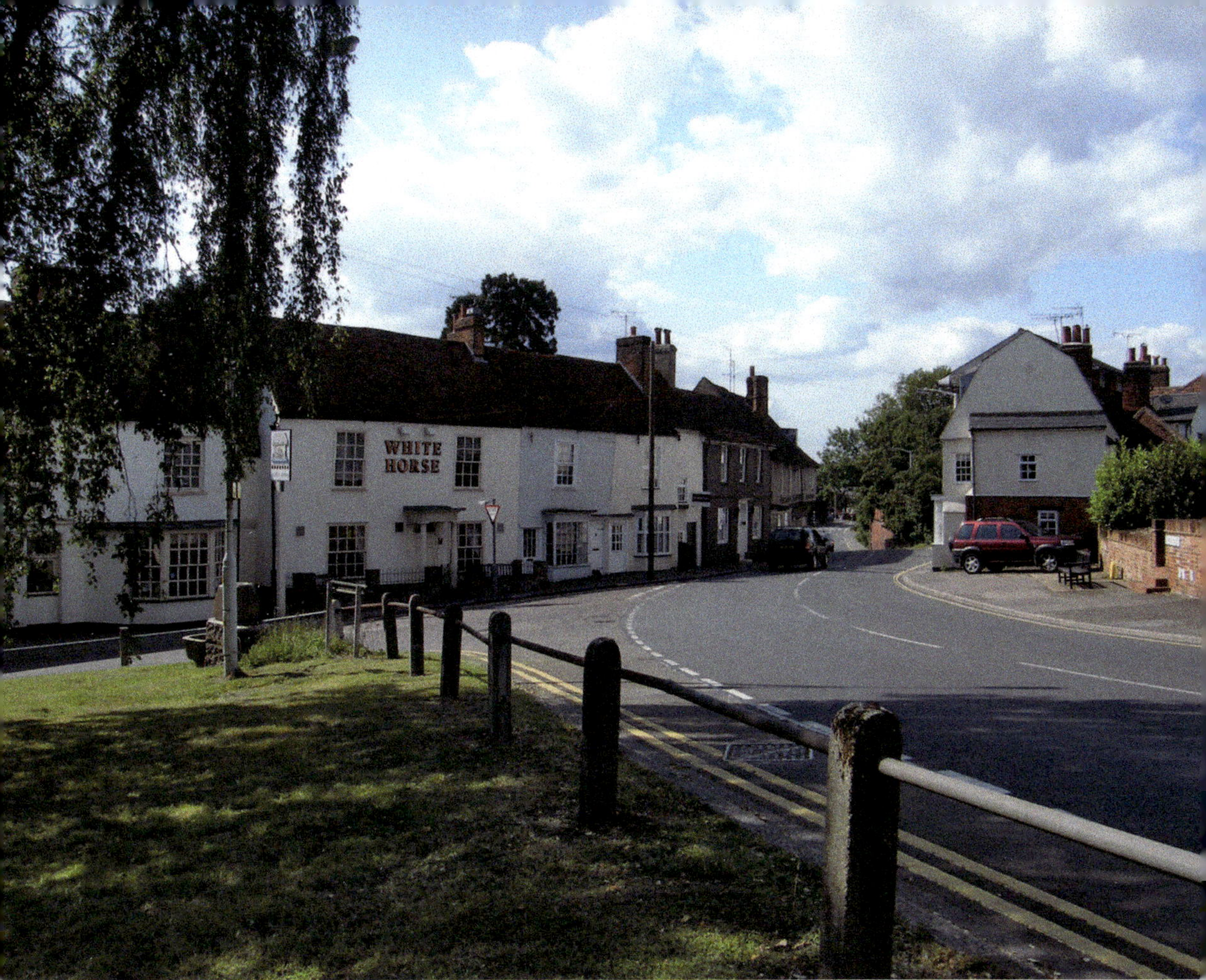

The White Horse, 2020.

He stopped off at the White Horse for the night and was never heard of again. Anne, his wife, who was pregnant at the time, was a strong, determined woman, and set out to find him. For years she followed every clue until, one day, she saw an article in a newspaper about a body being found in the garden of the White Horse by the new landlord who was digging the foundations for a wall. The authorities calculated that the body had been buried for ten years, which was about the time Anne's husband disappeared. She set out to investigate. By chance, while passing through Romford, she met a woman called Mary, who, surprisingly, had worked as a maid at the White Horse. She told Anne that the previous landlord, Mr Sewell, and the ostler, Mr Moses Drayne, were wicked and should be hanged. When Anne arrived at the inn she discovered that Mr Sewell had died of a fever but Mrs Sewell and Mr Drayne were still alive.

Anne found Mrs Sewell and questioned her, but her answers were so evasive that she contacted the authorities. After interrogating Mrs Sewell and Mr Drayne, they arrested them and charged them with murder. Mary, the maid, was questioned and she told the authorities that she had become suspicious that something was wrong when she went downstairs in the morning and was told that Mr Kidderminster had left. Later, she went into his bedroom and was surprised to find his clothes still in the wardrobe. When she asked about them, Mrs Sewell set about her and thrashed her. When Mr Sewell heard the commotion, he intervened and gave her twenty-five pounds to keep quiet. At the trial a cleaning lady gave evidence and said that when she was passing the pub early in the morning on the day in question she heard voices coming from the garden.

Two weeks before the trial, Mrs Sewell escaped justice by dying. Mr Drayne was found guilty and hanged. Mary was charged, convicted, and imprisoned. It is said that Mr Kidderminster haunts the pub, looking for his clothes.

35. The Saracen's Head

The Saracen's Head inn at 3 High Street is opposite Shire Hall. It was originally a staging post for travellers on their way from London to Harwich and was built in 1539. The inn was known for letting out chaises with their drivers, who were dressed in blue livery. The post boys would take the travellers to the next stage of their journey.

The Saracen's Head, 1942, showing the American Red Cross Club.

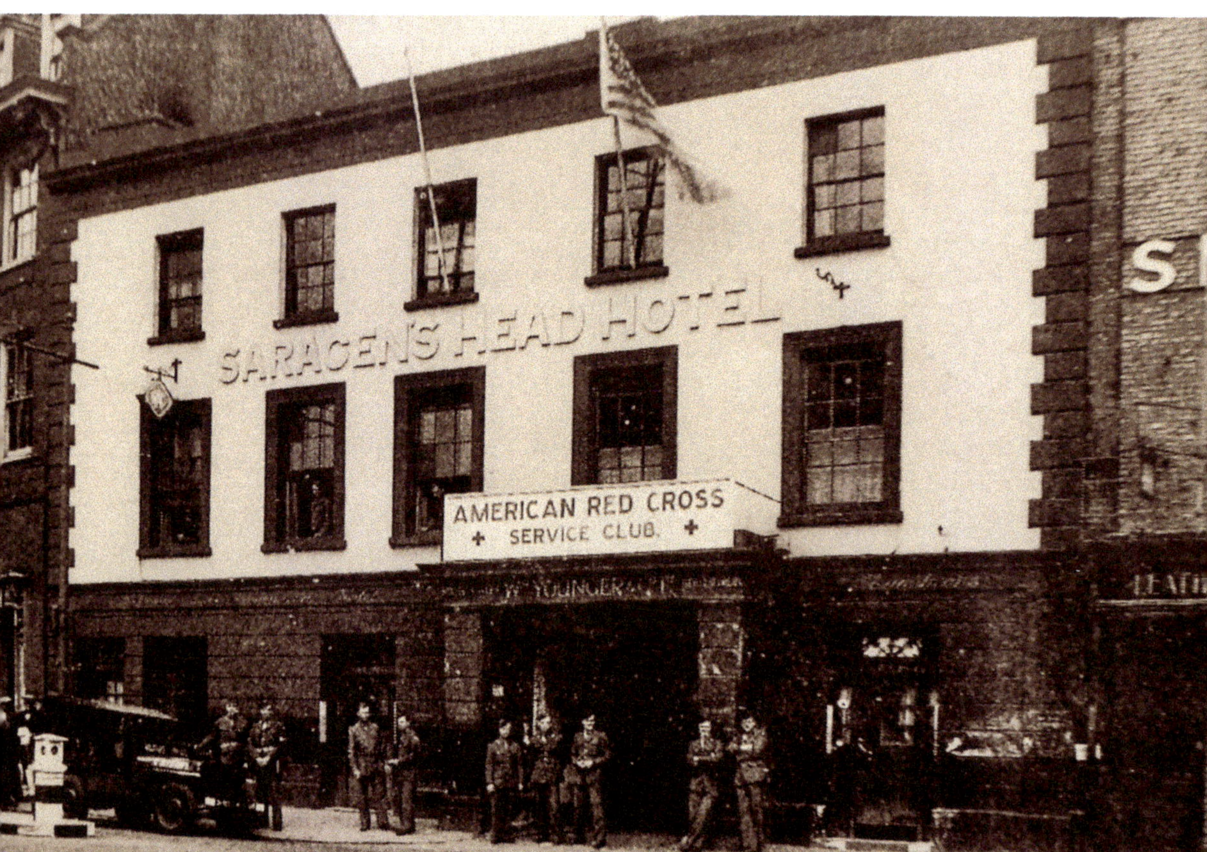

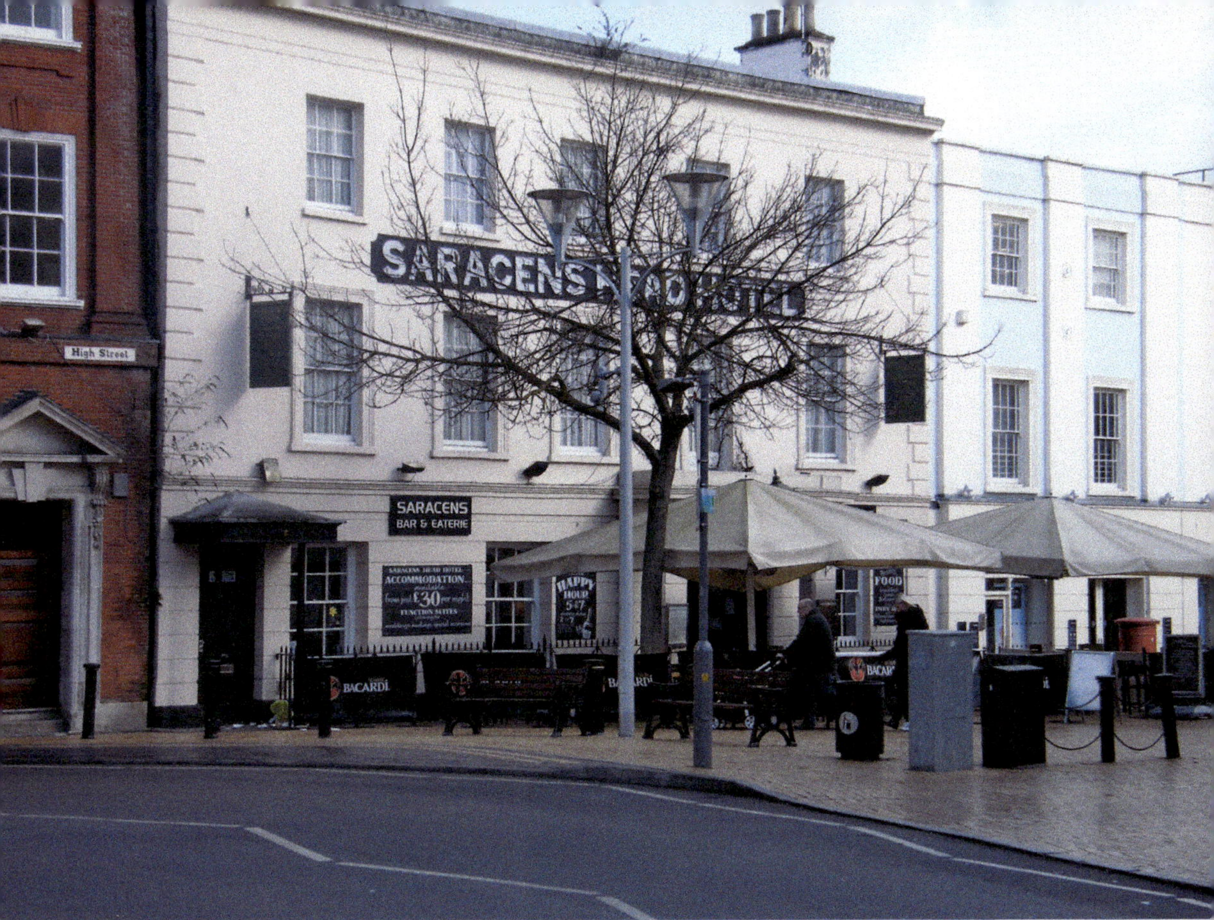

The Saracen's Head, 2013.

In 1718 a Mr Nichols bought the inn for £650 and started carrying out extensive alterations, but he ran out of money and was forced to sell the property to William Taylor. The inn was famous for its grand balls, which all the nobility from the district attended.

In 1724 Daniel Defoe mentions the inn in his *book Tour Through the Whole Island of Great Britain*. Anthony Trollope (1815–52) also stayed at the inn while carrying out his job as Inspector General for the Post Office and wrote part of *Barchester Towers* while staying there, and the story was published in weekly parts. One day, two clergymen were sitting at a table near him and he heard one say, 'Confound that Mrs Proudie. I wish she was dead.' Anthony Trollope leant across and said, 'Gentlemen, that happens next week!'

During the Second World War the American Red Cross Service Club, who were equivalent to our NAAFI, took over the inn so that American servicemen could drink cold beer, read American papers and socialise. The Americans had sixty-seven aerodromes in the East and had at least 200,000 personnel. Over the years many of the Americans who served here came back to reminisce but sadly they are becoming fewer and fewer.

36. Riverside Inn

Riverside Inn, formerly known as Springfield Mill, in Victoria Road was built in the seventeenth century. It was, as its name implies, originally a watermill but was converted into an inn. In my opinion it is one of the most beautiful buildings in Chelmsford sitting by the side of the river. Who would guess that it was the scene of a tragedy that involved the death of a baby.

In 1844, Chelmsford was rocked by the scandal of Elizabeth Belsham, who was having a child. Her partner, Stephen Dean, was convinced it was not his, so he threw her out. As most girls in that situation would do, she went home to her mother, where her son was born.

Her brother had just died and so she named her son after him. When her son was only nineteen days old, she decided to return to her partner, no doubt to try to convince him the boy was his. She took a lift on a mail cart that was on its way to Chelmsford, where she expected to find her partner in his favourite pub, the Beehive. The cart stopped at a pub in Runsell Green, where the landlady said at Elizabeth's trial that she saw the prisoner feed the baby with biscuits, although the baby was only under a month old. It was getting dark and Elizabeth was getting desperate to find her partner, so she hurried on to the Beehive, only to find her

Picture of Riverside Inn, 2020.

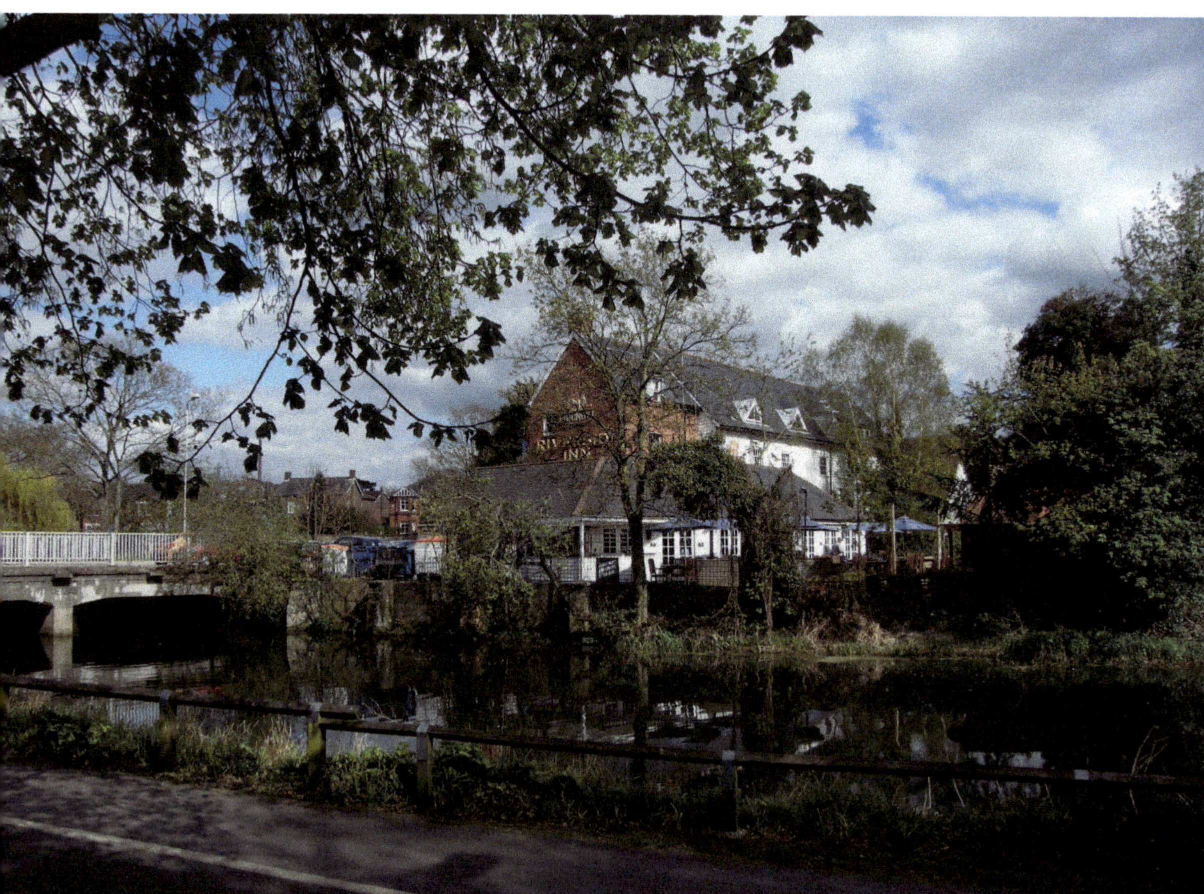

partner was not sitting in his usual corner. Cuddling her son in her arms she set off into the dark, rainy night to find him. Later, witnesses swore on oath that they had seen her in the King's Head but without the baby.

As it was now pitch black and she had not found her husband, she decided to stay at the Riverside Inn. The next morning, she changed her mind about seeing her partner and instead decided to make her way to a friend's house in Writtle. Before she did so, she wrote a note to her partner, explaining that their baby was dead.

It was a misty morning and Oliver Turner was walking along the river's pathway on his way to work when he saw something in the river. He stared harder and through the fog could just make out the body of a baby being battered against one of the bridge supports. In a panic, he raced into the Riverside Inn screaming for help. Hearing the shouting, Mr Joseph, who was having a quiet beer, sprang to his feet and the two of them rushed out into the river. They waded through the swirling water in the hope of saving the baby, but it was dead. They called the newly formed police force and Elizabeth was arrested. A post-mortem was carried out and after a long discussion it was decided that the baby had drowned. Even though there was no evidence of violence, Elizabeth was charged with murder.

The trial was held in the Shire Hall in July 1844, and a great crowd gathered outside, so much so that the court officials had to fight their way through to get to the court. The case looked clear-cut and the mob could not wait for the verdict and the subsequent hanging. They were to be disappointed, as she was defended by one of the best lawyers in the country who knew how to work a crowd. He maintained that she had felt dizzy through lack of food and had slipped in the mud by the river and dropped the baby accidentally. The jury was convinced and she was released, much to the crowd's disappointment.

37. The Spotted Dog

One of the greatest tragedies in Chelmsford, apart from the Second World War, occurred in the stables of the Spotted Dog in 1804. The inn was where 24 Tindal Street is today. A Hanoverian regiment was billeted in town after marching the miles from London on its way to Harwich before embarking for France. Every inn, church hall, stable and space had been taken over by them. Thirteen solders were billeted in the stables of The Spotted Dog, which had a latch on the outside and which was difficult to open from the inside. It is thought that as they settled down for the night, one of the soldiers, unable to sleep in the strange surroundings, lit his pipe and then, without thinking, knocked it out into the straw, which started to smoulder and then burst into flames. The soldiers, being in unfamiliar surroundings and in the dark, panicked and started shouting for help, but in German, which nobody understood. By the time somebody saw the flames

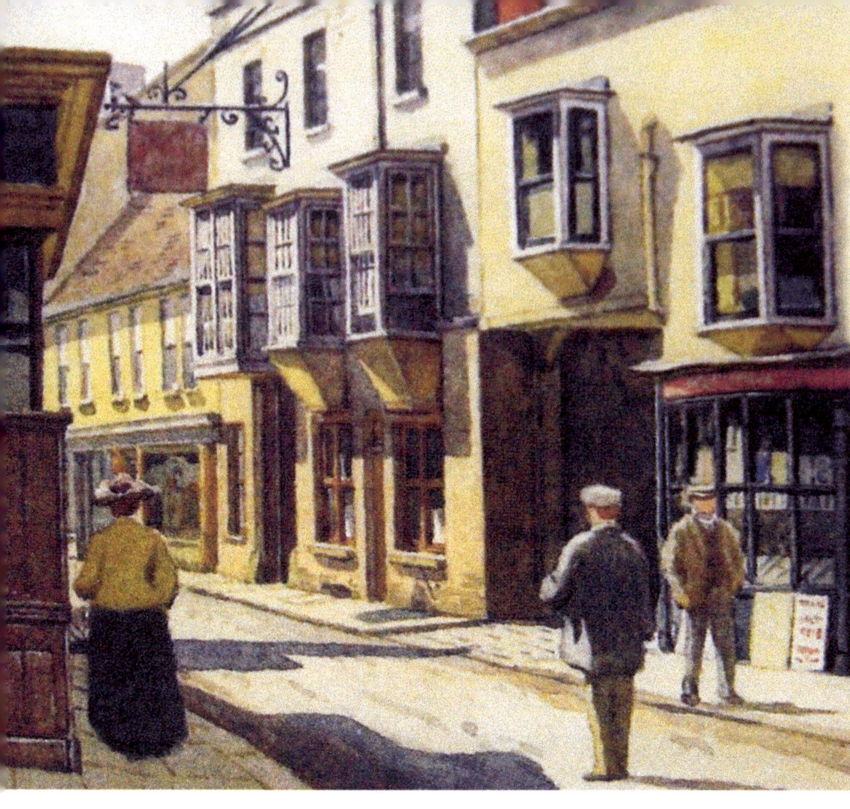

The *Spotted Dog*, a painting by Alfred Bamford. (Courtesy of Chelmsford Museum)

it was too late; all thirteen were burnt alive. Since then, it is said that the soldier that caused the fire returns and kicks boxes around in frustration.

The old public house saw its own maker in 1970 when it was demolished for a new development.

38. Tulip Public House

The Tulip public house's claim to fame is that it is the only public house in England with that name. It was originally owned by Mr Drake and was a farmhouse, but during the nineteenth century, farmers started to find that making a living from the soil was difficult. They were faced with cheap imports of wheat and grain from Canada and America and many British farmers turned to other ways of making a living. Mr Drake, to supplement his living, opened part of the farmhouse as a public house.

Other farmers in the 1890s supplemented their incomes by selling part of their land to the London Land Company, who divided the land up into small plots and sold these to Londoners who wanted to get out of the smoky city for weekends or holidays. The London Land Company organised train excursions and met the prospective buyers at the stations, and took them by a horse and cart to a marquee, where they were plied with food and drink for 2/6. When judged to be in the right mood they were taken out to see the plots. The nearest parcels of land to the stations were the more expensive. After purchasing the plot, for as little as £10, Londoners came down at weekends to the peace and tranquillity of the

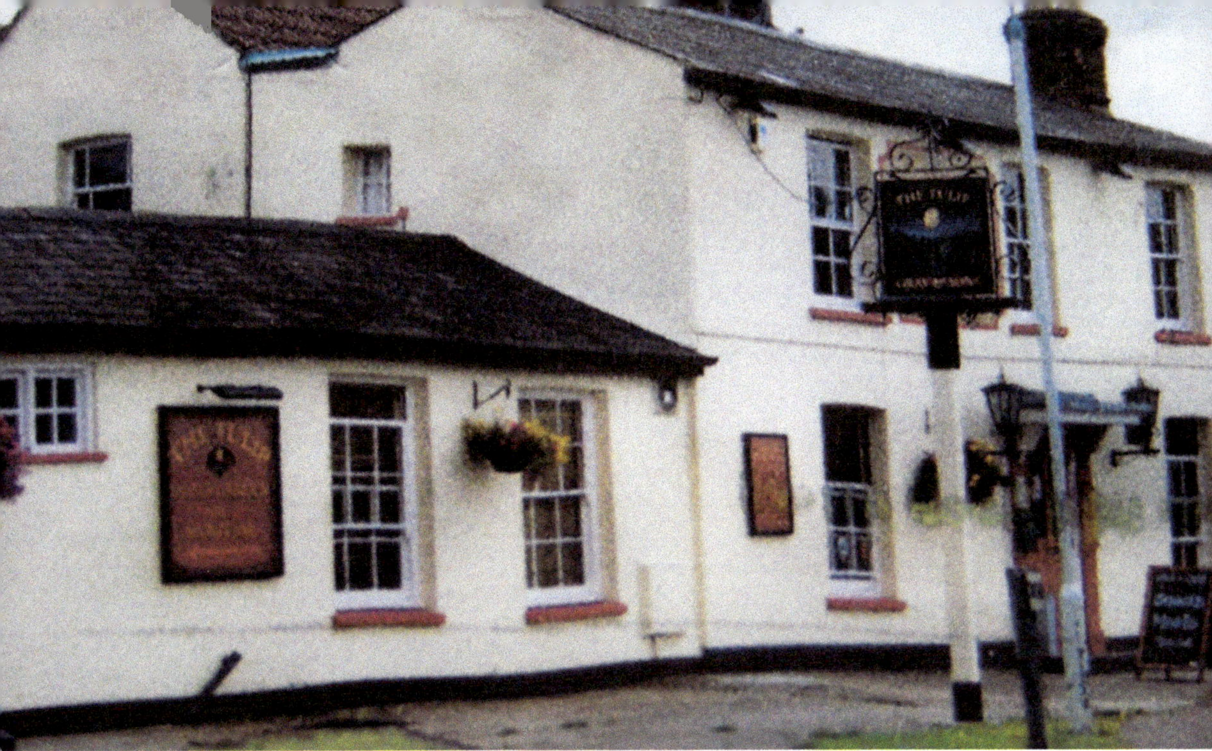

The Tulip, 2020.

countryside and would erect temporary shelters, like tents, old buses and, in one case, a ship's cabin. Then gradually some started building more permanent homes.

There was no sanitation, water, gas or electricity. They overcame these problems by burying their toilet waste and saving rainwater from the gutters. For heating and cooking they used paraffin or an open fire. The Water Board finally put standpipes in but every drop of water had to be collected and carried home. The pipes froze during the winter. In most cases a good community spirit developed and there was little anti-social behaviour and theft was almost unknown. The plotlanders would put a bag down at the bottom of the track with money in it for groceries that were delivered by horse and cart but the cash was never stolen.

During the Second World War, many Londoners came down in droves to their plots to escape the bombing and after the war, settled down on their plot.

There was a great need for housing when the war finished and one of the measures the government took was to introduce the New Towns Act of 1946, which set up New Town Corporations and gave them the power to compulsorily purchase the plots and build the New Towns.

39. The Hospital and Homes of St Giles'

Leprosy is a cruel and ancient disease which many people think has been eradicated, but it has not. There is a cure, but in 2016 there were 200,000 cases in the world. India accounted for most of these, followed closely by Brazil and Indonesia. America has between 150 and 200 cases a year.

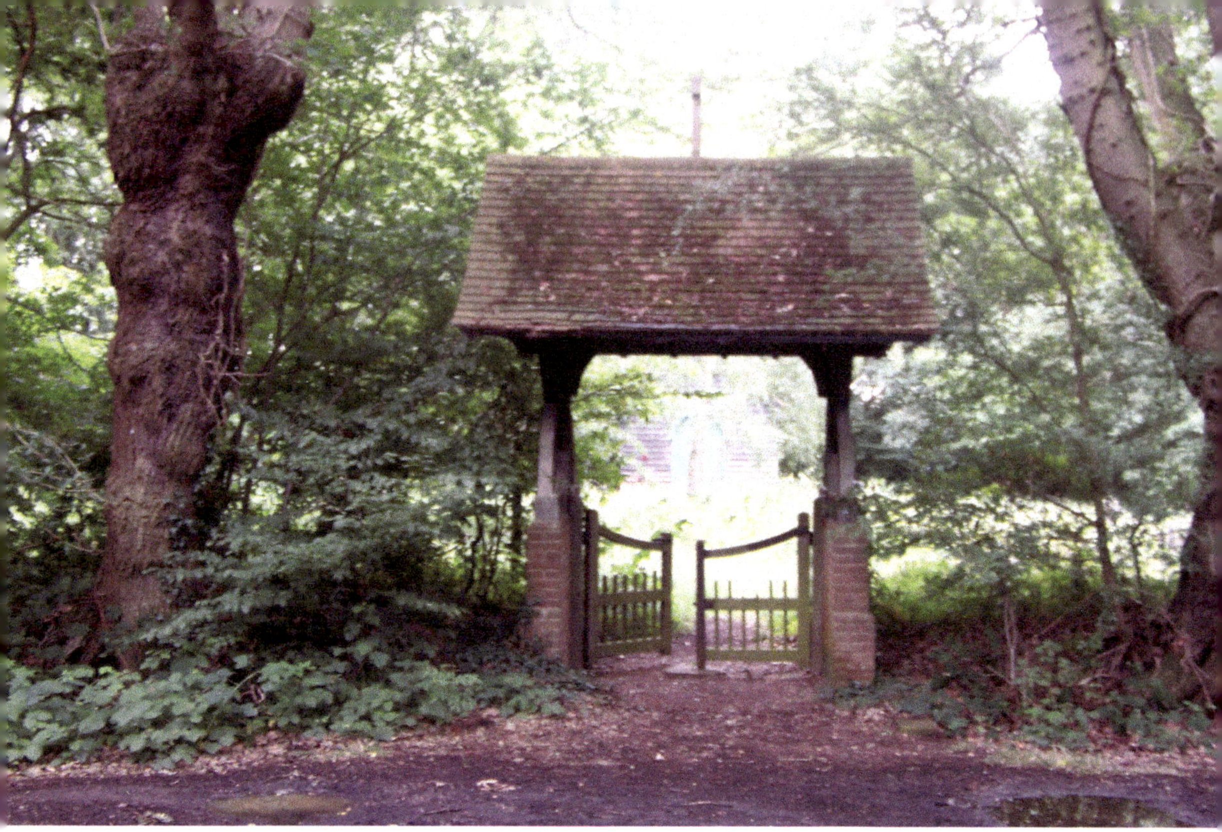

Above: The gates at St Giles' Cemetery.

Below: The Leper Cemetery.

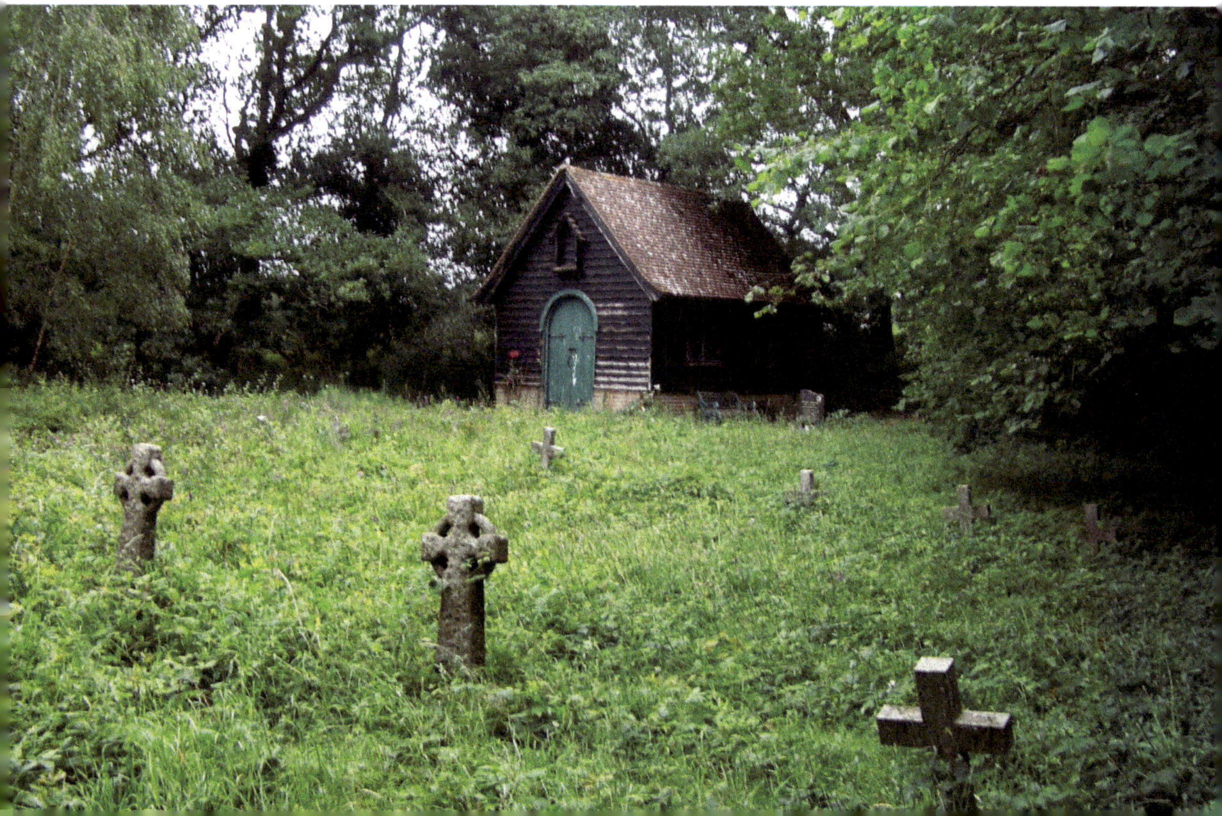

The illness was renamed Hansen's disease in 1873 after Gerhard Henrik Armauer Hansen, who discovered that the cause of the disease was mycobacterium leprae. Over the centuries, many leprosy hospitals were set up in this country. St Giles, in Moor Hall Lane, Bicknacre, was one of them but it no longer exists. However, the cemetery where the patients were buried when they died still does. In the late eighteenth century, 27 acres of land plus some farm buildings were purchased for the sum of £1,500 for a leper colony to be established. It was named St Giles' after the patron saint of the crippled and afflicted. Lord Strathcona donated £1,500 to help get the hospital established. In 1914, the staff consisted of two nurses from Guy's hospital and two monks.

Today, there is a cure that was discovered in 1982 and consists of a combination of three drugs taken for between six and twelve months. The drugs stop the disease but it does not reverse the damage that has already occurred.

Any patient that died in St Giles' was carried to the cemetery and a service held in the small building you can see in the picture. The patient was then interned in the churchyard.

40. Regent Cinema

Most old cinemas have gone through many changes over the years and started to decline when the majority of families bought televisions. At one time, people would go to the pictures at least once or twice a week. The highlight of the week for most children was Saturday morning pictures, where shouts of 'Look out behind you' could be heard as the baddy crept up behind the hero. The pictures normally showed cowboy films that would finish up with the hero about to tumble over a cliff. This was just to ensure that the audiences returned the following week.

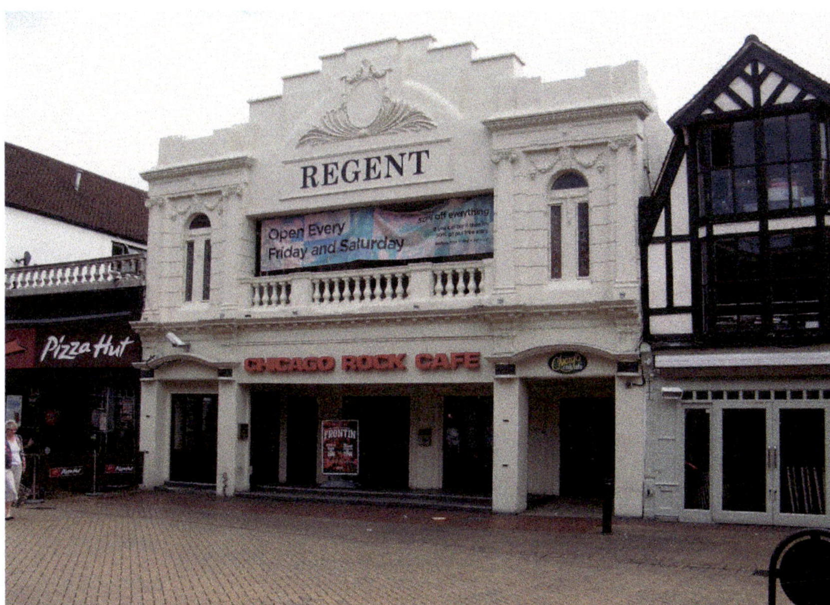

The Regent Cinema, 2020.

In Chelmsford, we are very lucky that the façade of the old Regent Cinema in 6 Moulsham Street is still intact and is now a Grade II listed building. It was designed by Francis Burdett Ward and was opened in 1913. It was built as a cine-variety house and had many shows as well as films. For three years, films and variety acts were put on, then, as films became more sophisticated and popular, the Regent became a full-time cinema in 1916. The large auditorium was richly decorated with fibrous plasterwork and had a balcony and two boxes on each side. Alterations were carried out in 1935 and in 1943 when it was taken over by Eastern Counties Cinemas Ltd and then, around 1959, Shipman and King bought it.

With the advent of mass television and falling attendance, it closed its doors on 6 September 1975 and became, as most cinemas did at that time, a bingo hall. This closed and became a night spot called the Chicago Rock Café, which has now closed.

41. Galleywood Racecourse

Galleywood Racecourse in Stock Road, opposite The Eagle public house, was once one of the oldest in the country. It is understood that there was a racecourse on the Common during the reign of Charles II (1660–80). There was a Grandstand but at a meeting in 1767, it mysteriously caught fire and burnt down. Luckily nobody was injured. Soon afterwards, a new grandstand was built, which could

The Grandstand Galleywood Racecourse, 1900s. (Copyright Chelmsford Museum)

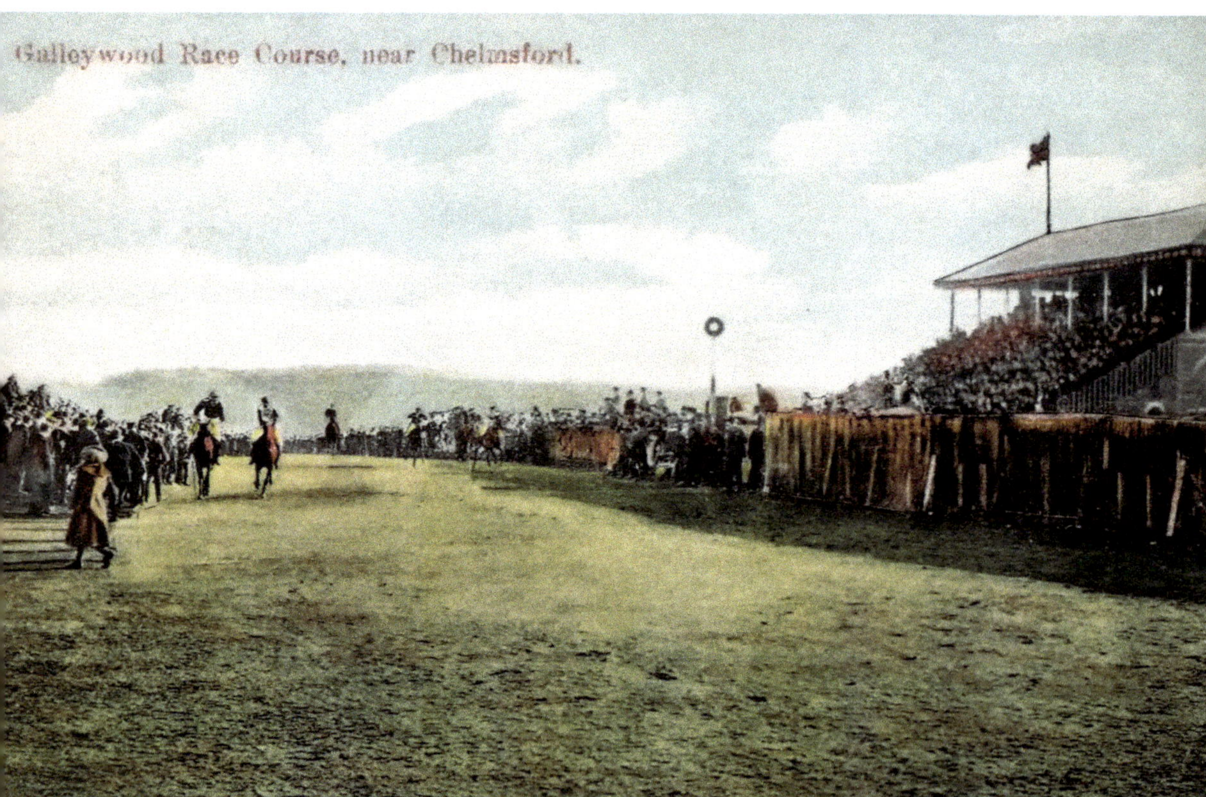

hold 1,000 spectators. Before it was built, the elite would stay in their carriages along the track and watch the races in comfort, drinking their champagne. The first recorded advertising for races was in *The Chelmsford Chronicle* in 1764. They reported that there was to be a three-day event and persons wishing to enter a horse had to register it at the Black Boy Inn in Chelmsford on the Saturday before the race. The course was not easy, as racehorses had to cross the road four times and race uphill to the winning post.

King George III liked a flutter and set up a race in 1770, called 'The Queen's Plate' with a prize of one hundred guineas, which in those days was a lot of money.

With the coming of the railway, racing at Galleywood became even more popular and punters flooded in from far and wide. Racehorse owners were pleased, for they could unload their horses nearer the course. Horse racing was not the only entertainment on race days. There was prize fighting, dog and bull baiting, card games, eating and drinking tents. Prostitutes plied their trade and, with so many drunks staggering about, the pickpockets did well. Marquees were erected and grand balls were held on the track and at the Black Boy Inn. Anybody who was anybody had to be there.

King Edward VII (1841–1910) loved gambling and attended the races. He must have caused a great stir amongst the regulars. During both world wars the course was used for military training. After the war racing began to diminish and in 1922, the Chelmsford Race Stand Company was put up for auction and taken over by Chelmsford Race Company, who revived racing and renovated the Grandstand so that it could hold 1,200 spectators. The revival of the track attracted hundreds of spectators who used every means of transport to attend. People came on foot, on coaches, special train excursions, cars and bicycles. Unfortunately, the numbers of people attending began to diminish and the course closed in April 1935. Part of the course can be seen today.

42. The Red Cow Temperance Hotel

The Red Cow was situated at the junction of Broomfield Road and Duke Street and was built before 1722. In 1867 it was owned by Writtle Brewery.

During Victorian times there was a great deal of drunkenness in Britain and Chelmsford in particular. The authorities were becoming worried that mothers and their children were being neglected by husbands who, once they had been paid, went down to the local public house and drank their wages away. In view of this trend, temperance organisations were established to prevent this behaviour. One of the earliest movements was inspired by an Irish professor of theology, John Edgar, who was so incensed by the drunkenness and negligence of families by drunken husbands that, as a protest, he poured his stock of whisky out of his window.

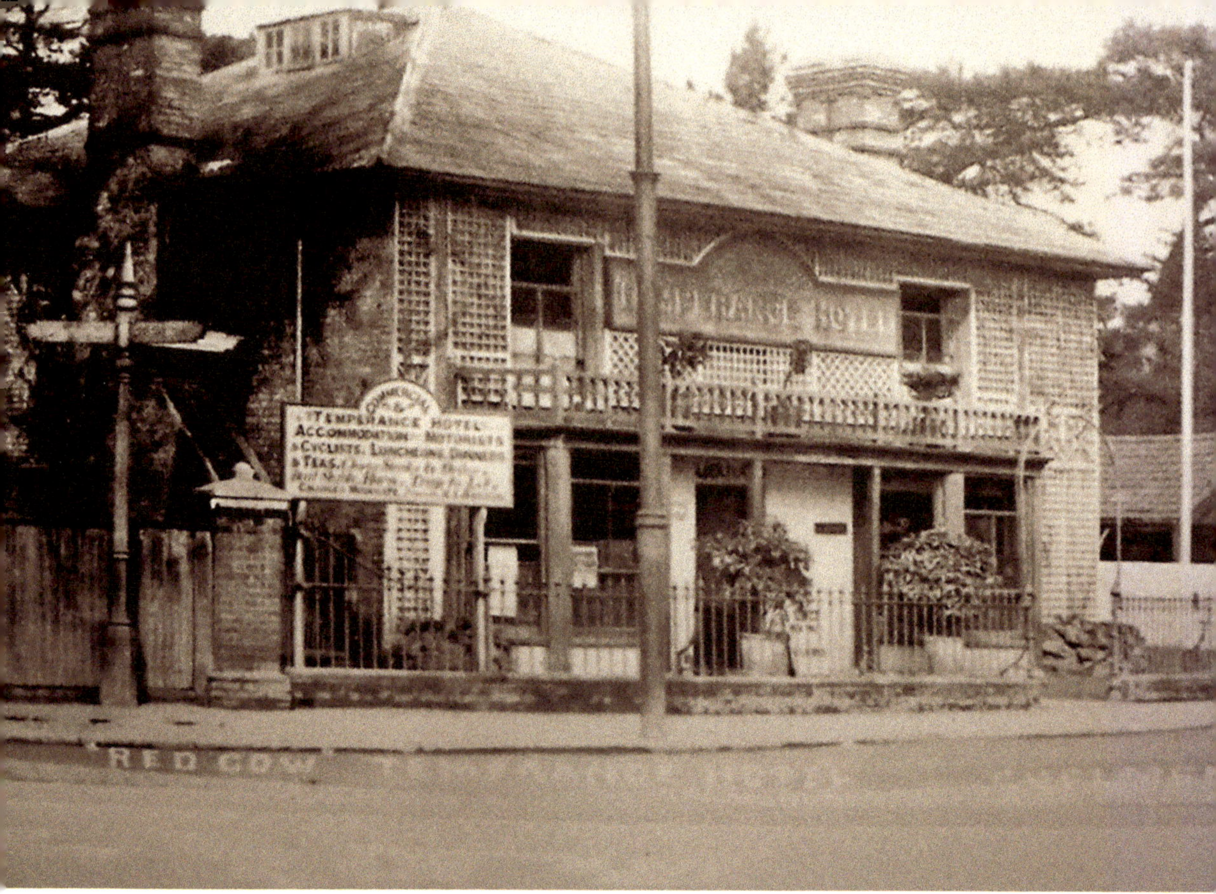

The Red Cow, 1900s. (Copyright Chelmsford Museum)

One of the first temperance movements was set up in Scotland and named the Glasgow and West Scotland Temperance Society. Other establishments, like the Church, Quakers and the Salvation Army, were foremost in the fight against drunkenness and tried to get people to sign the pledge not to drink. They tried to give alternatives to drinking and set up places where families could eat together, like the Red Cow. The first of these temperance hotels was set up in Preston and they soon spread throughout the country. To entertain their customers, they organised musical events, cycling, walking and holidays; anything to stop people drinking.

43. Riverside Leisure Centre

The original Riverside Centre was just a swimming pool, and was opened to the public in 1906 after having taken nine months to build. It was an open-air pool and had thirty dressing rooms and a place for customers to leave their bicycles, the popular means of transport in those days.

Most of the poorer homes in Chelmsford and throughout the country were without baths and by popular demand, in 1914, public baths were installed

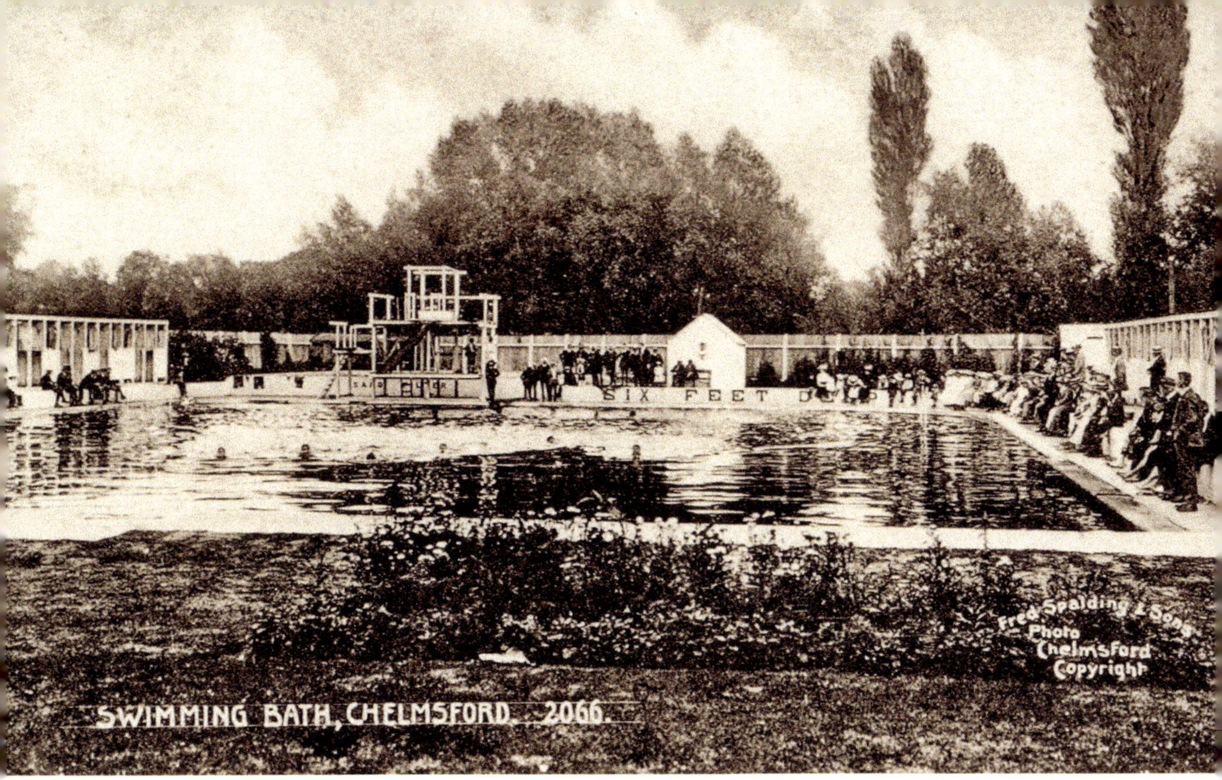

Above: Riverside Swimming Pool, 1906. (Copyright Essex Record Office)

Below: Riverside Leisure Centre, 2020.

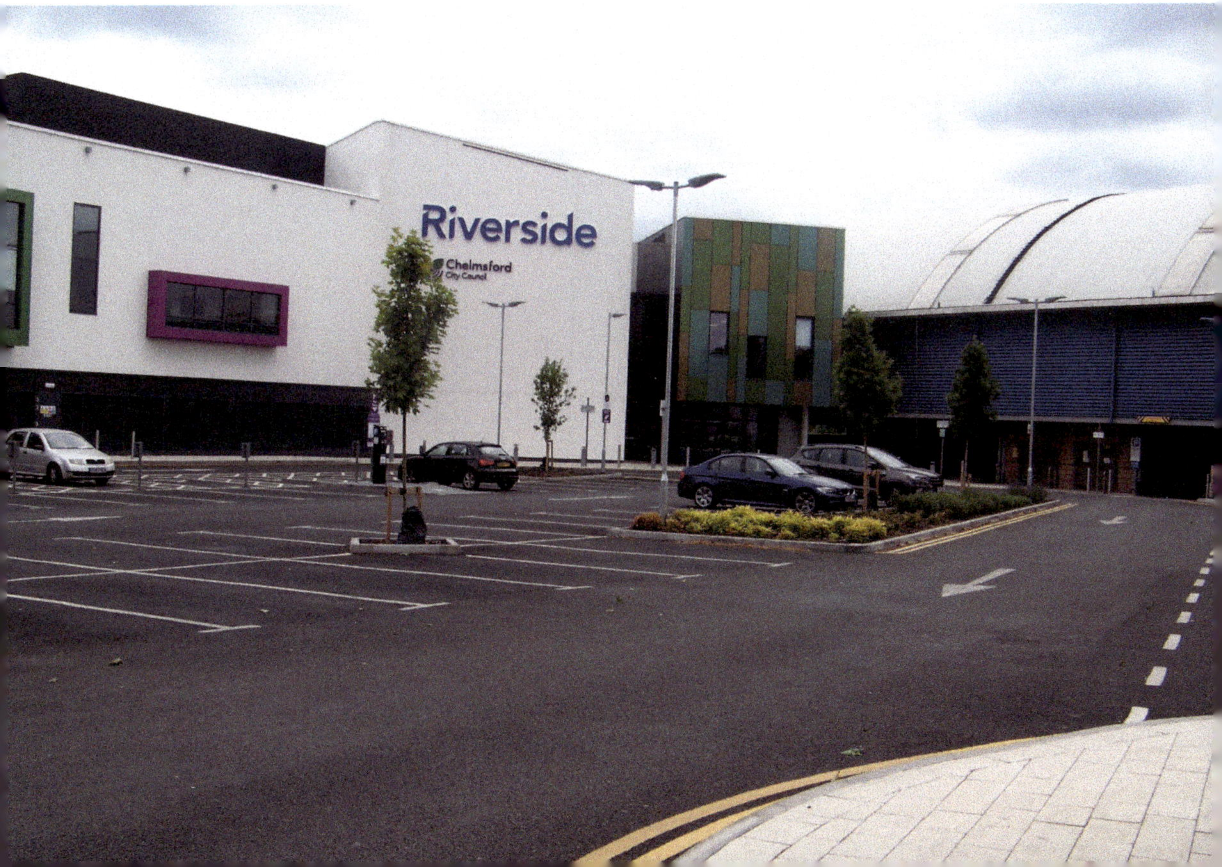

in Riverside. Whole families would troop along and have a weekly bath. An attendant controlled the water flow from outside the cubicle and the famous cry was 'A drop of hot please' and the attendant would turn the tap on.

4,000 people signed a petition to have an indoor swimming pool and as a result a pool and slipper bath were built in 1965. The project cost £279,500 and at that time to use the facilities it cost one shilling (5p) for an adult and six pence for a child. A learner pool was added in 1982 and later, in 1987, the building was refurbished and an ice rink, sports hall, four squash courts and a snooker hall were added. There was always a buzz of excitement on election nights when the hall was used for counting the votes and declaring the results. The hall was let out for other events, such as dog and art shows. Riverside was owned by the council but was run by a private firm. Chelmsford Council was the first to implement this form of management. The men's Chieftains ice hockey team and the women's team, the Cobras, were established in 1987.

The centre has recently undergone another major overhaul, which started in September 2017 and took twenty months to complete. The change involved two new swimming pools, a gym, sports hall and café. It did run over budget, as these projects often do, but the results look as if they are worth it.

44. The Three Compasses

The Three Compasses public house in Church Road, West Hanningfield, is one of the most picturesque in the district. Parts of it date back to 1425 and it is first recorded as an inn in 1738 when the landlady, Mrs Onton, put the first pint on the counter. Inside the cosy saloon is a sign listing all the names of the previous licensees that have served behind the bar. The present landlady, Rosemary Cotton,

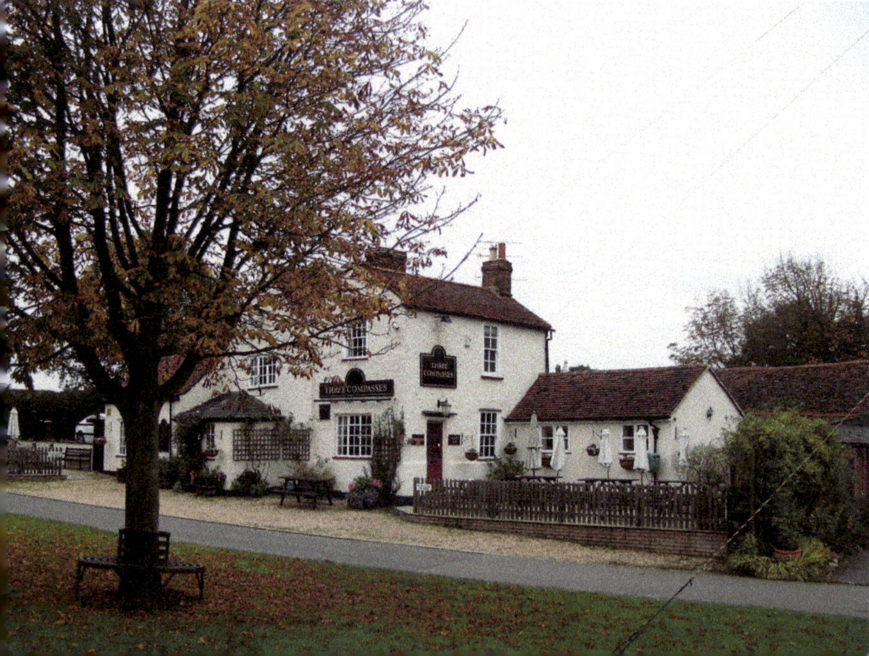

Three Compasses
public house.

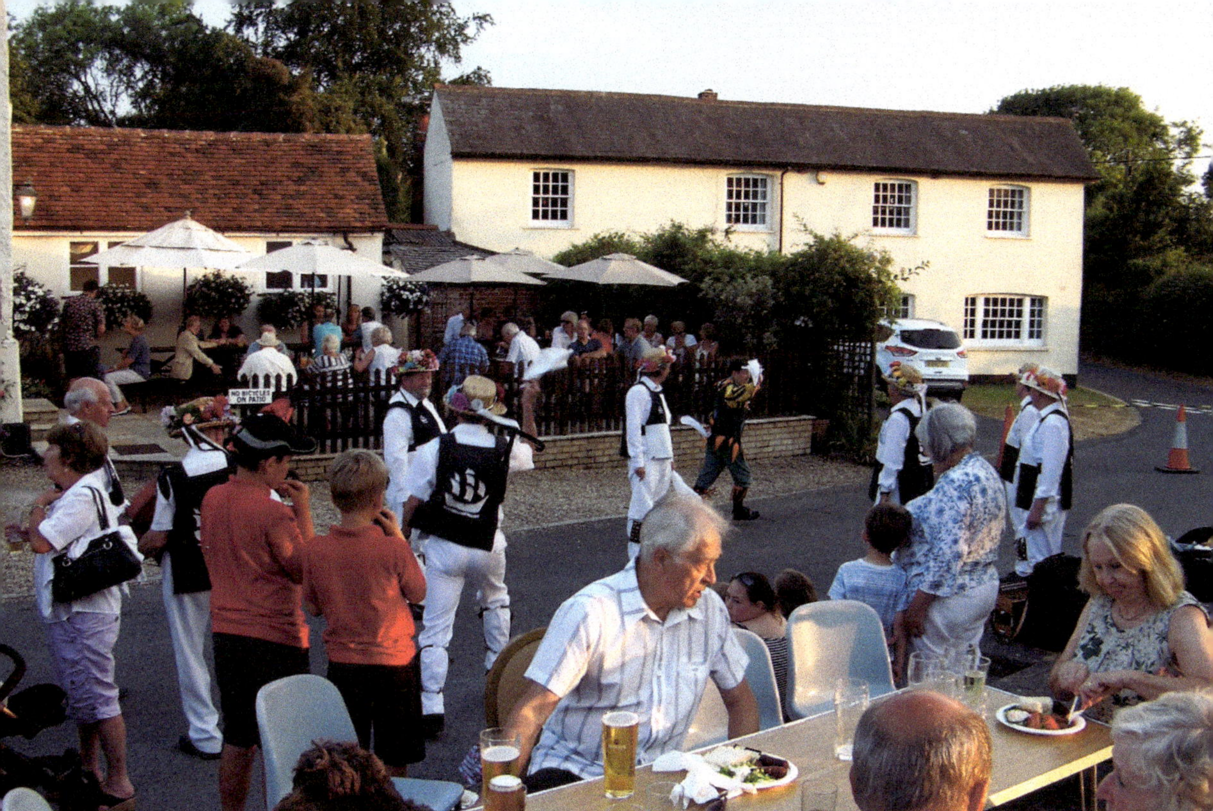

Morris dancers performing outside the Three Compasses.

has run the pub for nearly fifty years, first with her husband, Kenneth, and when he sadly died, by herself, until her son John joined her. On the wall hangs an aeroplane propeller, a tribute to Rose's husband who was a fighter pilot during the Second World War.

The public house is a Grade II listed building and is timber framed and plastered. The ceilings in the bars have low beams, which adds to the Three Compasses' charm. During autumn and winter there is always the warm glow of a log fire burning in the grate and during the summer Mrs Cotton helps to raise money for the village church restoration fund and holds a barbecue, which is well attended. One of the great attractions are the Morris dancers.

45. The Golden Fleece

A public house has stood on the site of the Golden Fleece in Duke Street since 1654. It was rebuilt in 1932. At one time, the wool trade was the backbone of the English economy and Chelmsford was one of the main wool areas, along with Yorkshire and the West Country. The Golden Fleece was a stopping place for wool traders on their way to Maldon to export their wool.

The history of wool is part of our past and even today the Lord Chancellor sits on a seat in Parliament stuffed with wool and which is known as the Woolsack.

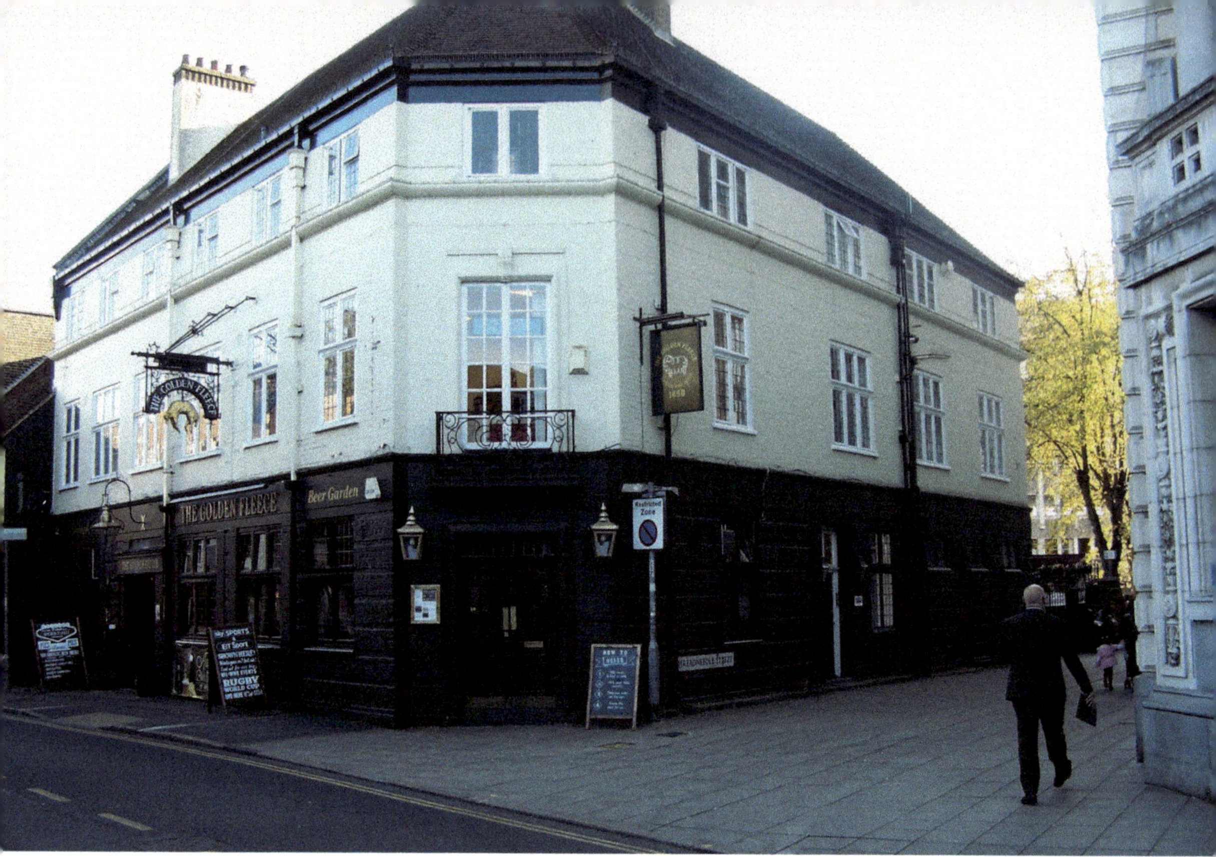

The Golden Fleece.

It is believed that even as far back as the Bronze Age, man had discovered how to weave wool into cloth and to use sheep's skins to keep warm. Before then, sheep were reared for meat and milk. By the time the Romans invaded Britain in 55 BC, there was already a thriving wool industry and by the eigth century it was being exported.

In March 1667, during Charles II's reign and a year after the Great Fire of London, a law was passed that bodies had to be buried in wool. There was a substantial fine if anyone broke this law. Previous to the Act, people were buried in yarn, 25 per cent of which came from France, our rivals. In 1699, the Wool Act was strengthened to include the complete ban on importing foreign wool and at that time it was illegal to attend church without a woollen hat.

46. The Black Boy Inn

One of the oldest inns in Chelmsford was the Black Boy, which was built during the sixteenth century but unfortunately demolished in 1857. As far as I can establish it stood on the corner of the High Street and Springfield Road, which is now a bank. The inn was once a staging post for travellers on their way to London, Harwich and Colchester. When the railway came to Chelmsford it rang

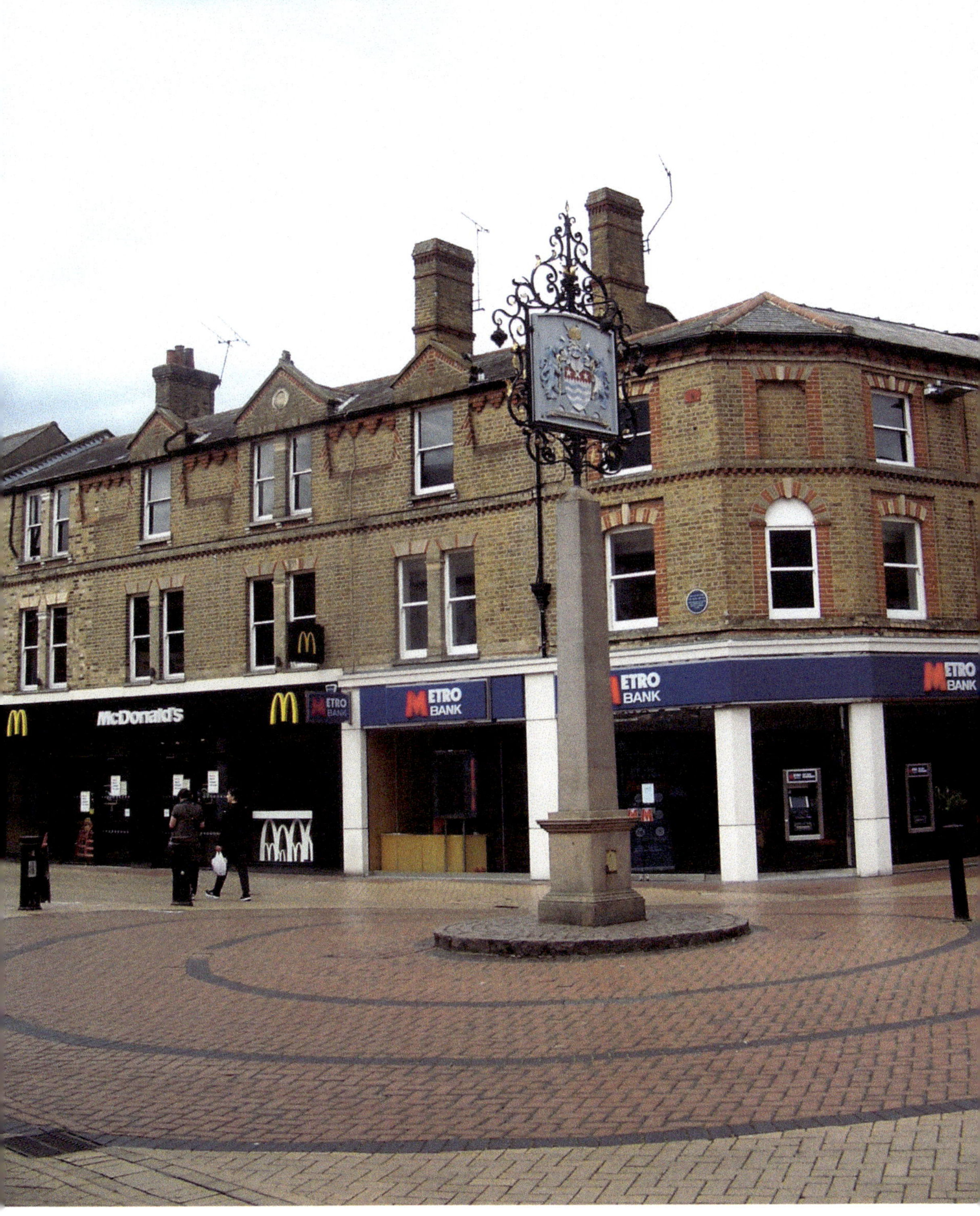

Site of the old Black Boy public house.

the death knell of the coaching inns, including the Black Boy. Trains were a much faster means of transport and much more comfortable.

The original name of the Black Boy was The Crown, which was owned by de Veres. During the seventeenth century The Crown was demolished and the Black Boy built in its place. It must have been a palatial building because it had a number of famous people stay in it. George IV, the Duke of Wellington and Charles Dickens stayed there, although Dickens was not very impressed with Chelmsford when he was covering the elections for *The Morning Chronicle*. He is reported to have said, 'Chelmsford was the dullest of places and has nothing to look at but two enormous prisons that could house the whole population.'

The Black Boy Inn had stables for over forty horses, twelve bedrooms and a large ballroom measuring 52 feet by 19. The Board of Guardians for the Poor Law used to meet in its rooms and at one time it was here that they decided to add five more parishes to their list. In 1777, the Chelmsford Tradesmen's Club started to meet regularly in the inn to discuss the commercial community and to hold auctions, which included the sale of the Rising Sun public house in Billericay in 1830. Eventually they moved to the Saracen's Head.

47. BBC Essex

Nothing has brought Essex together more than BBC Essex. Since its inauguration on 5 November 1986 it has entertained and informed the people of Essex. It is famous for its talk programmes, where listeners can express their views on a

BBC Essex, 2020.

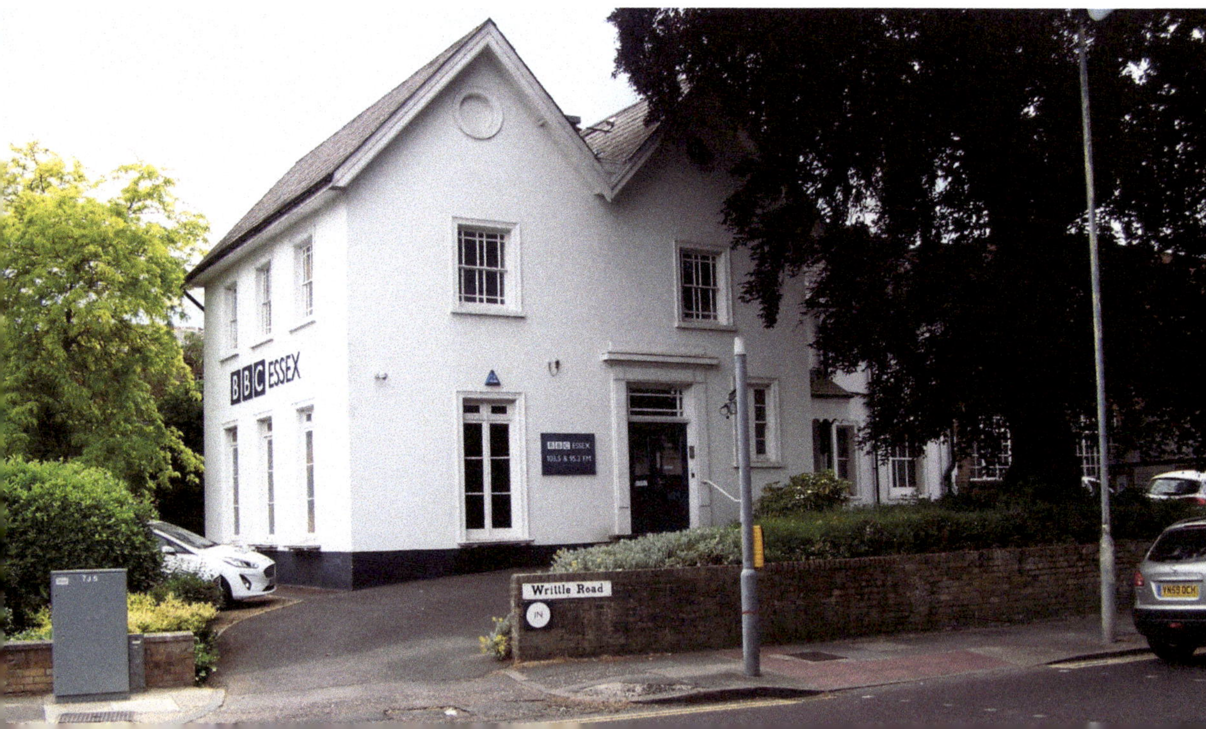

variety of subjects, its request programmes and, apart from the general news, it advises the public of items that affect the county.

It is housed in 198 New London Road, which is believed to date back to 1843, when it was leased to the Revd Hamilton but owned by Henry Kent, according to documents held at the Essex Records Office. At that time the house was called Falcon Villa and during the nineteenth century it was owned by a Mr Ling, who died in 1869.

Over the intervening years a number of firms and organisations have owned the property, including the AA, who occupied it until 1969, when an Electrical Engineering Company set up its head office in the building. It was followed by a firm of engineers, then finally, in 1984, BBC Essex bought it and started broadcasting.

48. The Priory Arch

The Priory Arch stands proudly in Priory Fields, Bicknacre, and has done so since the twelfth century. It is all that remains of the Priory that was occupied by the Black Cannon order of monks who followed the rules set out by St Augustine.

The Priory, Bicknacre.

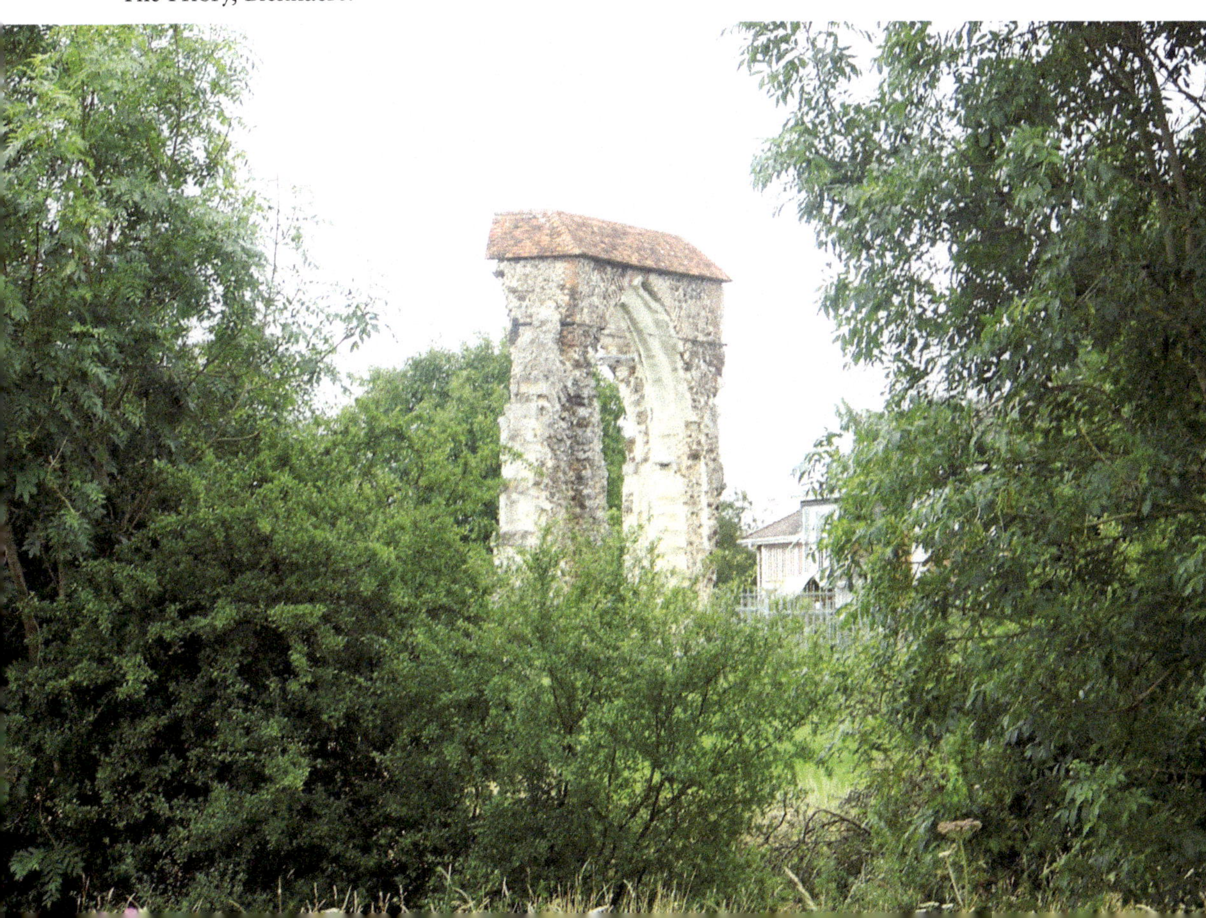

It was originally called Wodeham Priory until 1235 and was built to house fifteen monks. In 1507 the last prior died and the order was dissolved and, as was the law at that time, the priory and its lands, which consisted of the Manor of Bicknacre, farmland, acres of woodland and pastures, reverted to Henry VII. He did nothing with it and when Henry VIII came to the throne he issued a royal licence and the priory was linked up with St Mary's Hospital for £400. There were two conditions to granting the licence: a chaplain had to live in Bicknacre and to say prayers for the souls of the departed kings, and that on 27 and 28 October each year masses were to be heard and twenty pence given to the poor.

The Priory remained attached to St Mary's until Henry introduced the Dissolution of the Monasteries in 1536 and it gradually fell into neglect after he gave it to Henry Polsted. In 1548 it was sold to Sir Walter Mildmay, Chancellor to Elisabeth I.

In 1654 it was again sold to the Barrington family and after that it changed hands a number of times. The remains of the Priory were left to the elements until 1812, when the then owner carried out work to protect the last four arches.

In 1930 several wooden huts were built so that religious children from the East End of London could have a break in the country, but the Second World War put an end to that enterprise when the children were evacuated to escape the bombing. The huts were not wasted but were used for the army. After the war they were used for storage until they were finally pulled down.

49. St Michael and All Saints

St Michael and All Saints is probably the only church in Britain that is built in the middle of a racecourse. It is understood that there was a racecourse on Galleywood Common during the reign of Charles II (1660–80).

The church was built much later than the racecourse, having been erected in 1872, but it was an awkward course and jockeys had to steer their horses around the church, across a couple of roads before making for the grandstand. The last race was held in April 1935, just before the Second World War. The church is in a very secluded spot and is surrounded by a forest. Its tower, which is 131 feet high, stands tall and proud against the skyline. It once had pinnacles but today only the base remains.

Arthur Pryor of Hylands House was the instigator of the church, which was built to serve the people of Galleywood. It was consecrated by the Bishop of Rochester the year after it was built. It is constructed of striking, decorative brick. There are eight bells which were made by a firm in London and were rehung in 1926 when the bell frame was replaced. The area where the bells are rung is cordoned off with a glass screen.

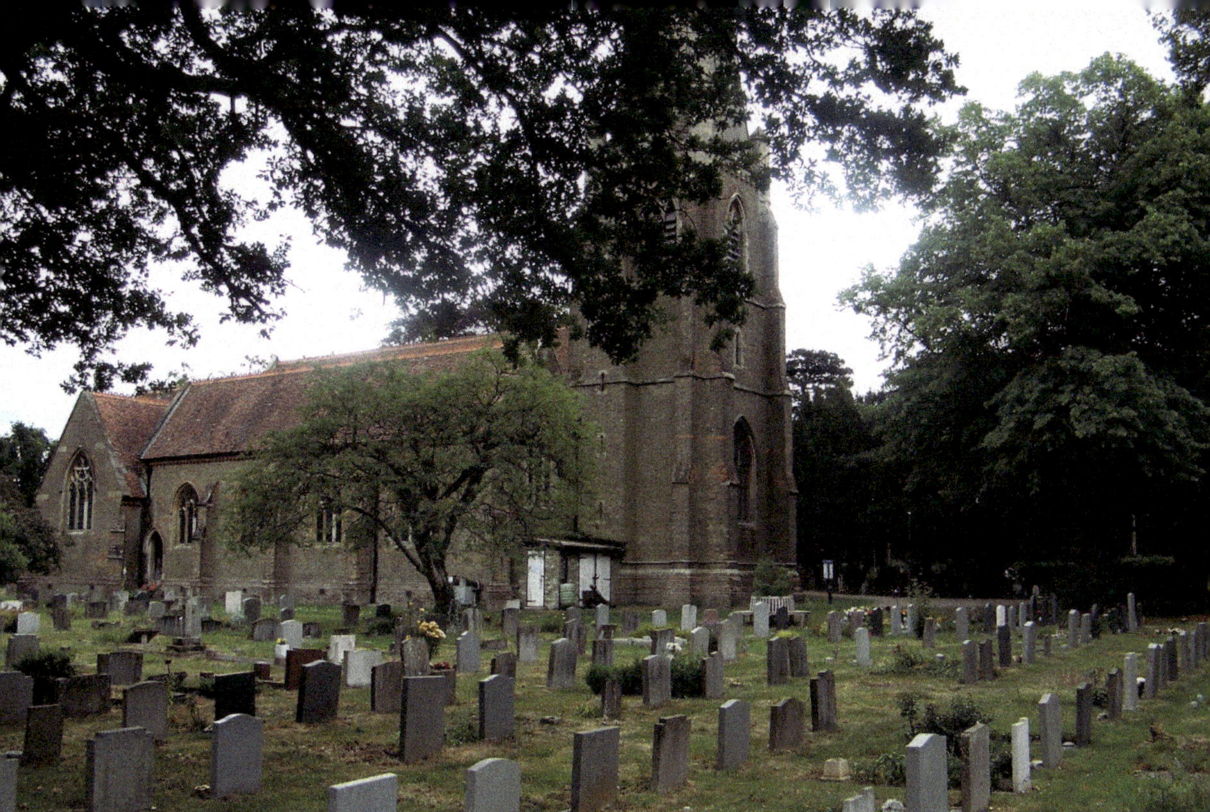

St Michael and All Saints, Galleywood.

The organ, which was built by Conacher and Co., began its life in another church and was transferred to St Michaels and All Angels in 1924.

The woods surrounding the church are very beautiful, with a serenity that makes them very popular with walkers.

50. St Peter's, Church Lane, South Hanningfield

It is thought that the north wall of the church was originally built in the late twelfth century because of its construction. It has been restored many times over the years and has had a number of additions; for example, the chancel is only 150 years old and is set slightly to one side. Some people think this is a weeping chancel, which depicts Christ on the cross with his head to one side. Another school of thought is that it was built that way to avoid the graves of two prominent families in the area, the Kings and the Langleys. The window facing the door is Norman and the roof beams are mediaeval. The bell tower is at the west end of the church, and was built during the fourteenth century and restored in 1888. The tower does not depend on the church for support but stands on its own. The tenor bell was cast by Anthony Bartlett, who, in the seventeenth century, had a famous bell-casting company in Whitechapel. Anthony's father cast many of the

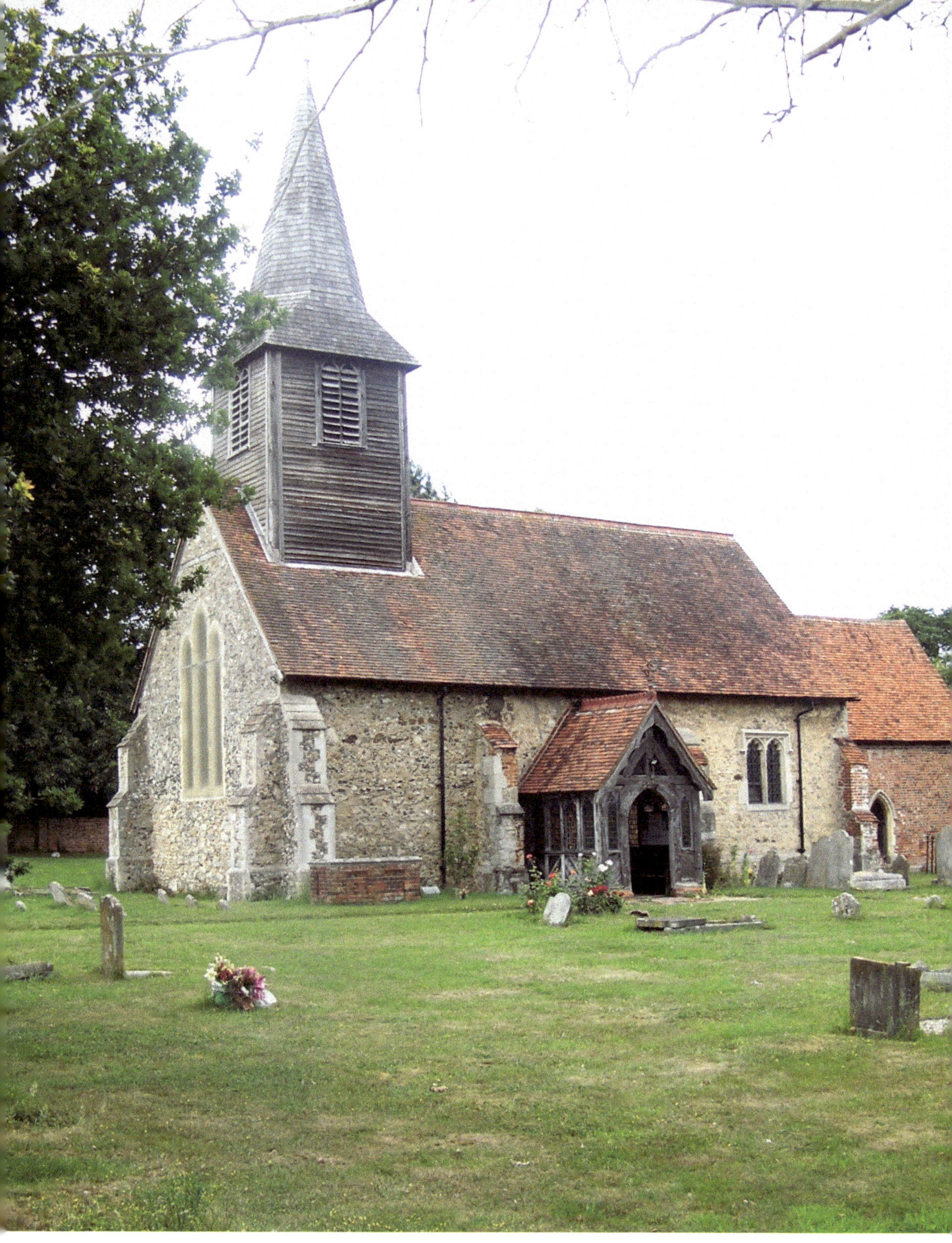

St Peter's.

bells in London churches but unfortunately a lot of them were destroyed in the Great Fire of 1666. Anthony was only a child when his father died in 1632 but the business was carried on by John Clifton for eight years until Anthony was old enough to take it over.

Many Norman churches were built on hills so they overlooked the countryside and were places of refuge from attackers and could be defended. The old solid door has marks in it which are thought to have been made during the English Civil War (1642–51) by musket balls. The original windows were high up and small so they gave more security. There is an example of this in the centre of the north wall. Later, as times became more peaceful, windows were built larger and lower down so they let in more light.

Many of the windows have remnants of the original glass, which were covered in whitewash during the puritan period of history. However, the Revd T. Devitt, during his spell of priesthood, spent ages removing the paintwork. One of the treasures of the church, which cannot be stored in it because of a spate of thefts, is an Elizabethan chalice dated back to 1562. It is now kept in the Victoria and Albert Museum in London.

The church has wonderful views over Hanningfield Reservoir and it is very pleasant and restorative to the spirit just to sit and enjoy.

Acknowledgements

I wish to express my gratitude to the following people, without whose help and patience this book would never have been written. I have made every effort to be as accurate as possible. Any mistakes are mine and mine alone and I apologise in advance for them.

Firstly, I must thank Nikki Embery, Jenny Stephens and the team at Amberley Publishing for all their help and understanding; my good friend Sylvia Kent, whose help and encouragement has been invaluable and who has written a similar book on Brentwood. I thank the staff of Chelmsford Museum, especially Mark Curteis, PhD. AMA FRNS, for their invaluable help. For the photographs of the police buildings I must thank Mick Berry and his team at the Essex Police Museum. I thank Lindsey Thompson, PR and Marketing Manager of King Edward VI Grammar School, for being so helpful and allowing me to use their photographs. The staff at Chelmsford County Girls' Grammar School and Elizabeth Murphy of New Hall School for giving permission to use their excellent old photographs. Peter Marriage, of Marriage's Flour, who was very helpful and allowed me to use their photographs. Also Liz Meer, of Gray & Sons Brewers.

There is one person who I must mention as without her patience, support and editing skills this book would never have been finished: my wife, Joan.